Cloud Computing and Virtualization

Scrivener Publishing
100 Cummings Center, Suite 541J
Beverly, MA 01915-6106

Publishers at Scrivener
Martin Scrivener (martin@scrivenerpublishing.com)
Phillip Carmical (pcarmical@scrivenerpublishing.com)

Cloud Computing and Virtualization

Dac-Nhuong Le
Faculty of Information Technology, Haiphong University,
Haiphong, Vietnam
Raghvendra Kumar
Department of Computer Science and Engineering, LNCT,
Jabalpur, India
Gia Nhu Nguyen
Graduate School, Duy Tan University, Da Nang, Vietnam
Jyotir Moy Chatterjee
Department of Computer Science and Engineering at GD-RCET,
Bhilai, India.

Scrivener
Publishing

This edition first published 2018 by John Wiley & Sons, Inc., 111 River Street, Hoboken, NJ 07030, USA and Scrivener Publishing LLC, 100 Cummings Center, Suite 541J, Beverly, MA 01915, USA
© 2018 Scrivener Publishing LLC
For more information about Scrivener publications please visit www.scrivenerpublishing.com.

Wiley Global Headquarters
111 River Street, Hoboken, NJ 07030, USA

For details of our global editorial offices, customer services, and more information about Wiley products visit us at www.wiley.com.

Limit of Liability/Disclaimer of Warranty
While the publisher and authors have used their best efforts in preparing this work, they make no representations or warranties with respect to the accuracy or completeness of the contents of this work and specifically disclaim all warranties, including without limitation any implied warranties of merchantability or fitness for a particular purpose. No warranty may be created or extended by sales representatives, written sales materials, or promotional statements for this work. The fact that an organization, website, or product is referred to in this work as a citation and/or potential source of further information does not mean that the publisher and authors endorse the information or services the organization, website, or product may provide or recommendations it may make. This work is sold with the understanding that the publisher is not engaged in rendering professional services. The advice and strategies contained herein may not be suitable for your situation. You should consult with a specialist where appropriate. Neither the publisher nor authors shall be liable for any loss of profit or any other commercial damages, including but not limited to special, incidental, consequential, or other damages. Further, readers should be aware that websites listed in this work may have changed or disappeared between when this work was written and when it is read.

Library of Congress Cataloging-in-Publication Data
ISBN 978-1-119-48790-6

Cover images: Pixabay.Com
Cover design by: Russell Richardson

Set in size of 11pt and Minion Pro by Exeter Premedia Services Private Ltd., Chennai, India

10 9 8 7 6 5 4 3 2 1

Contents

List of Figures

List of Tables

Preface

The idea of cloud computing isn't new, or overly complicated from a technology resources and Internet perspective. What's new is the growth and maturity of cloud computing methods, and strategies that enable business agility goals. Looking back, the phrase "*utility computing*" didn't captivate or create the stir in the information industry as the term "*cloud computing*" has in recent years. Nevertheless, appreciation of readily available resources has arrived and the utilitarian or servicing features are what are at the heart of outsourcing the access of information technology resources and services. In this light, cloud computing represents a flexible, cost-effective and proven delivery platform for business and consumer information services over the Internet. Cloud computing has become an industry game changer as businesses and information technology leaders realize the potential in combining and sharing computing resources as opposed to building and maintaining them.

There's seemingly no shortage of views regarding the benefits of cloud computing nor is there a shortage of vendors willing to offer services in either open source or promising commercial solutions. Beyond the hype, there are many aspects of the Cloud that have earned new consideration due to their increased service capability and potential efficiencies. The ability to demonstrate transforming results in cloud computing to resolve traditional business problems using information technology management's best practices now exists. In the case of economic impacts, the principles of pay-as-you-go and computer agnostic services are concepts ready for prime time. Performances can be well measured by calculating the economic and environmental effects of cloud computing today.

In *Cloud Computing and Virtualization*, Dac Nhuong Le *et al.* take the industry beyond mere definitions of cloud computing and virtualization, grid and sustainment strategies to contrasting them in day-to-day operations. Dac-Nhuong Le and his team of co-authors take the reader from beginning to end with the essential elements of cloud computing, its history, innovation, and demands. Through case studies and architectural models they articulate service requirements, infrastructure, security, and outsourcing of salient computing resources.

The adoption of virtualization in data centers creates the need for a new class of networks designed to support elasticity of resource allocation, increasing mobile workloads and the shift to production of virtual workloads, requiring maximum availability. Building a network that spans both physical servers and virtual machines with consistent capabilities demands a new architectural approach to designing and building the IT infrastructure. Performance, elasticity, and logical addressing structures must be considered as well as the management of the physical and virtual networking infrastructure. Once deployed, a network that is virtualization-ready can offer many revolutionary services over a common shared infrastructure. Virtualization technologies from VMware, Citrix and Microsoft encapsulate existing applications and extract them from the physical hardware. Unlike physical machines, virtual machines are represented by a portable software image, which can be instantiated on physical hardware at a moment's notice. With virtualization, comes elasticity where computer capacity can be scaled up or down on demand by adjusting the number of virtual machines actively executing on a given physical server. Additionally, virtual machines can be migrated while in service from one physical server to another. Extending this further, virtualization creates "*location freedom*" enabling virtual machines to become portable across an ever-increasing geographical distance. As cloud architectures and multi-tenancy capabilities continue to develop and mature, there is an economy of scale that can be realized by aggregating resources across applications, business units, and separate corporations to a common shared, yet segmented, infrastructure.

Elasticity, mobility, automation, and density of virtual machines demand new network architectures focusing on high performance, addressing portability, and the innate understanding of the virtual machine as the new building block of the data center. Consistent network-supported and virtualization-driven policy and controls are necessary for visibility to virtual machines' state and location as they are created and moved across a virtualized infrastructure.

Dac-Nhuong Le again enlightens the industry with sharp analysis and reliable architecture-driven practices and principles. No matter the level of interest or experience, the reader will find clear value in this in-depth, vendor-neutral study of cloud computing and virtualization.

This book is organized into thirteen chapters. Chapter 1, "Live Migration Concept in Cloud Environment," discusses the technique of moving a VM from one physical host to another while the VM is still executing. It is a powerful and handy tool for administrators to maintain SLAs while performing optimization tasks and maintenance on the cloud infrastructure. Live migration ideally requires the transfer of the CPU state, memory state, network state and disk state. Transfer of the disk state can be circumvented by having a shared storage between the hosts participating in the live migration process. This chapter gives the brief introductory concept of live migration and the different techniques related to live migration such as issues with live migration, research on live migration, learning automata partitioning and, finally, different advantages of live migration over WAN.

Chapter 2, "Live Virtual Machine Migration in Cloud," shows how the most well known and generally sent VMM-VMware is defenseless against reasonable assaults, focusing on their live migration's usefulness. This chapter also discusses the different challenges of virtual machine migration in cloud computing environments along with their advantages and disadvantages and also the different case studies.

Chapter 3, "Attacks and Policies in Cloud Computing and Live Migration," presents the cloud computing model based on the concept of pay-per-use, as the user is required to pay for the amount of cloud services used. Cloud computing is defined by different layer architecture (*IAAS, PAAS* and *SAAS*), and models (*Private, Public, Hybrid* and *Community*), in which the usability depends on different models. Chapter 4, "Live Migration Security in Cloud," gives different security paradigm concepts that are very useful at the time of data accessing from the cloud environment. In this chapter different cloud service providers that are available in the market are listed along with security risks, cloud security challenges, cloud economics, cloud computing technologies and, finally, common types of attacks and policies in cloud and live migration.

Chapter 5, "Solutions for Secure Live Migration," analyzes approaches for secure data transfer, focusing mainly on the authentication parameter. These approaches have been categorized according to single- and multi-tier authentication. This authentication may use digital certificate, HMAC or OTP on registered devices. This chapter gives an overview of Cloud security applications, VM migration in clouds and security concerns, software-defined networking, firewalls in cloud and SDN, SDN and Floodlight controllers, distributed messaging system, customized testbed for testing migration security in cloud. A case study is also presented along with other use cases: Firewall rule migration and verification, existing security scenario in cloud, authentication in cloud, hybrid approaches to security in cloud computing and data transfer, and architecture in cloud computing.

Chapter 6, "Dynamic Load Balancing Based on Live Migration," concentrates on ancient data security controls (like access controls or encryption). There are two other steps to help operate unapproved data moving to cloud services: Monitor for large internal data migrations with file activity monitoring (FAM) and database activity monitoring (DAM) and monitor for data moving to the cloud with universal resource locater (URL) filters and data loss prevention. This chapter gives an overview of detecting and preventing data migrations to the cloud, protecting data moving to the cloud, application security, virtualization, VM guest hardening, security as a service, identity as service requirements, web services SecaaS requirements, email SECaaS requirements, security.

Chapter 7, "Live Migration in Cloud Data Center," introduces the use of load balancing is to improve the throughput of the system. This chapter gives an overview of different techniques of load balancing, load rebalancing, and a policy engine to implement dynamic load balancing algorithm, some load balancing algorithms and VMware distributed resource scheduler.

In Chapter 8, "Trusted VMv-TPM," data center network architectures and various network control mechanisms are introduced. Discussed in the chapter is how resource virtualization, through VM migration, is now commonplace in data centers, and how VM migration can be used to improve system-side performance for VMs, or how load can be better balanced across the network through strategic VM migration. However, all the VM migration works in this chapter have not addressed the fundamental problem of actively targeting and removing congestion from oversubscribed core links within data center networks. The TPM can be utilized to enable outside parties to guarantee that a specific host bearing the TPM is booted into a confided in state. That is performed by checking the arrangement of summaries (*called estimations*) of the stacked programming, progressively delivered all throughout the boot procedure of the gadget. The estimations are put away in a secured stockpiling incorporated within the TPM chip and are in this way impervious to programming assaults, albeit powerless against equipment altering. This chapter presents a stage skeptic trusted dispatch convention for a generic virtual machine image (GVMI). GVMIs are virtual machine pictures that don't vary from the merchant-provided VM pictures (*conversationally known as vanilla programming*). They are made accessible by the IaaS suppliers for customers that plan to utilize a case of a VM picture that was not subject to any adjustments, such fixes or infused programming. The convention portrayed in this chapter permits a customer that demands a GVMI to guarantee that it is kept running on a confided stage.

Chapter 9, "Lightweight Live Migration," presents a set of techniques that provide high availability through VM live migration, their implementation in the Xen hypervisor and the Linux operating system kernel, and experimental studies conducted using a variety of benchmarks and production applications. The techniques include: a novel fine-grained block identification mechanism called FGBI; a lightweight, globally consistent checkpointing mechanism called VPC (virtual predict checkpointing); a fast VM resumption mechanism called VM resume; a guest OS kernel-based live migration technique that does not involve the hypervisor for VM migration called HSG-LM; an efficient live migration-based load balancing strategy called DC balance; and a fast and storage-adaptive migration mechanism called FDM.

Chapter 10, "Virtual Machine Mobility with Self Migration" discusses many open issues identified with gadget drivers. Existing frameworks exchange driver protection for execution and simplicity of advancement, and gadget drivers are a noteworthy protection of framework insecurity. Endeavors have been made to enhance the circumstance, equipment security methods, e.g., smaller scale bits and Nooks, and through programming authorized seclusion. Product frameworks don't uphold tending to confinements on gadget DMA, constraining the viability of the portrayed systems. Lastly, if applications are to survive a driver crash, the OS or driver se curity instrument must have a method for reproducing lost hardware state on driver reinitialization.

Chapter 11, "Different Approaches for Live Migration," studies the implementation of two kinds of live migration techniques for hardware-assisted virtual machines (HVMs). The first contribution of this chapter is the design and implementation of the post-copy approach. This approach consists of the last two stages of the processmigration phases, the stop-and-copy phase and pull phase. Due to the introduction of the pull phase, this approach becomes nondeterministic in terms of the completion of the migration. This is because of the only on-demand fetching of the data from the source.

Chapter 12, "Migrating Security Policies in Cloud," presents the concepts of cloud computing, which is a fast-developing area that relies on sharing of resources over a network. While more companies are adapting to cloud computing and data centers are growing rapidly, data and network security is gaining more importance and firewalls are still the most common means to safeguard networks of any size. Whereas today data centers are distributed around the world, VM migration within and between data centers is inevitable for an elastic cloud. In order to keep the VM and data centers secure after migration, the VM specific security policies should move along with the VM as well.

Finally, Chapter 13, "Case Study," gives different case studies that are very useful for real-life applications, like KVM, Xen, emergence of green computing in cloud and ends with a case study that is very useful for data analysis in distributed environments. There are lots of algorithms for either transactional or geographic databases proposed to prune the frequent item sets and association rules, among which is an algorithm to find the global spatial association rule mining, which exclusively represent in GIS database schemas and geo-ontologies by relationships with cardinalities that are one-to-one and one-to-many. This chapter presents an algorithm to improve the spatial association rule mining. The proposed algorithm is categorized into three main steps: First, it automates the geographic data pre-processing tasks developed for a GIS module. The second contribution is discarding all well-known GIS dependencies that calculate the relationship between different numbers of attributes. And finally, an algorithm is proposed which provides the greatest degree of privacy when the number of regions is more than two, with each one finding the association rule between them with zero percentage of data leakage.

Dac-Nhuong Le
Raghvendra Kumar
Nguyen Gia Nhu
Jyotir Moy Chetterjee
January 2018

Acknowledgments

The authors would like to acknowledge the most important persons of our lives, our grandfathers, grandmothers and our wives. This book has been a long-cherished dream which would not have been turned into reality without the support and love of these amazing people. They have have encouraged us despite our failing to give them the proper time and attention. We are also grateful to our best friends for their blessings, unconditional love, patience and encouragement of this work.

Acronyms

ACL	Access Control List
ALB	Adaptive Load Balancing
AMQP	Advanced Message Queuing Protocol
API	Application Programming Interface
ARP	Address Resolution Protocol
CAM	Content Addressable Memory
CCE	Cloud Computing Environment
CFI	Control Flow Integrity
CSLB	Central Scheduler Load Balancing
CSP	Cloud Service Provider
DAM	Database Activity Monitoring
DCE	Data Center Efficiency
DLP	Data Loss Prevention
DPM	Distributed Power Management
DRS	Distributed Resource Scheduler
DVFS	Dynamic Frequency Voltage Scaling
DHCP	Dynamic Host Configuration Protocol
ECMP	Equal-Cost Multi-Path
EC2	Elastic Compute Cloud
FAM	File Activity Monitoring
FGBI	Fine-Grained Block Identification
GVMI	Generic Virtual Machine Image
GOC	Green Open Cloud
HVM	Hardware Assisted Virtual Machine
HPC	Hardware Performance Counters
HIPS	Host Intrusion Prevention System
IaaS	Infrastructure as a Service
IDS/IPS	Intrusion Detection System/Intrusion Prevention System
IMA	Integrity Management Architecture
IRM	In-Lined Reference Monitors
ISA	Instruction Set Architecture
KVM	Kernel-Based Virtual Machine

KBA	Knowledge-Based Answers/Questions
LAN	Local Area Network
LLFC	Link Layer Flow Control
LLM	Lightweight Live Migration
LVMM	Live Virtual Machine Migration
MiTM	Man-in-the-Middle Attack
MAC	Media Access Control
NAC	Network Access Control
NRDC	Natural Resources Defense Council
NIPS	Network Intrusion Prevention System
OS	Operating System
ONF	Open Networking Foundation
PaaS	Platform as a Service
PAP	Policy Access Points
PDP	Policy Decision Points
PEP	Policy Enforcement Points
PUE	Power Usage Effectiveness
PDT	Performance Degradation Time
PMC	Performance Monitoring Counters
PPW	Performance Per Watt
RLE	Run-Length Encoding
SaaS	Software as a Service
SAML	Security Assertion Markup Language
SDN	Software-Defined Networks
SecaaS	Security as a Service
SLA	Service Level Agreements
SPT	Shadow Page Table
SFI	Software Fault Isolation
SMC	Secure Multi-Party Computation
SIEM	Security Information and Event Management
STP	Spanning Tree Protocol
S3	Simple Storage Service
TPM	Trusted Platform Module
TTP	Trusted Third Party
TCG	Trusted Computing Group
VDCs	Virtual Data Centers
VLB	Valiant Load Balancing
VPC	Virtual Predict Checkpointing
VM	Virtual Machine
VMM	Virtual Machine Migration
VMLM	Virtual Machine Live Migration
XSS	Cross-Site Scripting
WAN	Wide Area Network

Introduction

DAC-NHUONG LE, PHD

Deputy-Head, Faculty of Information Technology

Haiphong University, Haiphong, Vietnam

Contemporary advancements in virtualization and correspondence advances have changed the way data centers are composed and work by providing new mechanisms for better sharing and control of data center assets. Specifically, virtual machine and live migration is an effective administration strategy that gives data center administrators the capacity to adjust the situation of VMs, keeping in mind the end goal to better fulfill execution destinations, enhance asset usage and correspondence region, moderate execution hotspots, adapt to internal failure, diminish vitality utilization, and encourage framework support exercises. In spite of these potential advantages, VM movement likewise postures new prerequisites on the plan of the fundamental correspondence foundation; for example, tending to data transfer capacity necessities to help VM portability. Besides, conceiving proficient VM relocation plans is additionally a testing issue, as it not just requires measuring the advantages of VM movement, but additionally considering movement costs, including correspondence cost, benefit disturbance, and administration overhead.

This book presents profound insights into virtual machine and live movement advantages and systems and examines their related research challenges in server farms in distributed computing situations.

CHAPTER 1

LIVE VIRTUAL CONCEPT IN CLOUD ENVIRONMENT

Abstract

Live migration ideally requires the transfer of the CPU state, memory state, network state and disk state. Transfer of the disk state can be circumvented by having a shared storage between the hosts participating in the live migration process. Next, the VM is suspended at the source machine, and resumed at the target machine. The states of the virtual processor are also copied over, ensuring that the machine is the very same in both operation and specifications, once it resumes at the destination. This chapter is a detailed study of live migration, types of live migration and issues and research of live migration in cloud environment.

Keywords: Live migration, techniques, graph partitioning, migration time, WAN.

1.1   Live Migration

1.1.1   Definition of Live Migration

Live migration [1] is the technique of moving a VM from one physical host to another while the VM is still executing. It is a powerful and handy tool for administrators to maintain SLAs while performing optimization tasks and maintenance on the cloud infrastructure. Live migration ideally requires the transfer of the CPU state, memory state, network state and disk state. Transfer of the disk state can be circumvented by having a shared storage between the hosts participating in the live migration process. Memory state transfer can be categorized into three phases:

Push Phase: The memory pages are transferred or pushed to the destination iteratively while the VM is running on the source host. Memory pages modified during each iteration are re-sent in the next iteration to ensure consistency in the memory state of the VM.

Stop-and-copy Phase: The VM is stopped at the source, all memory pages are copied across to the destination VM and then VM is started at the destination.

Pull Phase: The VM is running at the destination and if it accesses a page that has not yet been transferred from the source to the destination, then a page fault is generated and this page is pulled across the network from the source VM to the destination. Cold and hot VM migration approaches use the pure stop-and-copy migration technique. Here the memory contents of the VM are transferred to the destination along with CPU and I/O state after shutting down or suspending the VM, respectively. The advantage of this approach is simplicity and one-time transfer of memory pages. However, the disadvantage is high VM downtime and service unavailability.

1.1.2   Techniques for Live Migration

There are two main migration techniques [1], which are different combinations of the memory transfer phases explained previously. These are the pre-copy and the post- copy techniques.

1.1.2.1   *Pre-Copy Migration*   The most common way for virtual machine migration (VMM) [2] is the pre-copy method (Figure 1.1). During such a process, the complete disk image of the VM is first copied over to the destination. If anything was written to the disk during this process, the changed disk blocks are logged. Next, the changed disk data is migrated. Disk blocks can also change during this stage, and once again the changed blocks are logged. Migration of changed disk blocks are repeated until the generation rate of changed blocks are lower than a given threshold or a certain amount of iterations have passed. After the virtual disk is transferred, the RAM is migrated, using the same principle of iteratively copying changed content. Next, the VM is suspended at the source machine, and resumed at the target machine. The states of the virtual processor are also copied over, ensuring that the machine is the very same in both operation and specifications, once it resumes at the destination.

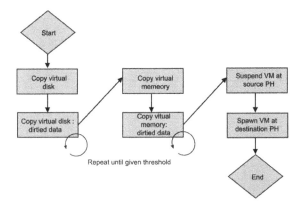

Figure 1.1   Pre-copy method for live migration.

It is important to note that the disk image migration phase is only needed if the VM doesn't have its image on a network location, such as an NFS share, which is quite common for data centers.

1.1.2.2 *Post-Copy Migration*   This is the most primitive form of VMM [3]. The basic outline of the post-copy method is as follows. The VM is suspended at the source PM. The minimum required processor state, which allows the VM to run, is transferred to the destination PM. Once this is done, the VM is resumed at the destination PM. This first part of the migration is common to all post-copy migration schemes. Once the VM is resumed at the destination, memory pages are copied over the network as the VM requests them, and this is where the post-copy techniques differ. The main goal in this latter stage is to push the memory pages of the suspended VM to the newly spawned VM, which is running at the destination PM. In this case, the VM will have a short SDT, but along performance degradation time (PDT).

Figure.1.2 illustrates the difference between these two migration techniques [3]. The diagram only depicts memory and CPU state transfers, and not the disk image of the VM. The latter is performed similarly in both the migration techniques, and does not affect the performance of the VM, and is therefore disregarded from the comparison. The "*performance degradation of VM migration technique*" in the pre-copy refers to the hypervisor having to keep track of the dirty pages; the RAM which has changed since the last pre-copy round. In the post-copy scenario, the degradation is greater and lasts longer. In essence, the post-copy method activates the VMs on the destination faster, but all memory is still located at the source. When a VM migrated with post-copy requests a specific portion of memory not yet local to the VM, the relevant memory pages will have to be pushed over the network. The "*stop-and-copy*" phase in the pre-copy method is the period where VM is suspended at the source PM and the last dirtied memory and CPU states are transferred to the destination PM. SDT is the time where the VM is inaccessible.

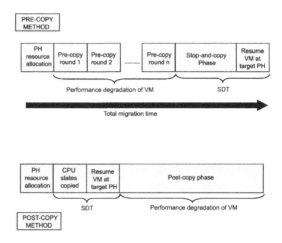

Figure 1.2 Pre- vs. Post-copy migration sequence.

1.2 Issues with Migration

Moving VMs [4] between physical hosts has its challenges, which are listed below.

1.2.1 Application Performance Degradation

A multi-tier application is an application [5] which communicates with many VMs simultaneously. These are typically configured with the different functionality spread over multiple VMs. For example, the database might be part of an application stored on one set of VMs, and the web server functionality on another set. In a scenario where an entire application is to be moved to a new site which has a limited bandwidth network link to the original site, the application will deteriorate in performance during the migration period for the following reason. If one of the application's member VMs are resumed at the destination site, any traffic destined for that machine will be slower than usual due to the limited inter-site bandwidth, and the fact that the rest of the application is still running at the source site. Several researchers have proposed ways of handling this problem of geographically split VMs during migration. This is referred to as the split components problem.

1.2.2 Network Congestion

Live migrations which take place within a data center, where no VMs end up at the other end of a slow WAN link, are not as concerned about the performance of running applications. It is common to use management links in production cloud environments, which allow management operations like live migrations to proceed without affecting the VMs and their allocated network links. The occurrence of some amount of SDT is unavoidable. However, such an implementation could be costly. In a setting where management links are absent, live migrations would directly affect the total available bandwidth on the links it uses. One issue that could arise from this is that several migrations could end up using the same migration paths, effectively overflowing one or more network links [6], and hence slow the performance of multi-tiered applications.

1.2.3 Migration Time

In a scenario where a system administrator needs to shut down a physical machine for maintenance, all the VMs currently running on that machine will have to be moved, so that they can keep serving the customers. For such a scenario, it would be favorable if the migration took the least time possible. In a case where the migration system is only concerned about fast migration, optimal target placement of the VMs might not be attained.

1.3   Research on Live Migration

1.3.1   Sequencer (CQNCR)

A system called CQNCR [7] has been created whose goal is to make a planned migration perform as fast as possible, given a source and target organization of the VMs. The tool created for this research focuses in intra-site migrations. The research claims it is able to increase the migration speed significantly by reducing total migration time by up to 35%. It also introduced the concept of virtual data centers (VDCs) and residual bandwidth. In practical terms, a VDC is a logically separated group of VMs and their associated virtual network links. As each VM has a virtual link, it too needs to be moved to the target PM. When this occurs, the bandwidth available to the migration process changes. The CQNCR-system takes this continuous change into account and does extended recalculations to provide efficient bandwidth usage, in a parallel approach. The system also prevents potential bottlenecks when migrating.

1.3.2   The COMMA System

A system called COMMA has been created which groups VMs together and migrates [8] one group at a time. Within a group are VMs which have a high degree of affinity; VMs which communicate a lot with each other. After the migration groups are decided, the system performs inter- and intra-group scheduling. The former is about deciding the order of the groups, while the latter optimizes the order of VMs within each group. The main function of COMMA is to migrate associated VMs at the same time, in order to minimize the traffic which has to go through a slow network link. The system is therefore especially suitable for inter-site migrations. It is structured so that each VM has a process running, which reports to a centralized controller which performs the calculations and scheduling.

The COMMA system defines the impact as the amount of inter-VM traffic which becomes separated because of migrations. In a case where a set of VMs, $\{VM_1, VM_2,.., VM_n\}$, is to be migrated the traffic levels running between them are measured and stored in matrix TM. Let the migration completion time for vm_i be t_i.

The VM buddies system also addresses the challenges in migrating VMs which is used by multi-tier applications. The authors formulate the problem as a correlated VM migration problem, and are tailored towards VM hosting multi-tier applications. Correlated VMs are machines that work closely together, and therefore send a lot of data to one another. An example would be a set of VMs hosting the same application.

1.3.3   Clique Migration

A system called Clique Migration also migrates VMs based on their level of inter-action, and is directed at inter-site migrations. When Clique migrates a set of VMs, the first thing it does is to analyze the traffic patterns between them and try to pro-file their affinity. This is similar to the COMMA system. It then proceeds to create groups of VMs. All VMs within a group will be initiated for migration at the same time. The order of the groups is also calculated to minimize the cost of the process. The authors define the migration cost as the volume of inter-site traffic caused by the migration. Due to the fact that a VM will end up at a different physical location (a remote site), the VM's disk is also transferred along with the RAM.

1.3.4   Time-Bound Migration

A time-bound thread-based live migration (TLM) technique has been created. Its focus is to handle large migrations of VMs running RAM-heavy applications, by allocating additional processing power at the hypervisor level to the migration process. TLM can also slow down the operation of such instances to lower their dirty rate, which will help in lowering the total migration time. The completion of a migration in TLM is always within a given time period, proportional to the RAM size of the VMs.

All the aforementioned solutions migrate groups of VMs simultaneously, in one way or another, hence utilizing parallel migration to lower the total migration time. It has been found, in very recent research, that when running parallel migrations within data centers, an optimal sequential approach is preferable. A migration system called vHaul has been implemented which does this. It is argued that the application performance degradation caused by split components is caused by many VMs at a time, whereas only a single VM would cause degradation if sequential migration is used. However, the shortest possible migration time is not reached because vHaul's implementation has a no-migration interval between each VM migration. During this short time period, the pending requests to the moved VM are answered, which reduces the impact of queued requests during migration. vHaul is optimized for migrations within data centers which have dedicated migration links between physical hosts.

1.3.5 Measuring Migration Impact

It is commonly viewed that the live migration sequence can be divided into three parts when talking about the pre-copy method:

1. Disk image migration phase

2. Pre-copy phase

3. Stop-and-copy phase

1.4 Total Migration Time

The following mathematical formulas are used to calculate the time it takes to complete the different parts of the migration. Let W be the disk image size in megabytes (MB), L the bandwidth allocated to the VM's migration in MBps and T the predicted time in seconds. X is the amount of RAM which is transferred in each of the pre-copy iterations.

The time it takes to copy the image from the source PM to destination PM is:

$$T_i = \frac{W}{L} \tag{1.1}$$

1.4.1 VM Traffic Impact

The following formulas have been provided to describe the total network traffic amount and total migration duration, respectively. The number of iterations on the pre-copy phase (n) is not defined here, but is calculated based on a given threshold in Table 1.1.

Table 1.1   Variables used in formulas in the VM buddies system

Variable	Description
V	Total network traffic during migration
T	Time it takes to complete migration
N	Number of pre-copy rounds (iterations)
M	Size of VM RAM
d	Memory dirty rate during migration
r	Transmission rate during migration

Another possible metric for measuring how impactful a migration has been, is to look at the total amount of data the migrating VMs have sent between the source and destination PMs during the migration process. This would vary depending on how the scheduling of the VMs is orchestrated.

1.4.2 Bin Packing

The mathematical concept of bin packing centers around the practical optimization problem of packing a set of different sized "items" into a given number of "*bins*." The constraints of this problem are that all the bins are of the same size and that none of the items are larger than the size of one bin. The size of the bin can be thought of as its capacity. The optimal solution is the one which uses the smallest number of bins. This problem is known to be NP-hard, which in simple terms means that finding the optimal solution is computationally heavy. There are many real-life situations which relate to this principle.

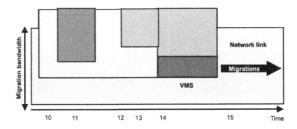

Figure 1.3   Bin packing in VM context.

In VM migration context, one can regard the VMs to be migrated as the items and the network links between the source and destination host as bins. The capacity in such a scenario would be the amount of available bandwidth which the migration process can use. Each VM requires a certain amount of bandwidth in order to be completed in a given time frame. If a VM scheduling mechanism utilized parallel migration, the bin packing problem is relevant because the start time of each migration is based on calculations of when it is likely to be finished, which in turn is based on bandwidth estimations. A key difference between traditional bin packing of physical objects and that of VMs on network links is that the VMs are infinitely flexible. This is shown in Figure 1.3. In this hypothetical scenario, VM_1 is being migrated between time t_0 and t_4, and uses three different levels of bandwidth before completion, since VM_2 and VM_3 are being migrated at times where VM_1 is still migrating. The main reason for performing parallel migrations is to utilize bandwidth more efficiently, but it could also be used to schedule migration of certain VMs at the same time.

1.5   Graph Partitioning

Graph partitioning refers [9] to a set of techniques used for dividing a network of vertices and edges into smaller parts. One appliance for such a technique could be to group VMs together in such a way that the VMs with a high degree of affinity are placed together. This could mean, for example, that they have a lot of network

traffic running between them. In graph partitioning context, the network links between VMs would be the edges and the VM's vertices. Figure 1.4 shows an example
of the interconnection of nodes in a network. The *"weight"* in the illustration could
represent the average traffic amount between two VMs in a given time interval, for
example. This can be calculated for the entire network, so that every network link
(*edge*) would have a value. The *"cut"* illustrates how one could divide the network
into two parts, which means that the cut must go through the entire network, effectively crossing edges so that the output is two disjoint subsets of nodes.

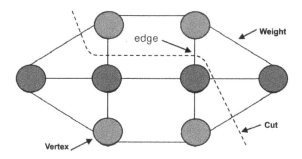

Figure 1.4   Nodes connected in a network.

If these nodes were MVs marked for simultaneous migration, and the sum of the
their dirty rate was greater than the bandwidth available for the migration task, the
migration will not converge. It is therefore imperative to divide the network into
smaller groups of VMs, so that each group is valid for migration. For a migration
technique which uses VM grouping, it is prudent to cut a network of nodes (*which
is too large to migrate all together*), using a minimum cut algorithm, in order to
minimize the traffic that goes between the subgroups during migration. The goal of
a minimum cut, when applied to a weighted graph, is to cut the graph across the
vertices in a way that leads to the smallest sum of weights. The resulting subsets of
the cut are not connected after this.

In a similar problem called the uniform graph partitioning problem, the number
of nodes in the resulting two sets have to be equal. This is known to be NP-complete
which means that there is no efficient way of finding a solution to the problem, but it
is takes very little time to verify if a given solution is in fact valid.

1.5.1   Learning Automata Partitioning

Multiple algorithms have been proposed for solving the graph partitioning problem
(see Figure 1.5). The time required to computationally discover the minimum cut is
very low, as there are few possibilities (*cuts over vertices*) which lead to exactly four
nodes in each subset. Note that the referenced figure's cut is not a uniform graph
cut resulting in two equal sized subsets, nor shows the weight of all the vertices. It
merely illustrates a graph cut.

To exemplify the complexity growth of graph cutting, one could regard two net-works, where one has 10 nodes and the other has 100. The amount of valid cuts and hence the solution space in the former case is 126, and 1029 for the latter. This clearly shows that a brute force approach would use a lot of time finding the optimal solution when there are many vertices. A number of heuristic and genetic algorithms have been proposed in order to try and find near-optimal solutions to this problem.

Learning automata is a science which divisions under the scope of adaptive con-trol in uncertain and random environments. Adaptive control is about managing a controller so that it can adapt to changing variables using adjustment calculations. The learning aspect refers to the way the controller in the environment gradually starts to pick more desirable actions based on feedback. The reaction from the en-vironment is to give either a reward or a penalty for the chosen action. In general control theory, control of a process is based on the control mechanism having com-plete knowledge of the environment's characteristics, meaning that the probability distribution in which the environment operates is deterministic, and that the future behavior of the process is predictable. Learning automata can, over time and by querying the environment, gain knowledge about a process where the probability distribution is unknown.

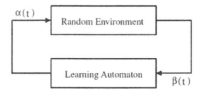

Figure 1.5   Learning automata.

In a stochastic environment, it is impossible to accurately predict a subsequent state, due to the non-deterministic nature of it. If a learning automata mechanism is initiated in such an environment, one can gradually attain more and more certain probabilities of optimal choices. This is done in a query-and-response fashion. The controller has a certain amount of available options, which initially have an equal opportunity of being a correct and optimal choice. One action is chosen, and the en-vironment responds with either a reward or a penalty. Subsequently, the probabilities are altered based on the response. If a selected action got rewarded, the probability of this same action should be increased before the next interaction (*iteration*) with the system, and lowered otherwise. This concept can be referred to as learning au-tomation.

The following is an example of how learning automation would work. Consider a program which expects an integer n as input, and validates it if $0 < n < 101$ and $n \bmod 4 = 0$. A valid input is a number between 1 and 100, which is divisible by 4. Now, let's say that the learning automation only knows the first constraint. Initially, all the valid options (1 - 100) have the probability value of 0.01 each, and the au-tomata choose one at random. A penalty or reward is received, and the probabilities are altered, with the constraint that

$$\sum_{x \in A} f_X(x) = 1 \tag{1.2}$$

where x is a valid option. After much iteration, all the numbers which the environment would validate should have an approximately equal probability, higher than the rest.

1.5.2   Advantages of Live Migration over WAN

Almost all the advantages of VM live migration [10] are currently limited to LAN, as migrating over WAN affects the performance due to low latency and network changes. The main goal of this chapter is to analyze the performance of various disk solutions available during the live migration of VM over WAN. When a VM using shared storage is live migrated to a deference physical host, end users interacting with a server running on the migrating VM should not sense notable changes in the performance of the server. Live migration is supported by various popular virtualization tools like VMware and Xen.

The following advantages of live migration over WAN have motivated us to devote a chapter to this area.

1. *Maintenance*: During the time of scheduled maintenance all the VMs running in the physical host are migrated to other physical host so that the maintenance work doesn't create an interruption to the services provided by the virtual machines.

2. *Scaling and Cloud Bursting*: Load balancing and consolidation can make best use of VMM over WAN. If the physical host gets overloaded beyond the capacity of hardware resources it will affect the performance of other VMs. So the VMs should be migrated (*cloud busted*) to physical hosts at other geographical locations to attain load balancing.

3. *Power Consumption*: VMs running on low populated hosts can be migrated to moderately load physical hosts at different locations. This allows the initial host to be shut down to reduce unnecessary power wastage.

4. *Disaster Recovery and Reliability*: During times of disaster the VM running on a physical host can be saved by migrating it to another physical host over WAN. When a physical host is corrupted or destroyed the VM can be recreated or booted at another mirror location by using the VM's shared disk and conguration file reducing the service downtimes.

5. *Follow-the-Sun*: It is a new IT strategy where a VM can be migrated between different time zones in a timely manner. This was designed for the teams working for a project round-the-clock. Team A works on a project during their working hours and the data is migrated to another location where team B will take care of the work during their work hours and migrate data to team A later.

1.6   Conclusion

Live migration is the technique of moving a VM from one physical host to another, while the VM is still executing. It is a powerful and handy tool for administrators to maintain SLAs while performing optimization tasks and maintenance on the cloud infrastructure. Live migration ideally requires the transfer of the CPU state, memory state, network state and disk state. Transfer of the disk state can be circumvented by having a shared storage between the hosts participating in the live migration process. This chapter briefly introduced the concept of live migration and the different techniques related to live migration, issues with live migration, research on live migration, learning automata partitioning and, finally, different advantages of live migration over WAN.

REFERENCES

1. Forsman, M., Glad, A., Lundberg, L., & Ilie, D. (2015). Algorithms for automated live migration of virtual machines. Journal of Systems and Software, 101, 110-126..

2. Akoush, S., Sohan, R., Rice, A., Moore, A. W., & Hopper, A. (2010). Predicting the performance of virtual machine migration. In Modeling, Analysis & Simulation of Computer and Telecommunication Systems (MASCOTS), 2010 IEEE International Symposium (pp. 37-46). IEEE.

3. Alamdari, J. F., & Zamanifar, K. (2012, December). A reuse distance based precopy approach to improve live migration of virtual machines. In Parallel Distributed and Grid Computing (PDGC), 2012 2nd IEEE International Conference (pp. 551-556). IEEE.

4. Anand, A., Dhingra, M., Lakshmi, J., & Nandy, S. K. (2012). Resource usage monitoring for KVM based virtual machines. In Advanced Computing and Communications (ADCOM), 2012 18th Annual International Conference (pp. 66-70). IEEE.

5. Arlos, P., Fiedler, M., & Nilsson, A. A. (2005, March). A Distributed Passive Measurement Infrastructure. In PAM (Vol. 2005, pp. 215-227).

6. Armbrust, M., Fox, A., Griffith, R., Joseph, A. D., Katz, R. H., Konwinski, A., ... & Zaharia, M. (2009). Above the clouds: A Berkeley view of cloud computing (Vol. 17). Technical Report UCB/EECS-2009-28, EECS Department, University of California, Berkeley.

7. Beloglazov, A., & Buyya, R. (2015). OpenStack Neat: a framework for dynamic and energy-efficient consolidation of virtual machines in OpenStack clouds. *Concurrency and Computation: Practice and Experience*, 27(5), 1310-1333.

8. Cerroni, W. (2014). Multiple virtual machine live migration in federated cloud systems. In Computer Communications Workshops (INFOCOM WKSHPS), 2014 IEEE Conference (pp. 25-30). IEEE.

9. Chadwick, D. W., Siu, K., Lee, C., Fouillat, Y., & Germonville, D. (2014). Adding federated identity management to OpenStack. *Journal of Grid Computing*, 12(1), 3-27.

10. Clark, C., Fraser, K., Hand, S., Hansen, J. G., Jul, E., Limpach, C., ... & Warfield, A. (2005). Live migration of virtual machines. In Proceedings of the 2nd Conference on

Symposium on Networked Systems Design & Implementation-Volume 2 (pp. 273-286). USENIX Association.

11. Rodriguez, Esteban, et al.(2017), Energy-aware mapping and live migration of virtual networks. *IEEE Systems Journal* 11.2,pp. 637-648.

12. Singh, G., & Gupta, P. (2016). A review on migration techniques and challenges in live virtual machine migration. In Reliability, Infocom Technologies and Optimization (Trends and Future Directions)(ICRITO), 2016 5th International Conference (pp. 542-546). IEEE.

13. Kansal, N. J., & Chana, I. (2016). Energy-aware virtual machine migration for cloud computing a firefly optimization approach. *Journal of Grid Computing*, 14(2), 327-345.

14. He, S., Hu, C., Shi, B., Wo, T., & Li, B. (2016). Optimizing Virtual Machine Live Migration without Shared Storage in Hybrid Clouds. In High Performance Computing and Communications; IEEE 14th International Conference on Smart City; IEEE 2nd International Conference on Data Science and Systems (HPCC/SmartCity/DSS), 2016 IEEE 18th International Conference (pp. 921-928). IEEE.

15. Al-Dhuraibi, Y., Paraiso, F., Djarallah, N., & Merle, P. (2017). Elasticity in Cloud Computing: State of the Art and Research Challenges. *IEEE Transactions on Services Computing*.

CHAPTER 2

LIVE VIRTUAL MACHINE MIGRATION IN CLOUD

Abtract

With a specific end goal to ensure that live migration of virtual machines is secure, there should be a verification method that secures the correspondence sheet between the source and final VMMs as well as the administration servers and specialists. The director ought to approach security arrangements that control viable migration of benefits that are allocated to different players required over the span of relocation. The alleged passage utilized by relocation must be secure and have arrangements set up to recognize sniffing and control of the information or movement state amid the migration stage. This should be possible by ensuring the vMotion parameter is scrambled effectively which right now is by all accounts in a condition of testing or needs broad additional items and checking. One imperative thing that can be set up is the partitioned virtual switches for vMotion.

Keywords: Virtualization, types, applications, virtualization system, machine.

2.1   Introduction

At the point when virtualization was first considered in the 1960s, it was referred to by software engineers and scientists as time sharing. Multiprogramming and comparative thoughts started to drive development, which brought about a few PCs like the Atlas and IBM's M44/44X. Mapbook PC was one of the primary supercomputers of the mid-1960s that utilized ideas such as time sharing, multiprogramming, and additionally shared fringe control. ChartBook was one of the quickest PCs mainly because a partition of OS forms from the executing client programs. The segment called the director dealt with the PC's handling of time, and passed additional codes along these lines, helping in the administration of the client program's guidelines. This was considered tobe the introduction of the hypervisor or virtual machine screen [1].

2.1.1   Virtualization

Virtualization [2] refers to the creation of a virtual version of a device or resource, such as a server, storage resource, network or even an operating system wherever the framework divides the resource into one or more execution environments. In other words, virtualization is a framework or methodology of dividing the resources of a computer into multiple execution environments, by applying one or additional concepts or technologies such as hardware and software partitioning, time-sharing, partial or complete machine simulation, quality of service, emulation and many others (see Figure 2.1).

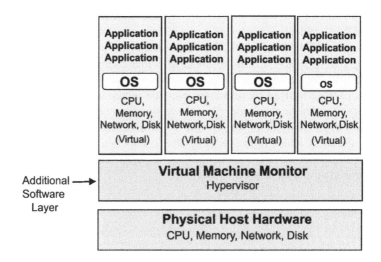

Figure 2.1   Simple representation of a virtualized system.

2.1.1.1 *Importance of Virtualization*   Live migration (LM) has many favorable circumstances. It gives the client adaptability and choices to bring down a working server midday, rather than around evening time or on weekends, overhaul the working framework, apply patches, and so forth; at that point it can be duplicated again during normal working hours. This is an extremely valuable idea; for example, operations administrators in server farms look at where they have huge workloads and move VMs around so the cooling framework is not working too hard in an attempt to simply keep a part of the data focus at the correct temperature. Virtualization is divided into two main parts: Process VM and System VM (see Figure 2.2).

2.1.1.2 *Benefits of Virtualization*

1. VM is acclimated to solidify the workloads of numerous underutilized servers to fewer machines, maybe a solitary machine (*server combination*).

2. Related favorable circumstances are reserve funds on equipment, natural costs, administration, and organization of the server foundation.

3. The need to run legacy applications is served well by VMs.

4. VMs can be utilized to give secure, segregated sandboxes for running VMs non-put stock in applications. Virtualization is a vital idea in building secure figuring stages.

5. VMs are utilized to make working frameworks or execute conditions with asset points of confinement, and given the right schedulers, ensure assets.

6. VMs can offer the figment of equipment, or equipment arrangement that you essentially don't have (for example, SCSI gadgets, different processors, and so on).

7. VMs are utilized to run numerous agent frameworks at the same time: unique forms, or completely extraordinary frameworks, can be on hot standby.

8. VMs accommodate effective investigation and execution observation.

9. VMs can disconnect what they run, with the goal of offering blame and mistake control. VMs make programming less demanding to move, consequently supporting application and framework versatility.

10. VMs are incredible instruments for examination and scholastic trials.

11. Virtualization can change existing agent frameworks to keep running on shared memory multiprocessors.

12. VMs are utilized to make self-assertive check situations, and may cause to some extremely innovative, successful quality affirmation.

13. Virtualization can make undertakings, for example, framework migration, reinforcement, and recuperation, less demanding and more sensible.

14. Virtualization is a successful method for giving twofold similarity.

2.1.2   Types of Virtual Machines

The types of virtual machines are process VMs and system VMs (see Table 2.1).

Table 2.1   Types of virtual machines

Process Virtual Machine	System Virtual Machine
Virtualizing software translates instructions	It provides a complete
from one platform to another platform	system environment
It helps execute programs developed for	Operating system + User Process
a difference operating system or difference ISA	Networking + I/O + Display + GUI
Virtual machine terminates when guest process terminates	Lasts as long as hot is alive

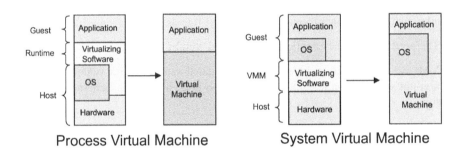

Figure 2.2   Types of virtual machines

2.1.3   Virtual Machine Applications

Virtual machine applications are given in Figure 2.3 and Table 2.2.

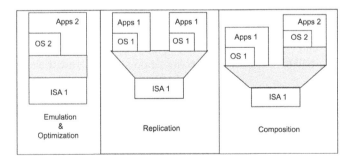

Figure 2.3   Virtual machine applications

Table 2.2   Virtual machine applications

Applications	Description
Emulation	It permits blend and match cross-stage convenience.
Optimization	It gives stage particular execution change. It is normally finished with imitating.
Replication	This permits having various VMs on a solitary stage.
Composition	Similar to replication yet shapes more mind-boggling yet adaptable frameworks.

Concert goal in migration:

1. Migration of VMs limits *"downtime"*.

2. One of the real execution objectives in migration is decrease of aggregate migration time of VMs.

3. It aides if there is no impedance with typical framework movement, which is an imperative objective of migration.

4. To limit arrange action is additionally an execution objective in migration.

2.2   Business Challenge

At first virtualization [3] was held onto as a strategy to combine numerous server applications on fewer servers in order to build usage and diminish vital necessities. Today, IT associations are looking past just server solidification. Today virtualization is being utilized to make more unique server farms.

LM powerfully dispenses and balances registering assets and accordingly encourages us to adjust the foundation to big business level business objectives. LM performs migrations without really intruding upon the administrations the VMs are giving and in this way lessening the extra work normally included with relocating VMs. Generally, the additional work includes first closing down the applications, at that point moving the VMs to new servers and lastly restarting the VMs and the applications that were shutdown. So by taking out this extra work, LM enhances adaptability and effectiveness in overseeing server farm assets.

Propelled server hubs are profited by LM by utilization of the following abilities:

1. Dynamic load balancing

2. No VM downtime during maintenance

2.2.1   Dynamic Load Balancing

Dynamic load balancing (DLB) [4] can change the mapping of employments to assets anytime, however there might be a cost related with the progressions. There are two fundamental sorts of DLB methods: preemptive and non-preemptive. In a preemptive calculation, the mapping of employments to physical assets may change while a vocation is running; however, with non-preemptive calculations, once work has begun the physical assets alloted to that occupation can't change. DLB redistributes undertakings amid execution, which normally moves assignments from vigorously stacked processors to gently stacked processors. Likewise, the DLB methods can be incorporated or conveyed. In a unified plan, all data is sent to a solitary basic leadership operator that chooses when stack adjusting will happen and which assignments will be moved. In circulated DLB, stack data is not shared internationally and all processors participate to choose when stack adjusting happens and which errands will be moved. One noteworthy favorable position of DLB is that the runtime conduct of the framework isn't known ahead of time. While these methods are great at expanding usage of all assets, there is a runtime overhead connected with social occasion data and exchanging errands to various processors.

2.2.2 No VM Downtime During Maintenance

Virtual machine nonitors were produced to better use the costly centralized computer equipment and its assets with the goal that numerous applications and servers could coincide on the same physical host. The inspiration for examining this field today is expanding significantly as more equipment is created with work in local virtualization support and more programming arrangements showing up.

Unwavering quality and an excess of entries are included in current virtualization innovation. The mission of basic applications doesn't endure downtime and partnerships can rapidly lose cash if their accessibility is influenced by upkeep, equipment or programming disappointment or malevolent action. Virtual machine innovation manages this test basically just by moving the virtual machine(s) from the physical host that necessitates upkeep onto other server equipment while the virtual machine is running and keeping up benefit accessibility. With the VMs running somewhere else there is no damage in doing a server shutdown, keeping in mind the end goal that the upkeep be done in a fast and undisturbed manner.

2.3 Virtual Machine Migration

Virtual machine migration (VMM) [8] is the process of moving a working/running virtual machine from one physical host to another physical host without interrupting the services provided by it. During migration the memory, CPU, network and disk states are moved to the destination host. The end users using the services provided by the virtual machine should not detect the notable changes. There are three types of migrations: cold migration, hot migration and LM. In cold migration, the virtual machine is rst powered off at the source node before migrating it to the destination node. CPU state, memory state and existing network connections in the guest OS are lost during cold migration. In hot migration, the virtual machine is suspended at the source node before migrating it to the destination node where it is resumed. Most of the OS state can be preserved during this migration.

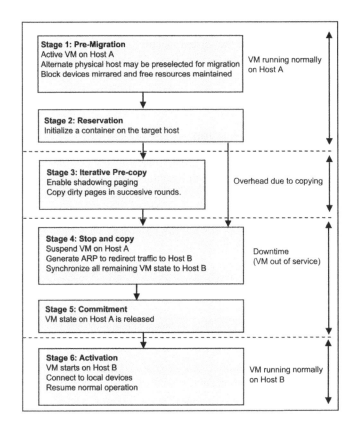

Figure 2.4   Xen live migration

In LM the hosted operating system is migrated along with CPU, memory and disk state from source to destination while the hosted OS is still in running state without losing the active network connectivity. The disk state migration is not necessary in the case of using shared storages like network-attached storage (NAS) or storage area network (SAN). Among the three migration techniques, LM is best suited to reduce notable downtime of services running on the virtual machine. By using LM, load on physical machines hosting several VMs can be decreased to a large extent. LM may increase the total migration time of the VM's running server applications.

In order to perform LM, hypervisor needs to move the memory state of the virtual machine from the source point to the destination physical machine. The crucial method used for migrating memory state is known as pre-copy, and is clearly explained. In pre-copy phase the memory state of virtual machine is copied to destination host in iterations. Unmodied or unused pages are moved in rst round and modied pages are moved in next nth round. Hypervisor maintains dirty bitmap to track modied pages. If predetermined bandwidth is reached or when bandwidth range is below 256 kb, pre-copy phase is terminated and stop-and-copy phase is initiated. In stop-and-copy phase the virtual machine is paused on source point host and modied pages are copied to destination host. The virtual host is resumed at the destination host and starts working as usual. The Xen LM timeline is shown Figure 2.4.

2.3.1   Advantages of Virtualization

Some of the advantages of virtualization are hardware abstraction and server consolidation where several small physical server machines can be efficiently replaced by a single physical machine with many virtual server machines. Virtualization is cost efficient. It eliminates the need of several individual physical server machines, thereby reducing the physical space, energy utilization, etc. A list of advantages associated with virtualization is shown in Table 2.3.

Table 2.3   Advantages associated with virtualization

No.	Description
1	Server consolidation and hardware abstraction
2	Proper resource utilization
3	Cost reduction
4	Low power consumption
5	Reduction of physical space
6	Global warming and corporate greenhouse gas reduction
7	Flexibility
8	High availability...

2.3.2   Components of Virtualization

Virtualization has two important components, namely the hypervisor [9], or virtual machine monitor and the guest. The hypervisor is responsible for managing the virtualization layer. There are Type-1 and Type-2 hypervisors. Type-1 and Type-2 hypervisors are shown below in Figure 2.5.

Type-1 hypervisor, which is also known as bare-metal hypervisor, runs directly above the host's hardware. It has direct access to the hardware resources. It provides greater exibility and better performance due to its design. Xen, Microsoft Hyper-V and VMware ESX are Type-1 hypervisors. Type-2 hypervisor works on top of the host machine's operating system as an application. For every virtual machine there is one virtual machine monitor to run and control them for this reason there is one virtual platform for each and every virtual machine to work. VirtualBox, VMware Player and VMware Workstation are examples of Type-2 hypervisors.

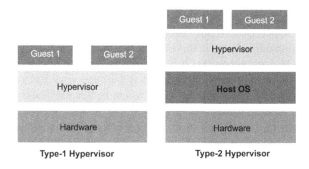

Figure 2.5   Type-1 and type-2 hypervisor

The guest is the virtual host that runs above the virtualization layer. The virtual host has its own operating system (OS) and applications. This guest operating system can be migrated from one physical host to another physical host.

2.3.3   Types of Virtualization

VMware, which is one of the world's biggest organizations currently gaining practical experience in virtualization, is essentially depicted as as "the partition of an administration asks for from the hidden physical delivery of that administration." What VMware focuses on with the expression "hidden delivery" of an administration is that the specific execution of the guideline started by a VM, for instance a processor asks for or a memory operation, is taken care of by an intermediary. The VM could conceivably know that this is occurring, contingent upon the method of virtualization utilized as a part of the framework. One can manufacture a virtualization stage in various diverse ways. With a specific end goal to fathom the distinctions and details behind each of them, there are some frequently utilized terms which require clarification:

- The guest is a virtual machine running on top of a virtualization infrastructure. The guest is usually, in itself, a fully functional OS.

- The host is a machine which delegates resources to a guest.

- The hypervisor is the abstraction layer between the physical hardware and the host. The hypervisor is usually referred to as a *"virtual machine manager"* (VMM). This is the proxy that carries out instructions on behalf of the guest. Virtualization can be classified into three types: full virtualization, paravirtualization and hardware-assisted virtualization.

2.3.3.1   Full Virtualization   This is outline astute, and the least difficult type of virtualization. A hypervisor is straightforwardly introduced onto the physical unit, which has at least one of each of the standard PC gadgets introduced: organize card, hard drive, processor, and memory (RAM). The hypervisor type utilized here is an uncovered metal hypervisor, which is also alluded to as "sort 1." The OS that the visitor utilizes is unmodified, and in this manner sees the gadgets as "genuine," which implies that the OS can't verify that it is being virtualized. Off camera, the visitor OS is allotted assets from the PM. The way that the hypervisor has guide access to the equipment can make this method of operation more adaptable and productive.

In any case, this virtualization mode depends on parallel interpretation of CPU guidelines between the visitor and host, as it reenacts all the hidden equipment to the visitors, which can effectively affect productivity regarding overhead. Full virtualization gives visitors an entire blueprint of a PC framework. On the off chance that security is of critical concern, it is prescribed to utilize a full virtualization suite, as it can give careful disconnection of running applications. The hypervisor can divide assets into pools, and it is regular practice to just enable one pool to a VM and just host one application for every VM. In the event that a PM is running numerous VMs, which together serve numerous applications, a security rupture event can cause a great deal of harm.

2.3.3.2 *Paravirtualization*

Along these lines, arranging virtualization depends on changing the OS of the visitor and including the hypervisor layer of the host. The hypervisor at that point exists between the host and the visitors. This requires a *"Type 2"* hypervisor, which is also called a facilitated hypervisor, and henceforth this kind of virtualization is otherwise called facilitated virtualization. It is basically a program that keeps running on the host OS. In this engineering, each VM can know that it is being run virtualized, as changes must be made on the visitor OS. With present day OS pictures, this happens naturally amid establishment. The asset demands from the visitor needs to experience the hypervisor on the host before achieving the physical assets, which can make it all the more overhead overwhelming. Be that as it may, since the VMM is little and straightforward in paravirtualization, visitors can frequently accomplish *"close local"* execution.

This implies VMs are near executing directions as quickly as a physical PC with similar details. The visitors don't keep running on copied gadgets, as in full virtualization, yet rather get to assets through extraordinary gadget drivers [5, 6]. In the x86 design (see Figure 2.6), there is the idea of benefit rings. A x86 OS normally keeps running in the most favored level, "ring-0", while ring-1, ring-2 and ring-3 are lesser advantaged modes (*"client level rings"*). An OS needs to play out its executions in ring-0. At the point when a VM starts such a guideline (*called a hypercall*), it is caught and executed by the hypervisor running close by the host OS, for the benefit of the visitor [7].

2.3.3.3 *Hardware-Assisted Virtualization*

Hardware-assisted virtualization is also called accelerated virtualization. This technique allows users to use unmodied operating system by using the special features provided by computer hardware. Both Intel and AMD started supporting hardware virtualization (VT-x/AMD-V) ever since 2006. In this technique, the virtual machine monitor runs on a root mode privilege level below the ring-0. That is, hardware virtualization creates an additional privilege level below ring-0 which contains hypervisor and leaves ring-0 for un-

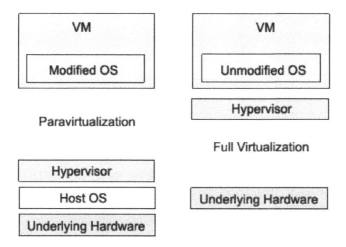

Figure 2.6   Simplified architecture of para- and full virtualization.

modied guest operating system. The protective ring structure of hardware-assisted virtualization is shown in Figure 2.7. CPUs manufactured before 2006 cannot take advantage of this system.

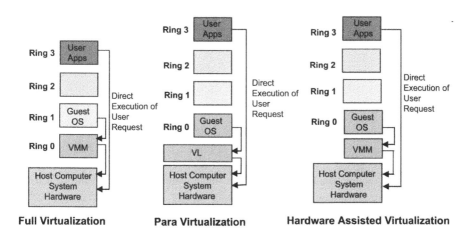

Figure 2.7   Types of virtualization.

2.4   Virtualization System

2.4.1   Xen Hypervisor

Xen, shown in Figure 2.8, is an open source hypervisor developed at the University of Cambridge computer science lab which supports both hardware-assisted virtualization and paravirtualization. It also supports LM of VMs. Xen is one of the VM1 type-1 or bare-metal hypervisors that are available as open source. Xen allows multiple operating systems to run parallel to host operating system. Xen is used for different open source and commercial applications such as server virtualization, desktop virtualization, infrastructure as a service (IaaS), security, and hardware and embedded appliances. Today Xen hypervisor is powering large clouds in production. The Xen hypervisor is responsible for handling interrupts, scheduling CPU and managing memory for the virtual machines.

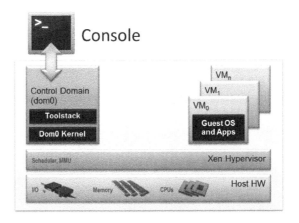

Figure 2.8   Xen architecture.

Dom0, or the Domain-0, is the domain in which Xen starts during the boot. From the Xen architecture which is shown in Figure 2.8 we can see that Dom0 is the privileged control domain which has direct access to the underlying hardware. The Dom0 has the toolstack which is a user management interface to the Xen hypervisor. Xen toolstack can create, manage and destroy VMs, or domUs, which are unprivileged domains. Xen supports hardware virtualization and paravirtualization. In hardware virtualization, unmodified operating systems can be used for the virtual machines, whereas paravirtualization requires modification to the operating system's kernel running inside virtual machines. Doing so will increase the performance of paravirtualized hosts. The host operating system should be Xen PV (paravirtualization) [10] enabled to create VMs. The Linux kernels before the 2.6.37 version are not paravirtualization enabled. Their kernels should be recompiled to enable paravirtualization. All the Linux kernels released after the 2.6.37 version are by default Xen PV enabled [13].

Xen allows VMs to migrate between hosts while the guest OS is running. This feature is called live migration. In Xen, the demons running in the `Dom0` of source and destination hosts takes the responsibility of migration. The memory and CPU states of the VM are migrated from source machine to destination machine by the control domain. The Xen hypervisor copies memory pages in a series of rounds using dynamic rate limiting and rapid page dirtying techniques to reduce the service downtime. The dynamic rate limiting algorithm adapts bandwidth limit for each pre-copy round and is used to decide when the pre-copy stage should end and stop-and-copy phase should start. The rapid page dirtying algorithm is used to detect the rapidly dirtied 2 pages and skip copying them in the pre-copy stage. Xen uses a microkernel design which consists of a small footprint and interface that is around 1 MB of size, making it more secure and robust than the other available hypervisors. Xen hypervisor is capable of running the main device driver for a system inside a VM. The VM that contains the main device driver and device driver can be rebooted leaving the rest of the system unaffected. This feature of Xen is called driver isolation. Driver isolation is a safe execution environment which protects the VMs from any buggy drivers. Xen is OS agnostic, which means different OSes, like NetBSD and OpenSolaris can be hosted.

Basically, Xen supports two types of virtual block devices named 'Phy' and 'file.' Phy is the physical block device which is available in the host environment whereas file is the disk image which is available in the form of a file in the host computer. The loop block device is create from the available image file and the block device is handled by the `domU`. Shared storage solutions like iSCSI use `Phy` and NFS use file [14].

2.4.2   KVM Hypervisor

Kernel-based virtual machine (KVM) is an open-source virtualization solution for Linux developed by Qumranet Inc., which was later acquired by Red Hat, Inc. It relies on the virtualization extensions in the Intel VT and AMD-V generation of processors to enable hardware-assisted virtualization capabilities in the host. KVM is implemented in the form of kernel modules which transform the Linux kernel into a bare-metal (`type-1`) hypervisor and allows unmodified OSes to run as VMs. It consists of a loadable kernel module (`kvm.ko`) that provides the core virtualization infrastructure and processor-specific modules, `kvm_intel.ko` and `kvm_amd.ko`, for the Intel and AMD processors respectively.

The KVM kernel module was merged with the mainline Linux kernel version 2.6.20 and has been part of the kernel since then, making it the default hypervisor in a Linux distro. This allows KVM to take advantage of the capability and support of the host Linux kernel for dealing with complex hardware and resource management tasks such as process scheduling, memory management, etc. Moreover, it also obtains full driver support from the kernel for devices like network cards, storage adapters, etc.

The architecture of KVM consists mainly of two components (Figure 2.9), a kernel and a user-space component. The kernel component is the KVM kernel module itself, which exposes the virtualization extensions to the user space via a character device `/dev/kvm`. The guest code is executed on the host hardware via this device node. KVM also adds a new guest mode of execution to the kernel and user modes on the host kernel for the execution of guest code. In this way, KVM provides the core virtualization infrastructure but does not perform any device emulation or VM management. This is handled by a user-space component which is the QEMU-KVM backend, a slightly modified QEMU (*Quick EMUlator*) process. It works similar to normal QEMU for device emulation, spawning VMs, migration of VMs, etc; but instead of completely emulating vCPUs, it implements them in the form of normal Linux threads on the host's user space and uses the guest execution mode. Each vCPU of the guests is implement as a Linux thread. This makes all guests running in this model look like normal Linux processes and the host kernel scheduler carries out the scheduling of these vCPU threads. One advantage of such an implementation of guests in the form of threads on the host kernel is that they can now be managed from the host for scheduling, setting priorities and affinities.

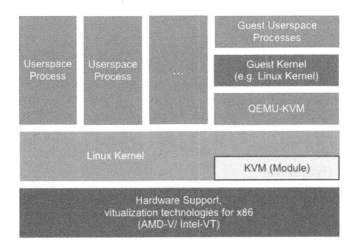

Figure 2.9   Architecture of KVM.

From this architecture, we can say that KVM is more of a virtualization infrastructure provider and the hypervisor here is actually a combination of KVM and QEMU.

2.4.2.1 KVM Management   Libvirt is the primary management library for KVM management. It provides an API which is used by tools such as `virt-install`, `virsh`, `virt-manager`, etc, to interact with the KVM/QEMU hypervisor for VM management and monitoring. It also enables these tools or applications to manipulate guests, automate management tasks and configure virtual storage and networks.

Overall, the complete virtualization capability is the combination of KVM, QEMU and libvirt.

2.4.2.2   *VirtIO* KVM supports paravirtualization as well as using the VirtIO API. Virtio is the Linux standard for a paravirtualization device and has been part of the kernel modules since version 2.6.25. The rationale behind using virtio was to have a common framework for hypervisors for paravirtualization of I/O devices. For now, virtio provides network, block and memory balloon paravirtualized drives in KVM to improve efficiency of I/O and allows adjusting memory availability to guest at runtime. The implementation is in user space (qemu-kvm), so no driver is needed in the host but the guests must have the virtio kernel drivers.

The KVM/QEMU hypervisor allows VMM [11] of running as well as stopped or suspended VMs across hosts. The actual process of migration is carried out by the qemu-kvm backend of the KVM/QEMU hypervisor.

Live migration in this model means moving a guest from one QEMU process and making it run on top of another at the destination host while the guest is still running on the source host. The content that is to be transferred here is the entire memory content as well as the state of each device that has been assigned to the guest by QEMU. Live migration requires that the QEMU is set up identically on both hosts. This is overcome by initiating the migration via the libvirt API, which helps performs checks to ensure successful migration [15].

The pre-copy migration algorithm is used for migration of memory state. Pre-copy requires dirty page tracking and this is provided to QEMU by KVM with the help of a migration bitmap. The bitmap constitutes one bit per page. At the commencement of migration, the memory pages are mapped as read-only and wait for the interrupt command by the first write operation at the destination. QEMU also maintains a bitmap using one byte per page. The KVM bitmap is merged with QEMU's before every memory transfer iteration (see Table 2.4).

Table 2.4   Kernel-based virtual machine features

No.	Features Description
1	Block migration for transferring disk state to the destination.
2	Encryption of data using TLS or SSH.
3	Data compression using utilities like gzip.
4	Tunneling of VM state through an external program.
5	Auto-convergence to force convergence during memory transfer.
6	Xor binary zero run-length-encoding (XBZRLE) compression to reduce VM downtime and total live-migration time when migrating VMs with write-intensive workloads.
7	Remote direct memory access (RDMA) live migration to make migration more deterministic uses the RDMA I/O architecture.

2.4.3   OpenStack

OpenStack is a Python-based open-source cloud platform which started as a joint venture by Rackspace Hosting and NASA in the year 2010, and OpenStack Kilo is the latest (11th) release (see Figure 2.10). It is a *cloud operating system that controls large pools of compute, network resources and storage throughout a data center, all managed through a dashboard that gives administrators control while empowering their users to provision resources through a web interface.* As mentioned, Open-Stack consolidates all the resources in a data center into pools of compute, storage and networking resources. These pools of resources can be managed either through a web-based dashboard, command-line interface tools or RESTful API. OpenStack is simple to implement, massively scalable and meets the needs of the cloud infrastructure regardless of size. The OpenStack architecture is a modular architecture meaning that it consists of multiple separate components working together. Moreover, in such architecture components can be replaced, removed or added without affecting the rest of the system.

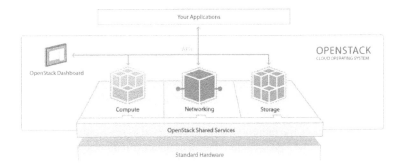

Figure 2.10   OpenStack architecture

2.4.3.1   OpenStack Services   OpenStack provides an IaaS solution through a set of interrelated services which can be integrated with each other using the service's API. Each service has multiple processes. For inter-process communication, an AMQP (advanced message queuing protocol) message broker is used. Also, the state of the services and other information corresponding to the cloud deployed is stored in a database. Administrators can choose, while deploying and configuring the OpenStack cloud, among several message brokers and databases such as RabbitMQ, Qpid, MySQL, MariaDB and SQLite. The OpenStack services with their project names are as follows: Compute, Networking, Storage, Image, Identity, Dashboard, Telemetry, and Orchestration.

2.4.3.2   Compute Service   The OpenStack compute service manages the life cycle of the instances (VMs) in an OpenStack environment. Its responsibilities include spawning, scheduling, migrating and decommissioning instances on-demand.

This service does not include any virtualization software but instead defines set of drivers that interact with the underlying hypervisor and its API such as libvirt for KVM/QEMU, XenAPI for XenServer, etc. The compute service comprises of an API service (*Nova Api*), core compute service (*Nova Compute*), a scheduler to select suitable compute host for an instance (*Nova Scheduler*), X509 certificate server (*Nova Cert*) and a mediator between the Nova Compute and the cloud database (*Nova Conductor*).

2.4.3.3 *Networking*   The networking service enables Network-Connectivity-as-a-Service for the other services such as Compute. Neutron provides layer-2 and layer-3 connectivity to instances. It uses either Linux bridging or Open vSwitch for layer-2 Ethernet connectivity and switching purposes. It has a pluggable architecture supporting many networking technologies and vendors. It also provides an API for defining network connectivity, and addressing, and configuring network services such as layer-3 forwarding, NAT, edge firewalls and IPsec VPN.

2.4.4 Storage

Storage for instances in OpenStack is of two types: ephemeral and persistent storage. Ephemeral storage is implemented as a filesystem on the Compute node in an OpenStack environment and is associated with the instance. This storage persists as long as the instance exists and is removed once the instance is terminated. Persistent storage, on the other hand, outlives the life of the instance and is available regardless of the instance's state. OpenStack provides two types of persistent storage: block storage (*Cinder*) and object storage (*Swift*).

The block storage service, Cinder, provides persistent block storage to running instances. These block devices, also called volumes, are pluggable and can be formatted, partitioned and mounted just like conventional disks or partitions. Swift is a multi-tenant object storage service. It is highly available, highly scalable and can manage large amounts of unstructured data objects via a RESTful, HTTP-based API. It uses a distributed architecture with no central control point, thereby providing greater scalability, redundancy and permanence. The objects are written to multiple hardware devices for ensuring data replication and integrity across the cluster. Swift storage can be used by Glance image service for storing VM images as well as by the Cinder service for backing up VM volumes.

2.4.4.1 *Image Service*   Glance image service provides discovery, registration, and delivery services for disk and server images. The ability to copy or snapshot a server image and store it away is the key feature of Glance. These stored images are used as templates while provisioning instances. Glance stores the disk and server images in various repositories, including the Swift object-storage system. It also supports multiple image formats, including `raw`, `vhd` (Hyper-V), `vdi` (VirtualBox), `qcow2` (QEMU/KVM), `vmdk` (VMware), etc.

2.4.4.2 *Identity Service*   Keystone is the default identity management system for OpenStack and is primarily responsible for providing authentication and authorization service for the users and the OpenStack services. It uses token-based authentication to authenticate and authorize an incoming request by checking against a catalog of users, domains, projects and roles. It also provides a catalog of API endpoints or URLs for all available OpenStack services.

2.4.4.3 Dashboard   This service provides a web-based management interface. It allows the cloud administrators and users to control their compute, storage and networking resources. For the cloud administrators, it gives an overall view of the state of the cloud and enables carrying out administrative tasks such as creating users and projects, modifying quotas for users, limiting resources for projects and so on. Horizon is a self-service portal for users, which can be used to provision resources, launch instances, configure networks, etc. It also provides an API which can be used by third parties for integration.

2.4.4.4 Telemetry Service   This service monitors and meters the OpenStack cloud for purposes like billing, benchmarking, scalability and statistical analysis. It operates by aggregating usage and performance data from across the services deployed in an OpenStack cloud. By doing so, Ceilometer provides an insight into the usage of the cloud across dozens of data points.

2.4.4.5 Orchestration Service   The OpenStack orchestration service, code-named Heat, allows application developers to explain and automate the redying of infrastructure in the form of templates. Heat orchestrates multiple composite cloud applications by using either the native HOT (heat orchestration template) format or the AWS (Amazon web services) CloudFormation template format, through both the OpenStack REST API and a CloudFormation-compatible Query API. The flexible template language can specify the configurations as well as detailed post-deployment activity to automate complete provisioning of the infrastructure, services and applications.

2.4.4.6 Migration of VMs in OpenStack   OpenStack provides different types of VM migration non-live migration (*also referred simply as "migration"*). This is performed by executing the "*nova migrates*" command. In this migration type, the instance is shut down and moved to another compute node chosen by the Nova Scheduler. The instance is rebooted at the destination. Live migration, or "*true live migration*," is the actual true seamless live migration which ensures almost no downtime of the instance. There are three different types of this live migration provided by OpenStack based on the storage used by the instance:

- *Shared storage-based live migration*: Both hypervisors have access to shared storage.

- *Block live migration*: Disk state is also transferred and hence no shared storage is required.

However, it is incompatible with read-only devices such as CD-ROMs and with `config_drive` enabled. Configuration drive (`config_drive`) is a special drive consisting of metadata that is attached to the instance upon booting. In volume-backed live migration the instances are backed by volumes rather than ephemeral disk and no shared storage is required. It is currently supported for libvirt-based hypervisors. OpenStack also provides an extension or an add-on called OpenStack Neat, which is an implementation of dynamic VM consolidation using live migration technique. The OpenStack Neat service has three components, namely, Global Manager, Local Manager and Data Collector. These components and the service, as a whole, can be integrated into existing OpenStack deployments and configured with custom algorithms as well for dynamic consolidation and placement of VMs.

2.4.5 Server Virtualization

Server virtualization facilitates the creation of multiple VMs in a single physical machine. The physical machine is termed the host and the VMs that run on the host are termed guests. The terms VMs and guests can be used interchangeably. Each VM is assigned its share of the host's physical resources (CPU, memory, disk, I/O, etc.) by a middleware called the hypervisor, which runs on the host.

2.5   Live Virtual Machine Migration

Defined in the simplest terms, live virtual machine migration is the transfer of VM/s from one physical machine to another with minimal or no service downtime (Figure 2.11).

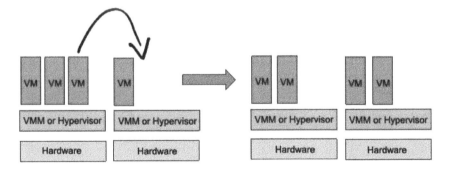

Figure 2.11   Virtual machine migration.

Migration Types: There are generally two basic types of migration which may be categorized as pre-copy and post-copy as discussed in the previous chapter. Following are some specific migration techniques:

Stop-and-Copy Migration: This type of migration is non-live migration [12]. This type of migration results in VM downtime. It works well for VMs under maintenance. The only positive aspect of this type of migration is that it provides a baseline to compare the total number of pages transferred and the total migration time.

Following are the details regarding stop-and-copy migration:

1. The source VM (*one that has to be migrated*) is stopped (*shut down*).

2. All the pages are copied over the network.

3. Finally, the destination VM is started.

4. This migration type has the longest service downtime.

5. This migration type has the shortest migration duration.

Demand Migration: This type of migration is based on post-copy based live VM migration. Following are the details regarding demand migration:

1. Initially all the critical and essential OS structures are copied over the network.

2. Then the destination VM is started.

3. Every page fault triggers copy of those pages over the network.

4. This migration type has the shortest service downtime.

5. This migration type has the longest migration duration.

Iterative Pre-Copy Migration: This type of migration combines pre-copy migration with a bounded iterative push phase. This migration type also involves a very short stop-and-copy phase. Following are the details regarding iterative pre-copy migration:

1. Iteratively copies pages over the network from source to destination.

2. Keeps copying pages until a particular threshold is reached, then stops source VM and further copies all the remaining pages, before finally starting the destination VM.

3. This kind of migration equally balances migration duration and service downtime.

2.5.1   QEMU and KVM

QEMU is software which provides machine emulation and virtualization. The program operates in different modes, including "*full system emulation*", where it is able to host a wide variety of machine types as guests. This is achieved by a recompiler in the QEMU software which translates binary code destined for one CPU type to another. QEMU also contains many emulators for other computer components, such as network cards, hard drives and USB. In other words, QEMU is a hypervisor which uses emulation to provide virtualization capabilities. KVM, which stands for kernel virtual machine, is a variant of the QEMU program and hence also a hypervisor. It is built into the Linux OS, and transforms the standard Linux kernel into a hypervisor, if activated. It runs guests as if they were processes on the host, which means they can be controlled like any other program. They are assigned process IDs with which KVM can interact. The KVM program can be started from the Linux command line, which could make one think it is a Type-2 hypervisor running "on top" of an OS, but the VMs on KVM actually run on bare metal, effectively making it a Type-1 (*bare-metal virtualization*). The discrepancy between which solutions lie within the different architectures can sometimes be unclear. KVM is reliant on the host having installed a processor which supports virtualization features, such as one from the "Intel VT" or the "AMD-V" series (see Figure 2.12).

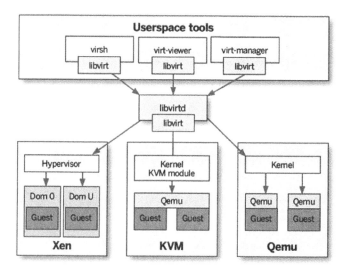

Figure 2.12   QEMU and KVM.

2.5.2 Libvirt

Libvirt is a Red Hat developed API and daemon for managing virtualization services (see Figure 2.13). It allows you to connect to VM remotely through the network and to launch VMs via the `virbr` command-line interface.

Libvirt can set up a virtual network switch on the host and have the guests connect to it and pass their network traffic through. The virtual switch is an optional feature. By default it performs NAT using the masquerade options, so that all VMs which connect to external sources will look like traffic sourced from the IP of the virtual bridge (`virbr0` interface by default). The switch program can also operate in "routed mode", where it puts VMs on a separate subnet, unknown to the host. In this mode, computers from the outside can access the VMs through a static route on on the host, which forwards traffic destined to the VMs to the bridge interface. A third option in Libvirt is to use an existing virtual switch on the host where a phys-

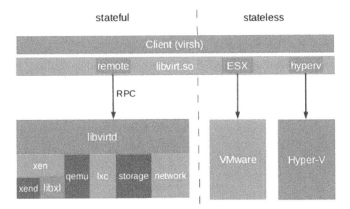

Figure 2.13   Libvirt architecture.

ical interface is connected. Each VM would then get a tap interface attached to the existing bridge. This is a virtual interface seen as a physical by the host, and as a switch port by the switch software. When setting up hosted virtualization on a Linux platform, it is common to use a combination of QEMU, KVM and Libvirt.

2.6   Conclusion

This chapter demonstrated how one of the most popular and widely deployed VMMs. VMware is vulnerable to practical attacks targeting its live migration functionality. These threats are cause for concern and require that applicable solutions be applied to each class of live migration threats. This chapter is in no way a criticism of virtualization technology, especially VMware. I personally am a follower and user of VMware technologies and this chapter is research in progress of security around virtual technologies, which should not be taken for granted. In order to make sure that live migration of virtual machines is secure, there needs to be an authentication algorithm that protects the communication pane not only between the source and destination VMMs, but also the management servers and agents. The administrator should have access to security policies that control effective migration of privileges that are assigned to various players involved during the course of migration. The so-called tunnel used by migration must be secure and have policies set up so as to detect sniffing and manipulation of the data or migration state during the migration phase. This can be done by making sure the VMotion parameter is encrypted correctly which at the moment seems to be in a state of testing or in need of extensive add-ons and monitoring. One important thing that can be established is setting up of separate virtual switches for vMotion that is kept aloof from other network objects and tasks. Also, vMotion takes place in cleartext by default and VMware encryption for vMotion is not fullproof, as evident from the tests conducted; administrators need to test vMotion before the production servers go online. Administrators can also try to incorporate tested encryption algorithms for VMotion to work securely. A timely audit of these parameters is necessary so as to reduce chances of breach that can occur during the migration. Management of virtual infrastructure should be done with a strict code of conduct. Security policies should be revisited. There should be a close monitoring of any changes to the virtualized systems, as while it is easy to execute changes, it is difficult to manage them. Any exploit like stolen guest VM can be used someplace else and if, for instance, it is a database server, nothing can stop the thief from stealing data. Furthermore, it is possible to look into limiting VM intervention by focusing on availability such that the application running on the VM is not affected due to intervention and data is not compromised. So basically to avoid integrity and confidentiality loss, we can focus on loss of availability. As any administrator understands, any vulnerability in network security could result in breach of data and intellectual property; but when it comes to VMM that involves full OS, any compromise to the network can also result in breach of VM monitor integrity. So to sum up, the approach towards securing a virtualized network needs certain add-ons to access control and a methodology that assures complete isolation from other network objects.

REFERENCES

1. Piao, G., Oh, Y., Sung, B., & Park, C. (2014). Efficient pre-copy live migration with memory compaction and adaptive VM downtime control. In Big Data and Cloud Computing (BdCloud), 2014 IEEE Fourth International Conference (pp. 85-90). IEEE.

2. Liu, H., Jin, H., Xu, C. Z., & Liao, X. (2013). Performance and energy modeling for live migration of virtual machines. *Cluster Computing*, 16(2), 249-264.

3. Hines, M. R., & Gopalan, K. (2009). Post-copy based live virtual machine migration using adaptive pre-paging and dynamic self-ballooning. In Proceedings of the 2009 ACM SIGPLAN/SIGOPS International Conference on Virtual Execution Environments (pp. 51-60). ACM.

4. Hu, B., Lei, Z., Lei, Y., Xu, D., & Li, J. (2011). A time-series based precopy approach for live migration of virtual machines. In Parallel and Distributed Systems (ICPADS), 2011 IEEE 17th International Conference (pp. 947-952). IEEE.

5. Hu, W., Hicks, A., Zhang, L., Dow, E. M., Soni, V., Jiang, H., ... & Matthews, J. N. (2013). A quantitative study of virtual machine live migration. In Proceedings of the 2013 ACM Cloud and Autonomic Computing Conference (p. 11). ACM.

6. Jain, R. (1990). *The art of computer systems performance analysis: techniques for experimental design, measurement, simulation, and modeling*. John Wiley & Sons.

7. Johnson, J. A. (2013). Optimization of migration downtime of virtual machines in cloud. In Computing, Communications and Networking Technologies (ICCCNT), 2013 Fourth International Conference (pp. 1-5). IEEE.

8. Joseph, C. T., Chandrasekaran, K., & Cyriac, R. (2014). A perspective study of virtual machine migration. In Advances in Computing, Communications and Informatics (ICACCI, 2014 International Conference (pp. 1499-1503). IEEE.

9. Kashyap, R., Chaudhary, S., & Jat, P. M. (2014). Virtual machine migration for back-end mashup application deployed on OpenStack environment. In Parallel, Distributed and Grid Computing (PDGC), 2014 International Conference (pp. 214-218). IEEE.

10. Kivity, A., Kamay, Y., Laor, D., Lublin, U., & Liguori, A. (2007). kvm: the Linux virtual machine monitor. In Proceedings of the Linux Symposium (Vol.1, pp. 225-230).

11. Law, A. M., Kelton, W. D., & Kelton, W. D. (1991). *Simulation modeling and analysis* (Vol. 2). New York: McGraw-Hill.

12. Lee, C. A. (2014). A Design Space Review for General Federation Management Using Keystone. In Proceedings of the 2014 IEEE/ACM 7th International Conference on Utility and Cloud Computing (pp. 720-725). IEEE Computer Society.

13. Khosravi, A., Nadjaran Toosi, A., & Buyya, R. (2017). Online virtual machine migration for renewable energy usage maximization in geographically distributed cloud data centers. *Concurrency and Computation: Practice and Experience*.

14. Bezerra, P., Martins, G., Gomes, R., Cavalcante, F., & Costa, A. (2017). Evaluating live virtual machine migration overhead on client's application perspective. In Information Networking (ICOIN), 2017 International Conference (pp. 503-508). IEEE.

15. Basu, D., Wang, X., Hong, Y., Chen, H., & Bressan, S. (2017). Learn-as-you-go with megh: Efficient live migration of virtual machines. In Distributed Computing Systems (ICDCS), 2017 IEEE 37th International Conference (pp. 2608-2609). IEEE.

CHAPTER 3

ATTACKS AND POLICIES IN CLOUD COMPUTING AND LIVE MIGRATION

Abtract

It is conceivable that cyberpunk/assailants bargain the respectability of a virtual machine's (VM's) operating system amid live migration (LM) in light of the fact that despite the fact that virtualization-based organizations have made programming that makes it simple to decrease server downtime and level burdens when there are vacillations over the servers, these products don't encode the information as it migrates from one server to another server. Concepts of different security paradigms are presented herein which are very useful at the time data is accessed from the cloud environment. Along with a list of different cloud service providers available in the market, this chapter also present topics such as security paradigms and issues, security risks, cloud security challenges, cloud economics, cloud computing technologies and, finally, common types of attacks and policies in cloud and live migration.

Keywords: Buffer overflows, heap overflows, DNS attacks, web based attack, man in middle attack.

Cloud Computing and Virtualization.
By Dac-Nhuong Le *et al.* Copyright © 2018 Scrivener Publishing

3.1 Introduction to Cloud Computing

This global network so-called internet, which came into existence in 1969 as a research project at the Advanced Research Projects Agency (ARPA) on behalf of the Ministry of Defense of the United State, was initially used for military and scientific purposesit was first commercialized in 1988 with services like email and telnet. So the Internet is the backbone of all these services which are provided by CSP. Some experts also say that the concept of cloud computing [1] was first conceived by the American computer scientist John McCarthy of MIT[1], who in the sixties stated that *"computation can be delivered as a public utility."*

Throughout its life span of 60 years, usage of computers has evolved spirally from centralized and sharable large size computers in 1970 to decentralized and small personal computers in 1999. Computing power has been distributed. In the 2010s, again based on the concept of cost-effective sharing, industries started to move toward a distributed center of compact machines for their computational needs. These centers were invisible to the end clients, so-called cloud computing. Cloud computing is based on internet computing that relies on the principle of sharing, in which the cloud computing idea of computing as a service comes true.

Cloud computing has evolved through various phases involving grid computing, utility computing and SaaS. Grid computing [2] can be defined as a collection of distributed computing resources with heterogeneous and non-interactive workload from multiple sites which are used collectively to reach a common goal. However, the scope of grid computing is very limited and is mostly used in scientific and research work. Utility computing involves the concept of metered services where users have to pay according to usage, which means commercialization of services (*e.g., traditional electricity and telephonic services*). This can be seen as the fulfillment of the prediction made by the scientists of ARPA regarding the utilization of a computer network, which was in the very early stages of development in 1969. So grid and utility computing are the foundation stones of cloud computing. The third phase of the cloud computing evolution was SaaS, which gained popularity in 2010, in which applications and data both reside on the vendor's site server; a client who wants to access the services connects with the remote server through an internet like social networking. So SaaS offers fully furnished applications using technologies like Java, Ajax, etc. SaaS is only part of the services provided by CSPs. Cloud computing is an umbrella term which also covers PaaS and IaaS.

Salesforce[2] took first step in 1999 by putting the idea of cloud computing in the market, and delivering its enterprise applications over the Internet using its website. Following that, the CSP giant Amazon came into existence in 2002 with a bunch of cloud-based services like computation and storage of big data with high level security. Thereafter, in 2006, Amazon provided its Elastic Compute Cloud (EC2) as commercial web services which offered reconfigurable compute capacity in the

---

[1] Massachusetts Institute of Technology
[2] Salesforce.com

Cloud. In 2009, Google started offering its cloud-based services, like Google Apps, which includes data storage, email at professional level, and many more shared services, e.g., calendar and spread data sheet, which is seen as a big milestone in the field of cloud computing. In February 2010, Microsoft launched Microsoft Azure, which provided both PaaS and IaaS. Microsoft Azure covers many cloud-based services, e.g., business analytics, data management, identity, access management and many more.

There is a lot of confusion about the exact definition of cloud computing. According to research study going back to 2008, there are a minimum of twenty-two definitions of cloud computing in common use. Many column writers and scientists, e.g., Michael Brown, Gartner, Rajkumar Buyya, and communities like Open Cloud Manifesto, have tried their best to frame the proper definition of cloud computing, but because of different people having different views, not a single canonical definition could be framed. Finally, in 2011, NIST (National Institute of Standards and Technology)[3] proposed a standard definition of cloud computing [3] which covers all the essential characteristics and models based on services and deployments.

In this preparatory chapter, we will review the fundamental concepts related to cloud computing. In this concern we will discuss the need for cloud computing, and the sequential method of cloud computing. The advancement of cloud computing came about due to fast-growing usage of the Internet among the people. Cloud computing is not a totally new technology; it is basically a journey through distributed, cluster, grid and now cloud computing. In fact, due to the rapid surge in Internet usage all over the globe, cloud computing has already been heading toward the IT industry. Cloud computing is transforming the computing landscape. Cloud concept and its computing process is the hot topic in the internet-centric and IT-market-oriented business place.

One thing is evident, IT business requires a targeted, clear discussion about how this new technonlogy's worldview will have an effect on associations, how it can be utilized with the current advancements, and the potential entanglements of exclusive innovations that can prompt secure and restricted decisions. Distributed computing needs a merchant who is an outsider through which a customer or an end client or a client can utilize the cloud given by a cloud service provider (CSP) on-request premise.

We also focus on the principles of cloud computing [4] and its related advances and virtualized, must give the PCs to be worked from physically conveyed parts a chance to like stockpiling, handling, information, and programming assets. Innovations like group, matrix and as of late distributed computing, have out-and-out permitted getting to colossal measures of figuring assets by incorporating registering and physical assets in a completely virtualized way, and have offered a single-view framework to the end client. The end clients utilize the figuring and physical assets in a utilitarian manner, which portrays a business structure for delivering administration and registering power on-request premise. What's more, as indicated by the

[3]https://www.nist.gov/

need of the client, CSPs have planned to deliver the administration and cloud clients need to pay the specialist organizations in light of their utilization, which signifies "pay-per-use" or "pay-as-you-go." As we examined previously, in electric matrix, the clients simply utilize the power which originates from the power stations and clients need to pay for the amount of power they have utilized. In like manner, under cloud computing conditions, clients are not required to know the hidden engineering that provides administration; they simply need to pay as per their utilization. Cloud is fundamentally a framework which is kept up by some cloud service providers and end clients are getting the administration on-request from the specialist co-op and they need to pay the required cash for its use. Specialist co-op mammoths like Amazon, Microsoft, Google, and IBM offer on-request asset and processing administration to the client at a cost.

Security Risks: Organizations which arrange their PCs [5] for cost-saving purposes by utilizing live virtual machine migration are helpless against programmers/aggressors. Since live virtual machine migration is generally new, it enables virtual machines to relocate between servers with practically zero administration downtime, and in this manner enables load to adjust over a few servers; the security of live virtual machine migration has not been widely looked into. It is conceivable that programmers/aggressors trade off the honesty of a virtual machine's working framework amid live migration in light of the fact that despite the fact that virtualization-based organizations have made programming that makes it simple for lessening server downtime and adjust loads when there are vacillations over the servers, these products don't encode the information as it moves from one server to another server. While a fleeting fix is to confine the arrangement utilized for migration from other system' movement or have the information encoded by utilizing some rumored equipment encryption programming, there is a pressing need to teach organizations and bring issues to light about this helplessness. To see how the security of virtual condition can be traded off, it is essential to think like an assailant. So this chapter gives a review of the sorts of assaults and how they function from the perspective of a penetration tester, programmer or displeased representative.

3.2   Common Types of Attacks and Policies

3.2.1   Buffer Overflows

This class of attack [6] involves data being written into a buffer which is greater than the allocated space of that buffer, resulting in corruption of memory inside a running process. The reason behind such an attack could be either a halt in the running process or call an injected malicious code as a result of buffer overflow.

3.2.2   Heap Overflows

This assault class happens in heap information range and is a sort of buffer overflow. As with buffer overflow, there is an off chance that an assailant supplies the application with information that is bigger than the span of the lump (*information obstructs in stack*), which causes the overwriting of metadata of the succeeding piece. Once more, the assailant information may contain vindictive code.

3.2.3   Web-Based Attacks

3.2.3.1   Fake Certificate Injection   An assailant goes about as a middle man between the site and the PC, endeavoring to get to that site. By using this type of attack, the attacker, much like a proxy server, after taking requests from an unsuspecting user, makes some (*possibly*) malicious changes and forwards the changed request to the target. But since the query has been tampered with, the user gets back a new location that the attacker wants him/her to go to (see Figure 3.1).

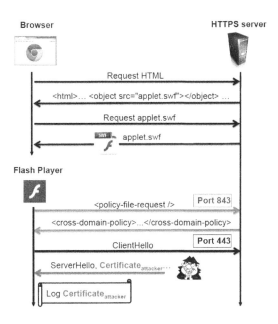

Figure 3.1   Fake certificate injection.

3.2.3.2   Cross-Site Scripting   Using this type of computer security vulnerability, an attacker (*malicious web user*) can inject malicious code into the web applications. Such vulnerability is usually used by the attacker to bypass access controls, for phishing attacks and browser exploits.

1. Type-1 XSS, or non-persistent, is a reflected vulnerability which shows up when server-side scripts instantly use the data provided by web clients without validating the received data, which can allow insertion of client-side code into dynamic web pages (see Figure 3.2).

2. Type-2 XSS, or persistent, is a second-order attack. This type of vulnerability occurs when the data provided by the user to the web application is stored persistently (*in database or file systems*), and is displayed on to the web page without being encoded using HTML.

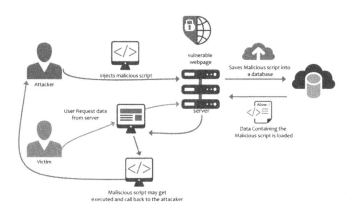

Figure 3.2   Cross-site scripting.

3.2.3.3 SQL Injection   At the point when info is given to a web application and translated as a SQL input, and the application answers back with a disappointing message, the aggressor can understand that the objective application is helpless against SQL infusion. In this sort of assault, the aggressor tries to get around the channels by testing out the shortcomings of the channels by questioning the channels tenaciously. So, essentially, SQL infusion happens when information is input into the SQL question motor that is not expected by the web client (see Figure 3.3).

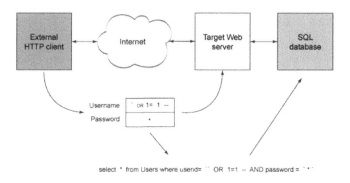

Figure 3.3   SQL injection.

3.2.3.4 Layer 2 Attacks   A large number of common threats need to be considered when securing a network, but a frequently overlooked area is the security of the LAN. When people think about security, often they're thinking specifically of the layers above Layer 2, but there's no reason to limit a security plan to these upper layers. A good security plan should account for all layers, from Layer 1 through Layer 7. This section takes a look at some of the most common Layer 2 attacks and how they operate (see Table 3.1 and Figure 3.4).

Table 3.1   Popular layer 2 attacks.

No.	Attack type
1	Spanning Tree Protocol (STP) Attacks
2	Address Resolution Protocol (ARP) Attacks
3	Media Access Control (MAC) Spoofing
4	Content Addressable Memory (CAM) Table Overflows
5	Cisco Discovery Protocol (CDP)/Link Layer Discovery Protocol Reconnaissance
6	Virtual LAN (VLAN) Hopping
7	Dynamic Host Configuration Protocol (DHCP) Spoofing

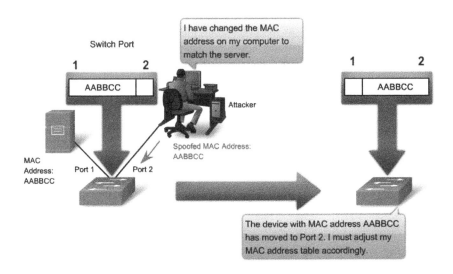

Figure 3.4   Layer-2 attacks.

Content Addressable Memory (CAM) Table or MAC Flooding: CAM table is essentially dynamic content addressable memory on an Ethernet switch and is in charge of accurately reverberating the edges out of pertinent port or else the switch is the same as a center point. On the off chance that an assailant gains power over any gadget that is associated with the Ethernet switch, he/she can assault the CAM table by MAC flooding which is defenseless in the plan of the switch when the switch has no more space to record MAC delivery to Port mapping amid its learning stage. So therefore, the switch loses its character and starts sending any received outlines out of all ports, similar to a center point.

Double Encapsulation Attacks: Such attacks are common in VLAN environments and so they are also referred to as VLAN hopping attacks. The transmitted frames are tagged with a *VTag* identifier so as to forward these frames to wrong the VLAN (see Figure 3.5).

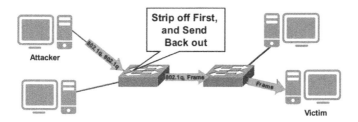

Figure 3.5   Double encapsulation attacks.

Multicast Brute Force Attacks: This assault utilizes the change's weakness to a tempest of multicast outlines. At the point when the switch gets such a tempest of multicast outlines quickly, it will attempt to compel the activity to the first VLAN; however, neglecting to do so results in outline holes to different VLANs, which may conceivably be vindictive (see Figure 3.6).

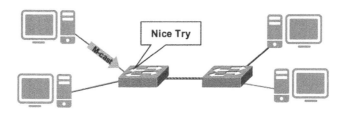

Figure 3.6   Multicast brute force attacks.

Spanning Tree Attacks: Spanning tree protocol (STP) is dependable in preventing exchanging or spanning circles that are the reason for communication storms, which can push the L2 systems to the brink of collapse. In STP, repetition is empowered to avoid arrange circles by allocating ports for utilization of limited MAC address confidence confidence. So in spreading over tree assaults, assailant can compel another decision which might be fixed by influencing its MAC to confidence higher than root connect confidence, and consequently trading off the whole system (see Figure 3.7).

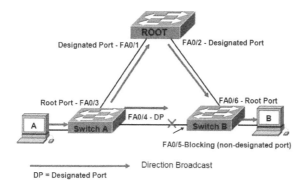

Figure 3.7   Spanning tree attacks.

Random Frame Attacks: This assault includes assailant arbitrarily fluctuating the fields of a parcel without changing the source and goal addresses. So, the assailant can convey undesirable noxious activity to private VLANs from conniving gadgets (see Figure 3.8).

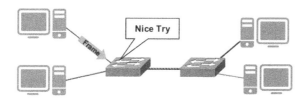

Figure 3.8   Random frame attacks.

3.2.3.5 Layer 3 Nonrouter Attacks   Assailant mostly utilizes ARP store harming as a method of assault for Layer 3 non-switch. Amid ARP communications, the convention has confidence in anything that it is told despite the fact that it might not have requested that data. The aggressor can convey ARP reserve refreshed with pernicious data by fashioning the substance making the casualty's machine terminate its own store. The aggressor can sniff, change and drop parcels by harming the default door and casualty's machine by influencing them to trust that his/hers is the asked for machine. So, essentially the assault is coordinated with TCP/IPv4 convention stack, which may require substitution [7, 8].

3.2.4   DNS Attacks

3.2.4.1 DNS Cache Poisoning Attack   This attack involves changing the values in the cache that contains previously looked up requests. So by controlling the name resolutions of the sites, the attacker could send unsuspecting users to fake sites without the users knowing the difference (see Figure 3.9).

3.2.4.2 Pharming Using the Host File While this is similar to DNS poisoning, the attacker makes changes to the host file rather than the DNS server. Since TCP/IP protocol consults the host file for resolving DNS names into IP addresses, by making any changes to this file, the user may get redirected to a fake site even though he/she is typing the correct URL [9].

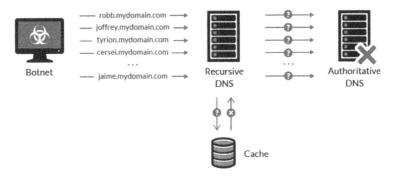

Figure 3.9   DNS attacks.

3.2.5   Layer 3 Routing Attacks

3.2.5.1 Route Table Poisoning Route table poisoning is inserting fake routes in the victim router's routing table by using outdated routing protocols like RIPv1 or IGRP that do not require authentication (see Figure 3.10).

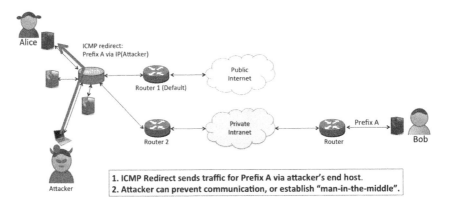

Figure 3.10   Layer 3 attacks.

3.2.5.2 *Source Routed Packets*   In this type of attack, the attacker changes the information in the source routing table of the packet itself, which causes the packet to select its own path to destination. So basically, the attacker modifies or poisons each router.

3.2.6 Man-in-the-Middle Attack (MITM)

If the integrity of the channel [7] used for communication between two devices or parties is not ensured along with the verification of the identity of the parties at both ends of this channel, then a MITM attack can easily be put into action. Some MITM examples include standard MITM ARP cache poisoning attack, SSL attack and iSCSI MITM. Such an attack is used to accomplish the following (see Figure 3.11):

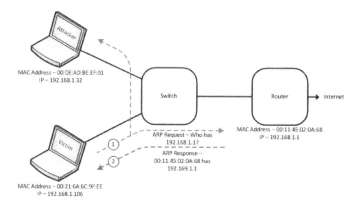

Figure 3.11   Man-in-the-middle attack.

- *Impersonate*: Attacker tries to impersonate the victim for intercepting messages and sends fake certificate to sender.

- *Eavesdrop*: Attacker tries to intercept and listen in on traffic by forcing it to pass by a hodgepodge of enabled NIC.

- *Modify*: Attacker can modify the message if he is able to decrypt the message to plain text.

- *Replay of Messages*: Similar to network injection attacks, the attacker who is able to listen in on the traffic can change the sequence of the packets making up the message by doctoring the sequence and hence causing the replay of packets due to incorrect sequencing.

- *Prevent Clock Synchronization*: Attacker may prevent synchronization of sender and receiver clocks [8] so as to listen in on the traffic as the synchronized clocks make it difficult to snoop around. Organizations, either big or small, never want their live systems to be interrupted if they are using virtualization technologies as that would defeat the whole purpose of high-availability features. But such organizations do fail to understand the security risks involved in live migration of VMs. While any or all of the above-mentioned vulnerabilities and attack classes would work in creating operational hazards with respect to the virtualized environment, there are certain known virtualization system attacks which have been documented [9, 10].

- *Management Server Attacks*: The management console can be exploited to gain login information and hence eventually access to the management server. Also, these attacks can allow the attacker to change privileges and gain elevated privileges [11, 12].

- *Admin VM Attacks*: These attacks result in denial of service, resulting in crashing admin VM. Passwords stored in cleartext can be obtained easily, which can lead to attackers bypassing authentication [13].

- *Guest VM Attacks*: Similar to admin VM attack, this attack can include gaining increased privileges, crashing VM, and executing rogue code with admin permissions [14].

- *Hypervisor Attacks*: Hypervisor can crash and attackers can easily jump between guests' VMs [15].

3.3 Conclusion

The cloud computing model is based on the concept of pay-per-use, as the user is required to pay for the amount of cloud services used. Cloud computing is defined by different layer architecture (IaaS, PaaS and SaaS) and models (private, public, hybrid and community), with different models of usability for the user. This chapter presented concepts of different security paradigms that are very useful at the time data is accessed from the cloud environment. A list of different cloud service providers available in the market, security paradigms and issues, security risks, cloud security challenges, cloud economics, major CSPs, cloud computing technologies and finally common types of attacks and policies in cloud and live migration were presented in this chapter.

REFERENCES

1. Beloglazov, A., Buyya, R., Lee, Y. C., & Zomaya, A. (2011). A taxonomy and survey of energy-efficient data centers and cloud computing systems. *Advances in computers*, 82(2), 47-111..

2. Beloglazov, A., Piraghaj, S. F., Alrokayan, M., & Buyya, R. (2012). *Deploying Open-Stack on CentOS using the KVM Hypervisor and GlusterFS distributed file system*. University of Melbourne.

3. Benini, L., Bogliolo, A., & De Micheli, G. (2000). A survey of design techniques for system-level dynamic power management. *IEEE transactions on very large scale integration (VLSI) systems*, 8(3), 299-316.

4. Benini, L., Bogliolo, A., Paleologo, G. A., & De Micheli, G. (1999). Policy optimization for dynamic power management. *IEEE Transactions on Computer-Aided Design of Integrated Circuits and Systems*, 18(6), 813-833.

5. Blackburn, M., & Grid, G. (2008). Five ways to reduce data center server power consumption. *The Green Grid*, 42, 12.

6. Bobroff, N., Kochut, A., & Beaty, K. (2007). Dynamic placement of virtual machines for managing sla violations. In Integrated Network Management, 2007. IM'07. 10th IFIP/IEEE International Symposium on (pp. 119-128). IEEE.

7. Bolch, G., Greiner, S., de Meer, H., & Trivedi, K. S. (2006). *Queueing networks and Markov chains: modeling and performance evaluation with computer science applications*. John Wiley & Sons.

8. Borodin, A., & El-Yaniv, R. (2005). *Online computation and competitive analysis*. Cambridge university press.

9. Han, Y., Chan, J., Alpcan, T., & Leckie, C. (2017). Using virtual machine allocation policies to defend against co-resident attacks in cloud computing. *IEEE Transactions on Dependable and Secure Computing*, 14(1), 95-108.

10. Tsai, S. C., Liu, I. H., Lu, C. T., Chang, C. H., & Li, J. S. (2017). Defending cloud computing environment against the challenge of DDoS attacks based on software defined network. In Advances in Intelligent Information Hiding and Multimedia Signal Processing: Proceeding of the Twelfth International Conference on Intelligent Information Hiding and Multimedia Signal Processing, Nov., 21-23, 2016, Kaohsiung, Taiwan, Volume 1 (pp. 285-292). Springer International Publishing.

11. Ahmed, R., Hussain, M., Rahmani, T. S., Mansoor, A., & Ali, M. L. (2017). Minimization of Security Issues in Cloud Computing. *Journal of Information Communication Technologies and Robotics Applications (JICTRA)*.(Formally known as Journal of Computer Science of NICE). ISSN 2226-3683, 3(1), 1-39.

12. Chase, J., Niyato, D., Wang, P., Chaisiri, S., & Ko, R. (2017). A Scalable Approach to Joint Cyber Insurance and Security-as-a-Service Provisioning in Cloud Computing. *IEEE Transactions on Dependable and Secure Computing*.

13. Ahmed, H. A. S., Ali, M. H., Kadhum, L. M., Zolkipli, M. F., & Alsariera, Y. A. (2017). A Review of Challenges and Security Risks of Cloud Computing. *Journal of Telecommunication, Electronic and Computer Engineering (JTEC)*, 9(1-2), 87-91.

14. Somani, G., Gaur, M. S., Sanghi, D., Conti, M., Rajarajan, M., & Buyya, R. (2017). Combating DDoS attacks in the cloud: requirements, trends, and future directions. *IEEE Cloud Computing*, 4(1), 22-32.

15. Hussain, S. A., Fatima, M., Saeed, A., Raza, I., & Shahzad, R. K. (2017). Multilevel classification of security concerns in cloud computing. *Applied Computing and Informatics*, 13(1), 57-65.

CHAPTER 4

LIVE MIGRATION SECURITY IN CLOUD

Abstract

Concerning the migrating security plan of virtual machines (VMs) in software-defined networks (SDNs), virtual machine migration is a fundamental ability that backs up the cloud versatility benefit. In any case, there is a major worry as to what happens to the security approach in relation to the relocated machine. As of late, SDNs have gained momentum in both the research field and industry. This is indicative of the awesome potential to be utilized in cloud server farms, especially for migration of VMs between areas. In a dispersed setting, where more than one physical SDN controller is utilized, especially in deferent system spaces, organizing security arrangements amid migration is a vital issue. In this chapter, we propose an alternate system; to be sent in a SDN domain that facilitates the versatility of the related security arrangement together with the moved VM.

Keywords: Software-defined networks, DMS, VMM, security, case studies.

4.1   Cloud Security and Security Appliances

Truth be told, cloud computing has upgraded its general security [1]. Centralization of framework in one area and simplicity of administration and control, detachment of virtual foundations and confinement of VMs were real enhancements in security in spite of the fact that they were simply solutions for moderation of a few assaults. Security is still an issue in light of the fact that not just the greater part of the customary assaults are not appropriate, but in addition some new cloud-particular assaults have been revealed. In this chapter, we endeavor to classify cloud-related security concerns and disclose the approaches which are most imperative for ensuring parts of the security apparatus (see Table 4.1).

Table 4.1   Cloud computing security risks

No.	Cloud computing security risk description
1	Investigative support
2	Regulatory compliance
3	Data location
4	Data segregation
5	Recovery
6	Privileged user access
7	Long-term viability

Security apparatuses, otherwise known as security middleboxes, are middle-person arranged gadgets that are intended to channel and investigate parcels. Firewalls and intrusion prevention system/intrusion detection system (IPS/IDS) are basic cases of security machines that are widely utilized as a part of server farms for ensuring them at the system level. In light of this, what kind of security apparatus will be utilized as a part of the eventual fate of cloud? Physical or Virtual? What's more, the appropriate response in view of this, is a crossbreed approach.

4.2   VMM in Clouds and Security Concerns

Data centers, also known as server farms, require a huge amount of hardware and infrastructure facilities. On the other hand, due to the fast growing technologies that data centers rely on and customers ask for, CSPs have to undergo major upgrades in every few years. Therefore, data centers need to make the best use of their facilities and this is exactly where virtualization can inevitably help. Server consolidation is a great example of virtualization's impact on improvement of data center efficiency.

Hypervisors have different features and capabilities depending on their vendor. As it has been found in the literature, there are three main features that most of them have in common according to VMware, which is the leader in virtualization technology; these features are high availability (HA), fault tolerance (FT) and live migration. The first and the second features are dependent on the last one.

Following is a brief description of the above-named features:

- *High Availability*: A technology that monitors all VMs constantly and in case of hardware failure immediately restarts the VMs on another server. This feature does not transfer the current state of VM and only loads the VM from the stored image in the storage unit.

- *Fault Tolerance*: This technology complements the previous feature. It runs identical copies of a VM in another place at the same time and in case of failure in origin location, duplicated VM will continue running without interruption. This feature is dependent on live migration of VM state.

- *Live Migration*: This feature provides the means, to transfer a VM and its running state from one server to another in real time.

VMM should be possible in two routes; inside a server farm or crosswise over different server farms that occasionally are situated in different mainlands. Notwithstanding the specified inspiration for migration that supplements different elements of hypervisor, there are more motivating forces to move a VM. One of the principle reasons and inspirations for VM migration is stack adjusting between servers. Once in a while an assignment needs more processor control and there are insufficient assets accessible in the server; in this circumstance, a migration to another server can take care of the issue. Periodical upkeep is another ordinary purpose of VM migration. Decreasing force utilization is dependably needed by server farms. It happens now and again that many separate devices have least load and it is conceivable to close down or rest them while exchanging some VMs to other servers; these migrations can altogether decrease control utilization and thusly server farm cost. Virtualization security difficulties can be classified as takes after:

- *Inactive VMs*: Normally VMs receive daily updates and security patches. VMs which are offine, are not able to receive those updates and become vulnerable when they go active. As a result, they turn into security threats for entire server.

- *VM Awareness*: All security solutions and appliances are not compatible with virtualized environment. The hypervisor security is also another concern that should be taken into consideration.

- *VM Sprawl*: VMs can be created with a click of a mouse. This is the key reason for the rapid growth of virtualization; however, not only can security not be achieved as easy as that, many security weaknesses can easily duplicate and spread all over the network. Each VM needs special care and administrator cannot apply the same solution to all VMs.

- *Inter-VM Traffic*: Traffic between the VMs is not visible to traditional physical layer security appliances. Hence, monitoring and management of that traffic can be performed by an appliance that is integrated into hypervisor.

■ *Migration*: When a VM migrates from one cloud to another, the security policies that are associated with that VM remain in the place of origin.

4.3 Software-Defined Networking

Software-defined network is a new paradigm in computer networks; however, the
idea of programmable network has been around for a long time. Emergence of programmable networks was due to the need of researchers to deploy new protocols and
ideas into the core network which was monopolized by big network companies such
as Cisco and Juniper. Before manifestation of programmable networks, control and
forwarding layers were tightly coupled to each other and implementation of network
hardware was mostly on application-specific integrated circuit (ASIC) chips. The
main property of ASICs is ultimate speed but their drawback is non-programmability.
Improvements in x86 processors and the popularity of using commodity hardware,
encouraged network researchers to find a way to decouple control and forwarding
layers, in order to deploy desired architectures and network control capabilities. To
achieve this, various approaches have been taken. Software routers and switches that
are installed on servers as well as virtualization technologies, added more flexibility to network architecture; in addition, testbeds enabled the researchers to perform
experiments and verification on their own prototype environment (see Figure 4.1).

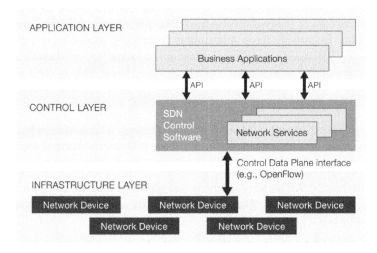

Figure 4.1   Software-defined networking architecture.

Eventually, researchers came up with the idea of role abstraction in networking
which led to emergence of SDN. SDN focuses on separation of control plane and
data plane when the control unit is centralized and manageable by third party application. In order to program those applications, the controller exposes an API;

however, programmability in SDN is not limited only to applications and the main improvement is that the control units are also programmable by data plane exposed APIs.

1. Data plane, also known as forwarding plane, is the layer on which infrastructure and particularly switches reside.

2. Control plane is in the middle; controllers that have a comprehensive view of the network and are able to control switches are placed there.

3. Management plane is on the top and applications which are replacements for many devices in traditional networks, such as middleboxes, load-balancers and etc., as well as some new business and management applications, are located on this layer. In order to make a connection between these layers, different APIs are used to provide programmable interface.

4.3.1 Firewall in Cloud and SDN

Network security that falls under architecture domain can affect cloud security. Firewalling is one of the solutions that has significant impact on improving network security. Firewall is a security appliance that filters packets and controls incoming and outgoing traffc [7]. Still, there is not enough information that gives us a clear view of firewall. Therefore, it is necessary to go another level deeper and define what are the main purposes and benefits of using these devices on which data centers invest a huge amount money. Middleboxes are essential intermediary devices in the network that mainly optimize performance and security of the network. Some of them, such as WAN optimizers and IDSs, specifically focus on one issue, respectively performance and security, and others can be helpful in both directions.

The term "*middlebox*" may mistakenly imply the physical existence of a separate device, whereas it can be a virtual appliance that is running on commodity hardware along with other functionalities or even as a software solution. The authors state that security appliances can be distinguished by their types. Active devices can filter and modify the traffic. Common examples of active devices are antivirus, content-filtering devices and firewalls. Passive devices basically monitor the network, and make reports and issue alerts whenever they detect a suspicious activity; like IDS. Another type of devices are preventative ones such as IPS or vulnerability assessment tools that unveil threats before an incident occurs. Finally, there are unified threat management (UTM) devices that integrate multiple security features into one box.

Knowing the place of firewall among all middleboxes allows higher accuracy in giving a definition of the firewall. As a result, firewalls are software or hardware components that separate a network into different security levels by enforcing rules. These rules specify access level as well as limitations of each network entity or program. According to NIST there are ten different firewall technologies for production networks and two types for individual hosts and home networks.

- *Packet Filtering*: Most basic feature on any firewall that specifies ACCEPT or DROP of a packet, based on information in the header.

- *Stateful Inspection*: Keeps track of connection states in a table called state table and inspects packets by matching their state with connection state.

- *Application Firewalls*: Stateful protocol analysis, it is also known as deep packet inspection. Allows or denies based on application behavior on the network.

- *Application-Proxy Gateways*: Another deep inspection method that act as a middleman between two hosts and prevents a direct connection.

- *Dedicated Proxy Servers*: Placed behind firewall because they have very limited firewalling features and acts as an intermediary between firewall and internal network.

- *Virtual Private Networking*: Using additional protocols in order to encrypt and decrypt traffic between two gateways or a host and a gateway.

- *Network Access Control*: Granting access to a client based on its credential and health check result.

- *Unified Threat Management*: Combination of multiple features like firewalling and intrusion detection in one system.

- *Web Application Firewalls*: A special type of application firewall used for protecting web servers.

- *Firewalls for Virtual Infrastructure*: Software firewalls that can monitor virtualized network traffic.

While firewalls usually protect the network to some extent, there are still some attacks that can pass through the firewall and reach the internal network. In order to protect the hosts in the network, there are firewalls designed to deploy particularly on host machines instead of network. Firewalls for individual hosts and home networks are as follows:

- *Host-Based Firewalls and Personal Firewalls*: Software firewalls that are installed on OS for servers and personal computers like Windows firewall. They can have other capabilities such as logging, intrusion prevention and application-based firewalling.

- *Personal Firewall Appliances*: Small hardware firewalls that are used in home or small offices. They have more advanced features than host-based firewalls and add another layer of protection.

In a cloud environment there are high capacity storage devices that store customers' information, plenty of high performance servers that handle different tasks and VMs that are running on top of servers. Virtual network inside servers and sophisticated physical network that connects the data center to the world are assets that should be protected very carefully. Firewalls are always deployed on the frontline of the network in order to safeguard the internal network. In a cloud, the network can be extremely complicated due to the huge number of servers and also VMs, which create a combination of virtual and physical traffic. Therefore, firewalling only on one layer cannot properly protect all assets. Moreover, virtual traffic is not visible to physical firewall. Co-tenancy of different customers on the same sever is another matter of contention because they may be owned by contender companies. Generally, different VMs in cloud are not considered as trusted by each other and there is a need for firewalling via VMs. In addition, security demands vary between different customers and in some cases, customized security services are demanded depending on the importance of their VMs. Thus, firewalling has to be applied in different layers from outside of data center to inside by physical firewalls with sophisticated features and within the virtual instances inside servers by virtual firewalls (or firewall that comes with hypervisor as a component). In our work, we considered both physical and virtual firewalls since they share same concepts in terms of access control, application filtering, stateful inspection and other technologies (*their difference is mainly in implementation*).

Firewalling in a pure SDN network is shifted to the application layer. SDN application firewalls are similar to virtual firewalls, from an implementation point of view, and are closer to physical firewalls, from the perspective of scope and functionality. In general, SDN firewalls can rule and protect the portion of the network that is controlled by SDN controller and they follow the main concepts of firewalling as traditional networks. However, it is very unlikely that we will see a pure SDN data center in the future; instead, it is more probable to have a hybrid architecture which is a combination of traditional network and SDN. Hence, virtual, physical and SDN firewalls will collaborate and protect the entire architecture.

Migrating security scheme of VMs in software-defined network VMMs is a necessary capability that supports cloud service elasticity. However, there is always a big concern about what happens to the security policy in relation to with the migrated machine. Recently, SDN has gained momentum in both the research field and industry. It has shown great potential to be employed in cloud data centers, particularly for inter-domain migration of VMs. In a distributed setting, where more than one physical SDN controller is used, particularly in different network domains, coordinating security policies during migration is an important issue. In this chapter, we propose a different framework, to be deployed in an SDN environment that coordinates the mobility of the associated security policy together with the migrated VM. We embedded our framework in a prototype application, called MigApp, which runs on top of the SDN controllers. Our function interacts with the VM monitor and other instance of MigApp through a messaging system to attain security migration. In order to evaluate our framework, we integrated our idea with the Floodlight controller and used it in a simulation environment.

Virtualization has become a commonplace in cloud computing data centers. Specifically, VM technology has recently emerged as a necessary building block for such an environment as it allows multiple tenants to share the similar infrastructure. The capability of VM migration brings multiple benefits such as high performance, improved manageability, and fault tolerance. While this mobility represents a valuable plus to the cloud computing model, it may introduce critical security flaws or violate the tenants' needs, if the security policy does not follow the VM to the destination after migration. Manual reconfiguration of security policies is not an acceptable solution as it is error prone and is inadequate for live VM migration. To the best of our knowledge, existing works on VM migration have not addressed security policy migration in SDN.

In this chapter, we address security policies mobility with VMs in IaaS cloud computing, and demonstrate how to solve security policy migration in SDN-based cloud. SDN is an emerging networking paradigm that aims at separating the control and data planes while offering logically centralized network's intelligence and state that are connected to the forwarding elements at the data plane. This architecture allows for a dynamic and flexible provisioning over data plane and facilitates network management in a value effective way. Particularly, the network administrator can program and manage multiple network devices based on business requirements without the need to deal with each network device separately. At the management plane, the administrator can specify various policies (*e.g., quality of service, security, etc.*) that are then utilized by a set of applications to program the controller through a northbound API. The controller, programs the forwarding devices at the information plane through a southbound API. The most popular protocol that offers an implementation of such an API is OpenFlow, maintained by the Open Networking Foundation (ONF). SDN provides new ways to solve age-old issues in networking while simultaneously enabling the introduction of sophisticated capabilities. For instance, GoGrid is an example of IaaS providers that have adopted an SDN approach to cloud architecture. The configuration and control is put into customers' hands so that they can design their own cloud platform with virtualized services, such as firewalls and load balancers, managed using the management console or a public REST API. In order to affect security groups, GoGrid implements security groups as global objects that are automatically synched across data centers. A recent IDC study projected that the SDN market will increase from $360 million in 2013 to $3.7 billion in 2016. There are several organizations worldwide, including Google, NDDI, and GENI, running and testing OpenFlow networks. A significant number of vendors, such as HP, Cisco, and IBM, are contributing by manufacturing SDN-enabling products.

Research initiatives supported by industry acknowledge the challenge and the importance of security context migration as a part of a cloud property mechanism. Many research initiatives have proposed to leverage the SDN paradigm to benefit cloud computing environments. Particularly, pa SDN strategy has been proposed to enable live and online migration of VM within and across multiple resource data centers. However, the reviewed solutions either circumvent the matter (*e.g., using traffic tunneling techniques*) or do not fully address it, if at all. In this chapter, we design and implement a framework for migrating security policies besides the VMs within the same data centers or between them based on SDN. Our solution, as opposed to vendor-specific ones, is meant to be open source, secure and practical with any SDN controller that provides a REST API and a virtual security appliance such as a firewall. To coordinate the migration, we propose to use a distributed messaging system, namely RabbitMQ. The latter relies on advanced message queuing protocol (AMQP), a highly scalable publish and subscribe message protocol that's increasingly used in cloud architectures (e.g., VMware vCenter Orchestrator 1). Thus, our main contributions are as follows:

1. Design of a novel framework, particularly MigApp, that enables the mobility of security policies during VMs migration in order to support cloud computing elasticity with an SDN-based architecture. The framework enables an east-west communication between management application inside and across data centers.

2. Implementation of the proposed framework in a prototype application integrated on the top of an existing OpenFlow controller, namely Floodlight.

3. Test and validation of the security policy migration and analysis of its performance using our framework deployed in a simulation and programming environment.

4.3.2   SDN and Floodlight Controllers

In SDN architecture, control planes of network devices are brought *"outside the boxes"* and they are logically centralized to facilitate configuration and management. Programming network devices is achieved by exchanging control messages between the controller and the switches. OpenFlow is an open standard network protocol that implements such control messages and provides a packet-forwarding abstraction to the controller for managing the behavior of network devices. The controller instructs the data plane on how to act on the incoming traffic flows. On the other side, switches inquire about the controller's decision regarding new incoming flow, inform about the occurrence of network events, or send statistics about the received traffic. When switches on a given network path receive the controller's decision as a set of flow rules, they update their flow tables with these entries in order to act on subsequent packets of the flow. In such a setting, security policies specified (*programmed*) at the management plane are applied by the controller at the switch level.

Floodlight is a Java-based open source SDN controller initially developed by Big Switch Networks and currently supported by a community of developers. A number of module applications can be developed and compiled within Floodlight so as to perform further functionalities. These modules make use of the Floodlight API to communicate with the controller. An example of a module application is the *Floodlight Firewall*. Floodlight exposes its own REST API as well as the one of its modules for northward communication with REST applications. REST stands for "representational state transfer" and it an architectural style for designing networked applications for distributed systems that run over the web. REST offers a scalable component interaction, general interface, and an independent components deployment while reducing latency, encapsulating legacy and systems enforcing security. It allows developing applications in any programming language (*Java, Python, etc.*) that communicate with the controller and its modules in a standard way. Once the controller is running, the modules running within it expose their REST API via a specific REST port to the management plane. Thus, any management application can send HTTP REST commands through the listening REST port in order to re-trieve information and invoke services from the controller or the supervised network. In this context, we built our MigApp as a REST application that uses REST API to retrieve and update data stored by the firewall module and to retrieve the network state. The firewall keeps the specified access control list (ACL) in a dedicated Flood-light storage that is consulted by the controller to take decisions on newly incoming flows. The rules/conditions in the Floodlight firewall module match a set of fields to their values, including switch id, the receiving switch port, the source and destination MAC and IP, and the protocol with the source.

4.4   Distributed Messaging System

In our solution, there's a need for a mechanism to coordinate the communication between the involved parties so that control messages and security policies can be changed. Constraints, such as security, reliability, and performance, have to be con-sidered while selecting the right mechanism. A nice characteristic of such a system is that the producer, consumer, and the broker do not have to necessarily reside on the same machine. In fact, as distributed applications, they are scattered around different machines. In RabbitMQ, the producers do not send messages directly to queues but to a specific entity called an exchange, which receives and pushes them to queues. Thus, one needs to first create an exchange, then create the queues, and finally bind the exchange to the queue. A binding is a relationship between an exchange and a queue which means that the queue is interested in messages from that particular exchange. The exchange must know what to do with a received message: either to append it to a specific or multiple queues, or even to discard it. The fate of a message is determined according to the exchange type, which can be direct, topic, headers or fanout. Moreover, among various messaging patterns, Publish/Subscribe is one of the most used patterns in which messages can be received by multiple users with a fanout change that broadcasts produced messages to all subscribers. On the other hand, in some cases, the users are supposed to selectively receive some messages. This means that one message should be delivered to a specific consumer, whereas another message is destined for another user, and so on. In this scenario, the direct change will be used in addition to an additional routing key parameter that deter-mines which consumer will receive which message. In our case, we use this latter exchange type so that any party only receives the messages intended for it.

With relation to the server's deployment, a RabbitMQ broker can be deployed in centralized settings where multiple clients connect to the same server. However, it is also possible to use a distributed architecture, where multiple brokers are clus-tered and federate in order to confirm measurability and reliability of the messaging service and to interconnect multiple administrative domains. Particularly, a shovel may be used to link multiple RabbitMQ brokers across the Internet and provide more control than federation. The latter deployment allows dealing with inter-data-center security rules migration. With respect to security, RabbitMQ supports encrypted SSL connection between the server and the client and has pluggable support for various authentication mechanisms. Thus, these specific features enable strengthening of the security of our framework by only allowing authorized MigApps and hypervisors to produce and consume messages and protecting the underlying communications. In the next section we discuss our approach in more detail.

4.4.1   Approach

We assume cloud data centers deployed according to the SDN strategy. In such a setting, an SDN controller is in charge of controlling and configuring a set of OpenFlow-enabled switches. In the following, we detail the design, implementation, and deployment of our framework.

4.4.2   MigApp Design

In order to address the need for security rules migration, we designed our solution as a distributed REST application that communicates with other MigApp instances and the hypervisor through a distributed messaging system, namely RabbitMQ. MigApp uses the REST API of Floodlight and its modules, particularly the firewall module, in order to retrieve the matching ACL rules at the source of the migration or to update them at the destination. In our migration scenario, MigApp at the source of migration receives a request from hypervisor and starts a communication with the peer application that resides at the destination side. The source MigApp, identifies the rules which correspond to the migrating VM, from the source firewall. Then, the two MigApps exchange the rules while coordinating the migration of VM through communication with hypervisors. This supervision ensures that the VM does not start running at the destination before the rules migration. At the end, the source MigApp deletes unnecessary rules and sends a message to the hypervisor in order to let the VM run at the destination place. As far as the communication through messaging is concerned, we designed various types of structured messages that contain the information needed for successfully coordinating the firewall rules migration. Each type of message is associated with a numerical identifier that identifies the message purpose.

4.5   Customized Testbed for Testing Migration Security in Cloud

Cloud computing is widely deployed all over the globe and its popularity is growing due to the benefits that it offers to both service providers and users. As the rate of adaptation to the cloud increases day by day, cloud security is becoming more important. Multi-tenancy is one of the main points of concern in cloud. Migrations are essential for cloud elasticity and security of the data center and VMs should be preserved during and after migrations. There are many other examples that highlight the importance of security research in cloud.

In order to conduct a research, a test environment is a must for researchers. Benchmarking an application performance, testing the compatibility of a new protocol or analyzing the security of a new feature, all are examples that need a testbed for evaluation. On the other hand, testing security on real-world cloud environments is not a good idea. First of all, a real cloud needs a huge amount of money and time to deploy and it may not be safe to conduct a security testing on a production network. Furthermore, running multiple tests may need reconfiguration of the entire network that obviously takes more time in a real network. Thus, simulation environments are a good alternative for real employments, because they are cost effective, safe and flexible.

To model a real network behavior, there are two ways that are known as Simulation and Emulation, and each one has pros and cons. A network simulator is usually a piece of software that models network entities and the interactions between them, by using mathematical formulas. Simulators are typically used in research for studying and predicting network behavior and performance analysis. Most simulator model network devices, have links between them and generate network traffic within the same program [6]. Discrete-event simulation that models system operations as a sequence of events in time is widely used in network simulators. Another simulation method is to use a Markov chain, which is less precise but faster than discrete-event simulations. There are many commercial and open-source network simulators with various features.

Network emulator is a piece of software or hardware to test and study a network that imitates the behavior of a production network. Emulators normally do not simulate endpoints such as computers; and therefore, computers or any type of traffc generator can be attached to emulated network. Normally, in emulation actual firmware runs on general purpose hardware. As a result, it is possible to run live applications and services on an emulated network which usually is not feasible in a simulation. Hardware-based network emulators are more expensive and more accurate than software-based ones and are commonly used by service providers and network equipment manufacturers. Although, both simulators and emulators are applied for testing network performance, they are used for different purposes based on the capabilities that each of them offers. For example, simulators are good for scalability and performance tests while emulators can be used to test network applications and real services. Nevertheless, both simulators and emulators are crucial in network research.

Network and cloud simulation has been around for a while. However, most of the network simulators are not capable of cloud modeling. On the other hand, most of the existing cloud simulators focus on performance benchmarking, cost effectiveness evaluations and power consumption assessments. Hence, a majority of them lack modeling security boxes such as firewall, IPS and security services like VPN. Furthermore, in some experiments a real running VM and actual services which imitate the behavior of a real network are necessary. At the time this chapter was written, a free cloud simulator which mimics middleboxes and real services in simulations is not available. Hence, we decided to prepare a distributed testbed based on GNS3, which is mainly a network simulator. In order to use GNS3 for cloud, we introduced an architecture that models the deployment of standard data centers on a small scale but with real running services and security features. We also equipped the testbed with a set of free network and testing utilities that facilitate many experiments. In addition, we focused on VM migration in cloud and first designed a migration framework and then improved it to a security-preserving migration framework. In summary, out goal was to:

1. Design and deploy an architecture that introduces the way to use GNS3 for simulating multiple data centers on multiple host machines.

2. Design and implement a framework for migrating VMs on the testbed by improving the features in VirtualBox.

3. Design and implement a framework to migrate firewall rules in the case of migration.

4.5.1 Preliminaries

In this section we introduce different software programs that are used to make the testbed. Hardware that was used in a set-up environment is explained.

Graphical Network Simulator (GNS3)[1] is open-source software that prepares the environment for emulating Cisco and Juniper routers in a simulated network. Dynamics, Oracle VirtualBox and QEMU are three main back-end components that GNS3 uses to emulate different network OSes. GNS3 acts as a front-end system with a GUI that enables the user to make arbitrary network. GNS3 is mainly used for training purposes and network labs. We used GNS3 as the base layer of our cloud testbed.

VirtualBox:[2] is a free x86 and AMD64/Intel64 virtualization software. It is used in GNS3 for emulating Juniper JUNOS. We used VirtualBox to make VMs in our cloud environment and benefited from features that VirtualBox offers for migration to make a testbed for VM migration in a simulated data center environment.

Wireshark:[3] Using a tool to capture and analyze packets is a must in network and security researches. Wireshark is an open-source, multi-platform network packet analyzer that can perform a live capture of network traffic. Captured traffic can be saved and analyzed offline. Wireshark can be used with GNS3 to analyze the packets that pass through each interface. Interface can be a network device port or even a host NIC. Wireshark offers various filters which we frequently used in our tests.

TFTP/SFTP Server: Trivial file transfer protocol (TFTP) is a protocol to transfer files and is supported by many commercial routers and firewalls in order to read/write configuration data from/to their flash memory. We used a TFTP server in source, to read firewall configuration and extract the rules that have to be migrated and another server in destination to insert the rules into firewall.

---

[1]/www.gns3.com/
[2]www.virtualbox.org/
[3]www.wireshark.org/

4.5.2   Testbed Description

In this section we explain our testbed architecture, environment setup and network design for two data centers with a 3-tier deployment model. We also introduce some tools as well as optional software applications that can facilitate network configuration and tests.

Migration Framework: Migration of a VM from one physical server to another can be done in two different ways. These methods are based on the features that are provided by VirtualBox. Below, each method with its features is explained.

4.5.2.1   *Live Migration by Teleporting*   Teleporting is a feature of VirtualBox that enables live migration of a VM state. However, it has some conditions and limitations that have to be considered. The first limitation is that the migration can be done between two VMs with the same configuration. An important condition for migration is that both of the VMs have to be running at the migration moment; this means that a VM in destination of the migration [5] should be running and ready to receive the running state from source VM. The state is sent through a TCP/IP port and it starts from the destination side by listening to the port. Then, source VM sends its running state to the listening VM and stops that process (VM is still running). Whereas teleporting supports multi-platforms, some errors may occur when CPU of the source and the destination machines have different architectures. The last and most important condition for teleporting is a shared storage that keeps both source and destination VMs. It implies that even though the source and the destination can be two separate physical machines, they need to have access to a shared storage and both of the mentioned VMs have to reside on that shared storage device. Access to the shared storage can be achieved by implementing network file system (NFS) or server message block (SMB)/common internet file system (CIFS).

Although in many real-world data centers, live migration is similar to what is offered by teleporting in VirtualBox, a shared storage between data centers is not always available. Normally, shared storage is available between servers that are located within the same data center. Hence, we propose another way to migrate a VM without having access to a shared storage media by using snapshots.

4.5.2.2   *Migration by Moving Snapshots*   Snapshot is another feature that VirtualBox offers for saving and restoring the current state of a running VM. By default, this feature is not meant to be used for VM migration, however we utilize it in our migration framework. Snapshot is the preservation of the current running state of a VM. This state revert back in the future or immediately after taking the snapshot. When a snapshot is taken, three things are saved to the disk:

- *All VM Configurations*: A small XML file that contains complete copy of the VM settings and configurations.

- *Hard Disk Image*: A file that contains the state of all virtual disks that are attached to the VM. Note that this file is a differencing image, and is not the entire virtual hard disk image.

- *Memory State*: An image from the memory of running VM that can be as large as the size of VM memory.

There are two ways of migrating the VM and its state by using snapshots. The first way is freezing the VM in the source location and migrating it to the destination in one shot [11]. Obviously, this takes quite a long time (depends on the entire VM size), which may not be acceptable for a VM migration process. In our migration framework, we leveraged snapshot features and moved the VM and its state from source to destination in two steps. In the first step, the source machine sends a copy of the VM virtual hard disk to the destination place. Obviously, sending the virtual hard disk can take a long time but this is not a problem, because meanwhile, VM is running in the source location. When the VM virtual hard disk is completely received by the destination, the source machine freezes the VM state by taking a snapshot from the running VM. As mentioned earlier, snapshot creates a file that contains difference images from the virtual hard disk in addition to two other files that contain VM configurations and memory state, respectively. In the second step, the source machine sends the snapshot to the destination machine. When the VM snapshot has been received in the destination location and the VM connection to the destination network established properly, VM starts running and resumes all the processes that were stopped before migration. At this point, the source storage is allowed to wipe out the VM. Although the VM transfer is not a live migration, it has a short downtime and more importantly, it does not need a shared storage between source and destination machines. All the steps in the migration process can be verified by a tool that checks the correctness of each step, and either passes or reverts to the migration process. An extension to this framework is a security-preserving migration framework, which is explained in Chapter 12.

4.6   A Case Study and Other Use Cases

In this section we first discuss some use cases of our cloud testbed [4] and then we study a VM migration case from one data center to another. Our testing environment has a flexible architecture that enables the user to test various types of security scenarios for different purposes. For instance, one of the features that can be added to the testbed is network-based IPS 7 devices. IPS is a security appliance that monitors the network activities and blocks/stops malicious activities after detecting them. Much research can be conducted to evaluate the impact of using IPS on the performance of data centers and finding methods which can optimize it. Another possible use case could be testing site-to-site or client-to-site VPN from different locations and then investigate how the IPsec connection can be affected by VM migration or firewall rule changes. Moreover, various scenarios can be designed to test the compliance of SSL VPN, which is also supported by this testbed. It is worth mentioning that, although VPN can significantly improve the security of a remote connection, misconfiguration of it can backfire and turn VPN into an attack vector. Principally, this testbed architecture can be used as a testing environment in network and cloud security research or as a training appliance for security labs and online classes.

4.6.1   Case Study: Firewall Rule Migration and Verification

We now explain the migration case study. We assume that the migration can be initiated and controlled by a network admin or an automated program. This migrator not only moves the VM, but also is responsible for migrating the firewall rules. Thus, the security of VM and data centers can be preserved after migration. In this case study we deploy a typical three-tier cloud of web applications: A web tier that implements the presentation logic, application server tier which implements the presentation logic, application server tier that implements the business logic, and a back-end database tier. A possible implementation would be to deploy a VM per each tier [12]. The tenant has also specified a firewall policy for each VM group as follows:

1. Web group allows any host to connect on ports 80 (http) and 443 (https),

2. Application group allows only web services to connect to port 8000,

3. Database group allows only application services to connect to port 3306,

4. All the above groups allow the corporation network (CorpNet) to connect on port 22 (ssh).

4.6.2   Existing Security Issues in Cloud Scenarios

Traditionally data was stored on users' own premises so data owner need not to worry about the data, but now in the current era of cloud computing [3] where a huge amount of data is stored in unknown remote locations, several security issues need to be addressed. Cloud computing is a way to enhance capabilities and capacity dynamically with minimal investment in terms of infrastructure, technology and software licensing. Despite so many advantages, customers are least willing to use cloud in the case of confidential data. The most important reason behind this is security. Based on the IDC (International Data Corporation) enterprise survey security is depicted as the main challenge, followed by availability and performance.

Security in itself is broad term which covers numerous aspects. CSA (*Cloud Security Alliance*) has identified as *Notorious Nine* computing threats for 2013 as follows:

1. Data Breaches, in which VMs on the same server can extract the valuable information from others using a side channel attack but this attack, can be mitigated using encryption.

2. Data Loss, in which attackers can delete or modify user data. A possible solution for this is to keep a backup of data but it will increase the exposure of data to breaches.

3. Account or Service Traffic Hijacking, in which if attackers gain access to user credentials so they can easily monitor your activities and transactions and redirect the user to any sites. A possible solution for this is two-step authentications.

4. Insecure APIs and Interfaces.

5. Denials of Service, in which, availability and response time are major factors from the point of view of end users. If it is not possible for attackers to entirely shut down user application then they may create a cause which increases the processing time, which is not tolerable. With virtualization, a single machine can be divided into many VMs, which is a possible solution for denial of service.

6. Malicious Insiders, who may be employees, contractors or business partners.

7. Abuse of Cloud Services, like a bad guy using a cloud service to interrupt an encryption key too difficult to crack on a standard computer.

8. Insufficient Due Diligence, that is, organizations embrace the cloud while not fully understanding the cloud environment and associated risks and therefore users don't fully utilize the Cloud resources.

9. Shared Technology Vulnerabilities; Cloud service providers use shared infrastructure in terms of CPU caches and memory that was not designed to offer strong isolation.

Hence, as the IDC survey reveals, security is a major concern for Cloud with 87% of the vote, and in the specific field of security, data security in terms of data breach and loss are the top two points which need to be addressed carefully.

4.6.3   Authentication in Cloud

Authentication is a process which decides the legitimate users by verifying the details provided by the end users. In most applications, one-tiered traditional credential authentication (e.g., user name and password) is used but it is not safe enough in the case of cloud (see Figure 4.2). It is very necessary to provide strong authentication for executing important transactions over the Internet. Authentication is the first phase depicted which needs to be passed by the users to gain access over resources there; after proper authorization, data is transmitted over network securely. To improve the security, multi-tier or multi-factor authentications should be used in the cloud. Multi-factor authentications, upon the principal of something we know already, e.g., stored password, and something recently provided by the Cloud side automated server to us, e.g., secret code to registered devices. Various factors defined by NIST which should be incorporated into the authentication system are:

- *Something user knows*: Shared secrets are the information users share with the trusted cloud services provider. Since it may be a password which is stored in the memory, it is called as something that is known rather than something one has. This method covers only single level of authentication which is the weakest form because the password is entered using a keyboard in the system, hence vulnerable to keyboard logging or shoulder surfing attacks [13, 14].

- *Something user has*: Registered device or something which users have with them at the time of authentication, e.g., mobile or keys.

- *Something user is*: Personal attributes which uniquely belong to the user only, e.g., voice or fingerprints, iris and retinal scanning, facial expression, thumbprints, DNA and many other things.

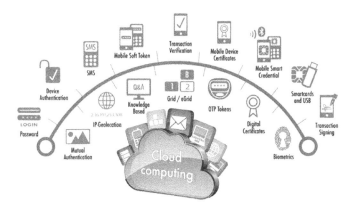

Figure 4.2   Authentication in Cloud.

A strong authentication system must incorporate all three factors to resist the attacks mentioned below:

- *Man-in-the-middle*: In this attack, a malicious attacker situates himself/herself in between client and verifier to intercept and alter the data flows between them.

- *Verifier impersonation attack*: An attack where the attacker impersonates the verifier in an authentication protocol, usually to learn a password.

- *Password guessing attacks*: Here the attacker usually guesses the password in repeated login trials.

- *Replay attack*: Here an attacker records and reruns some portion of the last good protocol run to the verifier.

- *Eavesdropping*: Here the attacker illegally listens to or intercepts the private communication, such as phone call or fax transmission.

- *Session hijacking*: This occurs when a session token is sent to a client browser from the web server following the successful authentication of a client logon by guessing the session token.

Authentication in Cloud [2, 9, 10] is provided in various ways, e.g., SMS OTP (one-time password), telephony OTP, e-mail OTP, static PIN, pluggable USB, user's known password, KBA (knowledge-based answers/questions), Digital certificate, federated IDs (a token is issued in trusted languages, i.e., SAML- security assertion markup language) that validates the user's identity.

4.6.4   Hybrid Approaches for Security in Cloud Computing

A single technique can't offer in-depth security in Cloud [1, 8], it really requires a strong authentication, data integrity and confidentiality. Various approaches are discussed below which give different tiers of authenticity in order to ensure security.

1. Puzzle solving pattern and time is stored and validated by local server and if the user is authenticated, begins accessing the cloud services. Although this scheme ensures two-tier authentications, it is static in nature; if an unauthorized person once identified the stored pattern, he/she could easily break the security.

2. Diffie-Hellman with digital signature for providing two-tier authentications. But digital signature uses so many parameters, which is why it's heavy enough and also requires a proper key management.

3. Hash Message Authentication Code in which key, message and hash function is concatenated along to ensure authentication. This approach describes only single-tier authentication that is weak in the case of cloud computing.

4. Diffie-Hellman Key Exchange Mechanism for the connection establishment and elliptic curve cryptography for data encryption. Traditional one-tier authentication which is vulnerable to security attacks.

5. RSA Algorithm for encryption/decryption which is followed by the process of digital certification. This algorithm ensures only single-tier authentication using digital certification, which raises a problem of key management.

4.6.5   Data Transfer Architecture in Cloud Computing

User sends requests to the cloud services using a web browser, so first he/she will redirect automatically to an account authentication server. Account authentication server (Figure 4.3) first asks the user about his/her stored authentication details; these details may be anything, e.g., credential login/password supported by OpenNebula cloud, digital certificate X.509 supported by Eucalyptus and Nimbus open-source cloud. After first step of verification, if server supports for multi-factor authentication, it will continue to ask queries by sending some pin or password to registered device that will be reentered by the user; if given information is correct he/she will be redirected to the cloud storage with generated cookies. Now data transfer takes place between end user and cloud storage securely using the proper encryption method for providing confidentiality [15].

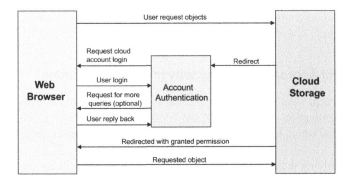

Figure 4.3   Data transfer after authentication in cloud.

4.7 Conclusion

Various approaches for secure data transfer have been analyzed that focus mainly on the authentication parameter. These approaches have been categorized on single- and multi-tier authentications. These authentications may use digital certificate, HMAC or OTP on registered devices. This chapter presented an overview of concepts related to security; Cloud security and security appliances, VM migration in clouds and security concerns, software-defined networking, firewalls in cloud and SDN, SDN and Floodlight controllers, distributed messaging system, customized testbed for testing migration security in cloud. The case studies included: Firewall rule migration and verification, existing security issues in cloud scenarios, authentication in cloud, hybrid approaches to security in cloud computing and data transfer architecture in cloud computing.

REFERENCES

1. Cardosa, M., Korupolu, M. R., & Singh, A. (2009). Shares and utilities based power consolidation in virtualized server environments. In Integrated Network Management, 2009. IM'09. IFIP/IEEE International Symposium (pp. 327-334). IEEE.

2. Chase, J. S., Anderson, D. C., Thakar, P. N., Vahdat, A. M., & Doyle, R. P. (2001). Managing energy and server resources in hosting centers. *ACM SIGOPS Operating Systems Review*, 35(5), 103-116.

3. Chen, Y., Das, A., Qin, W., Sivasubramaniam, A., Wang, Q., & Gautam, N. (2005). Managing server energy and operational costs in hosting centers. *In ACM SIGMETRICS performance evaluation review* (Vol. 33, No. 1, pp. 303-314). ACM.

4. Chung, E. Y., Benini, L., Bogliolo, A., Lu, Y. H., & De Micheli, G. (2002). Dynamic power management for nonstationary service requests. *IEEE Transactions on Computers*, 51(11), 1345-1361.

5. Clark, C., Fraser, K., Hand, S., Hansen, J. G., Jul, E., Limpach, C., ... & Warfield, A. (2005, May). Live migration of virtual machines. In Proceedings of the 2nd Conference on Symposium on Networked Systems Design & Implementation-Volume 2 (pp. 273-286). USENIX Association.

6. Feller, E., Rilling, L., & Morin, C. (2012). Snooze: A scalable and autonomic virtual machine management framework for private clouds. In Proceedings of the 2012 12th IEEE/ACM International Symposium on Cluster, Cloud and Grid Computing (ccgrid 2012) (pp. 482-489). IEEE Computer Society.

7. Feller, E., Rohr, C., Margery, D., & Morin, C. (2012). Energy management in IaaS clouds: a holistic approach. In Cloud Computing (CLOUD), 2012 IEEE 5th International Conference (pp. 204-212). IEEE.

8. Deshpande, U., & Keahey, K. (2017). Traffic-sensitive live migration of virtual machines. *Future Generation Computer Systems*, 72, 118-128.

9. Abali, B., Isci, C., Kephart, J. O., McIntosh, S. K., & Sarma, D. (2017). U.S. Patent No. 9,619,259. Washington, DC: U.S. Patent and Trademark Office.

10. ALAmri, S. M., & Guan, L. (2016). Exploring the Firewall Security Consistency in Cloud Computing during Live Migration. In Proceedings of the 7th International Conference on Computing Communication and Networking Technologies (p. 40). ACM.

11. Sun, D., Zhang, J., Fan, W., Wang, T., Liu, C., & Huang, W. (2016). SPLM: security protection of live virtual machine migration in cloud computing. In Proceedings of the 4th ACM International Workshop on Security in Cloud Computing (pp. 2-9). ACM.

12. Huang, T., Zhu, Y., Wu, Y., Bressan, S., & Dobbie, G. (2016). Anomaly detection and identification scheme for VM live migration in cloud infrastructure. *Future Generation Computer Systems*, 56, 736-745.

13. Devine, W. M., Gottimukkala, S., Huynh, L. T., Joseph, D., Law, M. S., & Overby Jr, L. H. (2017). U.S. Patent No. 9,715,401. Washington, DC: U.S. Patent and Trademark Office.

14. ALAmri, S. M., & Guan, L. (2016). Exploring the Firewall Security Consistency in Cloud Computing during Live Migration. In Proceedings of the 7th International Conference on Computing Communication and Networking Technologies (p. 40). ACM.

15. Gu, J., Hua, Z., Xia, Y., Chen, H., Zang, B., Guan, H., & Li, J. (2017). Secure Live Migration of SGX Enclaves on Untrusted Cloud. In Dependable Systems and Networks (DSN), 2017 47th Annual IEEE/IFIP International Conference (pp. 225-236). IEEE.

CHAPTER 5

SOLUTION FOR SECURE LIVE MIGRATION

Abstract

Virtualization is one of the key parts of IaaS (infrastructure as a service)cloud offerings and private clouds, and it is progressively being used in portions of the back end of PaaS (platform as a service) and SaaS (software as a service) providers too. Virtualization is additionally, naturally, a key technology for virtual desktops, which are conveyed from private or public clouds. This chapter gives an overview of detecting and preventing data migrations to the cloud, protecting data moving to the cloud, application security, virtualization, VM guest hardening, security as a service, identity as service requirements, web services SECaaS requirements, email SECaaS requirements, security assessment SECaaS requirements, intrusion detection SECaaS requirements, SIEM SECaaS requirements, encryption SECaaS requirements, business continuity and disaster recovery requirements and network security SECaaS requirements.

Keywords: Security as a service, virtual machine guest hardening, application security, data migrations, access management services.

5.1   Detecting and Preventing Data Migrations to the Cloud

A common situation organizations face with the cloud is managing storage data [1]. Many organizations report individuals or corporate units moving sometimes sensitive data to cloud services without the approval or perhaps notification of IT or security. Aside from ancient data security controls (*like access controls or encryption*), there are two other steps to help operate unapproved data moving to cloud services:

1. Monitor for large internal data migrations with file activity monitoring (FAM) and database activity monitoring (DAM).

2. Monitor for data moving to the cloud with URL filters and data loss prevention (DLP).

5.1.1   Internal Data Migrations

Before data can move to the cloud it is required to be pulled from its existing repository. Database activity monitoring can search when an administrator or other user pulls a group of data sets or replicates a database, which could indicate a migration.

5.1.2   Movement to the Cloud

A combination of URL searching (*web content security gateways*) and data loss prevention (DLP) can find data moving from the enterprise into the cloud. URL filtering permits you to observe (*and prevent*) users connecting to cloud services. Since the executive interfaces for these services generally use totally different addresses than the consumption aspect, the user can distinguish between anyone accessing an executive console versus a user accessing an application already hosted by the service provider. Look for a tool that gives a cloud services list and keeps it up to date, instead of one that requires creating a custom classification, and also the user managing the destination addresses. Far more prominent is the use of DLP tools. DLP tools look at the particular data/content being transmitted, not simply the destination. So the user can generate alerts (*or blocks*) supported by the classification of the data. As an example, the user can permit corporate private data to go to an endorsed cloud service but block similar content from moving to an unapproved service. The insertion purpose [2] of the DLP solution can verify how successfully data leakage can be detected. For instance, availability of cloud solutions to different users (*e.g., employees, merchants, customers*) outside of the company network environment avoids or nullifies any DLP solutions if they are inserted at the company boundary.

5.2   Protecting Data Moving to the Cloud

In both public and private cloud deployments, and throughout the various service models, it's necessary to protect data in transit. This includes:

1. Data moving from ancient infrastructure to cloud service providers, as well as public/private, internal/external and alternative permutations.

2. Data moving between cloud service providers.

3. Data moving between instances (*or alternative components*) inside a given cloud. There are three options (*or order of preference*):

   - *Client/Application Encryption*: Data is encoded on the endpoint or server before being sent over the network or is already stored in a appropriate encrypted format. This includes nearby client (*agent-based*) encryption (*e.g., for stored files*) or encryption coordinated in applications.

   - *Link/Network Encryption*: Regular network encryption techniques, including SSL, VPNs, and SSH, can be either hardware or software. End to end is ideal yet may not be viable in all architectures.

   - *Proxy-Based Encryption*: Data is transmitted to an intermediary machine or server that encodes before sending it further on the network. It is typically the most popular possibility for integrating with legacy applications but isn't generally recommended.

5.3 Application Security

Cloud environments [3], especially public cloud environments, by virtue of their flexibility and openness challenge several fundamental assumptions about application security. Some of these assumptions are well known, however, many are not. This section is meant to provide guidance on how distributed cloud computing influences security over the time period of an application, from configuration to operations to ultimate decommissioning. This guidance is for all partners (*including application designers, technical management security professionals and operations personnel*) on how to best relieve risk and manage assurance once coming up with cloud computing applications.

Cloud computing is a specific challenge for applications over the layers of SaaS, PaaS and IaaS. Cloud-based software applications require a configuration rigor similar to an application connecting to the raw Internet; the security must be provided by the application without any assumptions being made concerning the external environment. In any case, the threats that applications are going to be exposed to during a cloud environment are quite like those experienced in a traditional data center. This creates the necessity for rigorous practices that have to be followed once developing or migrating applications to the cloud.

This application security domain has been classified into the following areas of focus:

1. Secure SDLC (*general practices for secure software development life cycle and nuances specific to the Cloud*).

2. Authentication, compliance, authorization – Application Security Architecture in the Cloud.

3. Identity and also the consumption of identity as it relates to Ccloud application security.

4. Entitlement procedures and risk-based access management as it relates to cloud encryption in cloud-based applications.

5. Application approval management (policy authoring/upgrade, enforcement).

6. Application penetration testing for the Cloud (*general practices and subtleties particular to cloud-based applications*).

7. Monitoring applications within the Cloud.

8. Application authentication, consistence, and risk management and also the repercussions of multi-tenancy and shared infrastructure.

9. The distinction between avoiding malicious software and providing application security.

5.4   Virtualization

Virtualization is one of the key parts of IaaS cloud offerings and private clouds [4], and it is progressively used in portions of the backend of PaaS and SaaS providers too. Virtualization is additionally, naturally, a key technology for virtual desktops, which are conveyed from private or public clouds (see Figure 5.1).

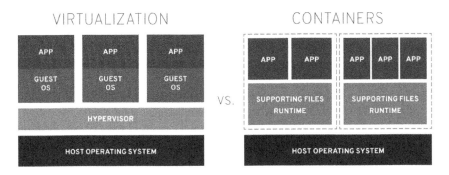

Figure 5.1   Virtualization vs. Containers

The advantage of virtualization is well known, including multi-tenure, better server utilization, and data center solidification. Cloud providers can accomplish higher density, which translates to better margins, and enterprises can use virtualization to capital expenditure on server hardware as well as increase operational potency.

However, virtualization carries with it all the security concerns of the OS running as a guest, along with new security considerations about the hypervisor layer, and additionally new virtualization threats, inter-VM assaults and blind spots; and performance considerations arising from CPU and memory utilized for security, and operational complexness from *"VM sprawl"* as a security matter. New issues like instant-on gaps, data commingling, the issues of encrypting VM images, and leftover data destruction are coming into focus. While there are several types of virtualization [5], by far the most well-known one is the virtualized OS, which is, the focus for this domain (see Table 5.1).

Table 5.1   Virtualization-related security issues

No.	Virtualization-related security issue description
1	VM guest solidifying
2	Hypervisor security
3	Inter-VM attacks and blind spots
4	Performance considerations
5	Operational complexness from VM sprawl
6	Instant-on gaps
7	VM encryption
8	Data mixing together
9	VM knowledge destruction
10	In-motion VMs

5.5 Virtual Machine Guest Hardening

Proper hardening and security of a VM instance, as well as firewall (*inbound/outbound*), HIPS, web application assurance, antivirus, file integrity monitoring, and log monitoring are often delivered via software in every guest or utilize an inline VM joined with hypervisor-based APIs.

Hypervisor Security: The hypervisor has to be locked down and solidified using best practices. The primary issues for enterprises and virtualization users ought to be the proper management of configuration and operations and also physical security of the server hosting the hypervisor.

Inter-VM Attacks and Blind Spots: Virtualization has a great effect on network security. VMs can communicate with each other over a hardware backplane, instead of a network. Thus, standard network-based security controls are blind to the present traffic and can't perform monitoring or inline blocking. Inline virtual appliances facilitate solving this problem; another approach to the present issue is hardware-assisted virtualization, which needs API-level integration with hypervisors and virtualization management system. Migration of VMs is an additional concern. An attack situation could be the migration of a malicious VM in a trusted zone, and with ancient network-based security controls, its misconduct will not be noticed. Installing a full set of security tools on each individual VM is another way to add a layer of protection.

Performance Concerns: Installing security software intended for physical servers onto a virtualized server may result in severe degradation in execution, as some security tasks like antivirus checking are CPU-intensive. The shared environment in virtualized servers prompts resource contention. Particularly with virtual desktops or high-density environments, security software has to be virtualization-aware or it has to perform security functions on a solitary VM to support alternative VMs.

Operational Complexity from VM Sprawl: The ease with which VMs can be provisioned has prompted an increase in the number of requests for VMs in typical enterprises. This creates a larger attack surface and will increase the percentage of misconfigurations or operator mistakes, opening a security hole. Policy-based management and use of a virtualization management framework is essential.

Instant-On Gaps: The ease with which VMs are often stopped or started, combined with the rate at which threats change, creates a circumstance where a VM can be safely configured once it's turned off, but by the time it's started again, threats have evolved, leaving the machine vulnerable. Best practices incorporate network-based security and "*virtual patching*" that inspects activity for known attacks before they can get to a recently provisioned or newly started VM. It is also prudent to enforce network access control (NAC)-like capabilities to isolate stale VMs until their tenets and pattern files are updated and an output has been run.

VM Encryption: VM images are susceptible to theft or modification once they are dormant or running. The solution to this issue is to encrypt VM images at all times, yet there are performance issues at this time. For high security or controlled environments, the execution cost is worth it. Encryption must be joined with administrative controls, DLP, and audit trails to keep a snapshot of a running VM from "*getting away into the wild*," which might provide the attacker access to the data in the VM snapshot.

Data Commingling: There is concern that diverse categories of data (or VMs hosting different categories of data) might be intermixed on the constant physical machine. In PCI terms, we allude to this as a mixed-mode deployment. We prescribe using a combination of VLANs, firewalls, and IDS/IPS to confirm VM isolation as a mechanism for supporting mixed-mode arrangements. We also suggest using data categorization and policy-based management (e.g., DLP) to keep this. In distributed computing environments, all tenants within the multi-tenant virtual environment might potentially share the lowest common divisor of security.

VM Data Destruction: When a VM is moved from one physical server to another server, enterprises need affirmations that no bits are abandoned on the disk that could be recovered by another user or once the disk is de-provisioned. Zeroing memory/storage or encryption of all data are solutions to this issue. Encryption keys ought to be stored on a policy-based key server far from the virtual environment. Additionally, if a VM is migrated while it is running, it might be at risk itself during the relocation if encryption, or proper wiping, isn't used.

VM Image Tampering: Pre-configured virtual appliances and machine images might be misconfigured or may have been messed with before you start them.

In-Motion VM: The distinctive ability to move VMs starting with one physical server to another is an essential quality for audits and security monitoring. In several cases, VMs can be migrated to another physical server (*regardless of geographic location*) while not creating an alert or trackable audit trail.

1. Users should identify which types of virtualization the cloud provider uses, assuming any.

2. Implementers should think about a zoned approach with production environments separate from test/development and sensitive data/workloads.

3. Implementers should think about performance once testing and installing VM security tools, as performance differs widely. Virtualization-aware server and system security tools are also necessary to consider.

4. User should evaluate, arrange, and refine the permitting agreements with major merchants in virtualized environments.

5. Implementers should secure every virtualized OS by using hardening software in every guest occurrence or use an inline VM joined with hypervisor-based API's 140.

6. Virtualized operative systems should be increased by inherent security measures, utilizing third party security technology to provide stratified security controls and lessen dependency on the platform provider alone.

7. Implementers should make sure that secure by default configurations take after or exceed obtainable industry baselines.

8. Implementers should encode VM images when not being used.

9. Implementers should investigate the efficacy and feasibility of isolating VMs and creating security zones by type of use (*e.g., desktop vs. server*), production stage (*e.g., advancement, production, and testing*), and affectability of data on partitioned physical hardware components like servers, storage, etc.

10. Implementers should ensure that the security vulnerability evaluation tools or services cover the virtualization technologies used.

11. Implementers should consider executing data automated discovery and labeling arrangements (*e.g., DLP*) organization-wide to enhance the data classification and management between VMs and environments.

12. Implementers should consider fixing VM images very still or protect newly spun-up VMs till they can be patched.

13. Implementers should comprehended which security controls are in place external to the VMs to ensure administrative interfaces (*web-based, APIs, etc.*) exposed to the users.

Requirements:

1. VM specific security mechanisms implanted in hypervisor APIs must be used to provide granular observing of traffic crossing VM backplanes, which can be obscure to conventional network security controls.

2. Implementers must redesign the security approach to reflect upcoming security issues of virtualization.

3. Implementers must encode data accessed by VMs utilizing policy-based key servers that store the keys independently from the VM and the information.

4. Users must know the multi-tenancy circumstances concerning their VMs where regulatory issues may warrant segregation.

5. Users must accept the pedigree and integrity of any VM image or format starting from any third party, or better yet, create their own VM occurrences.

6. Virtualized operative systems must embrace firewall (*inbound/outbound*), antivirus, host intrusion prevention system (HIPS), network intrusion prevention system (NIPS), file integrity monitoring, web application protection and log monitoring, and so on. Security countermeasures can be delivered through software in each guest virtual instance or by utilizing an inline VM consolidated with hypervisor-based APIs.

7. Providers must clean any reinforcement and failover systems while deleting and wiping the VM images.

8. Providers must have a coverage mechanism in place that provides evidence of detachment and raises alerts if there is a breach of isolation.

5.6   Security as a Service

Cloud computing [6] represents one of the most critical shifts in information technology the industry has encountered. Reaching the point where processing functions as a utility has incredible potential, promising sweeping innovations. One such innovation is the centralization of security assets (eee Figure 5.2). The security industry has perceived the advantage of a standardized security system for both the providers and consumers. With regards to a cloud service level agreement amongst providers and consumers, a standardized security system is a document that specifies how and where security services are given. With the maturation of security offerings supported standard frameworks, cloud consumers have perceived the need to centralize computing data for providers and consumers. One of the developments of the maturity of Cloud as a platform for commercial operations is the appropriation of security as a service (SECaaS) on a worldwide scale, and therefore the recognition of how security can be upgraded. The global implementation of security as an outsourced artifact will eventually minimize the disparate fluctuations and security voids. SECaaS looks at company security from the Cloud as what separates it from most of the other work/analysis on cloud security. Transcendentally, cloud security discussions have concentrated on how to migrate to the Cloud and how to confirm confidentiality, integrity and location. Availability is maintained when using the Cloud. SECaaS looks from the other side to secure network and data within the cloud as well as hybrid and traditional venture networks via cloud-based services. These network systems may be in the Cloud or more generally hosted within the user's premises. A case of this might be facilitated spam and AV filtering.

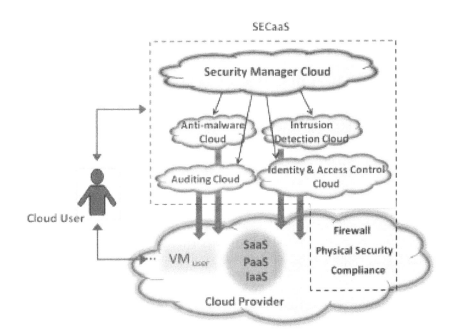

Figure 5.2   Security as a service.

5.6.1   Ubiquity of Security as a Service

Clients are both excited and nervous at the possibilities of cloud computing. They are energized by the opportunities to reduce capital expenses and excited for an opportunity to divest infrastructure management and highlight core competencies.

Most of all, they are energized by the agility offered by the on-demand provisioning of processing resources and the ability to adjust information technology with business systems and needs more readily. However, clients are also very worried about the security risks of cloud computing and therefore the loss of direct control over the security of systems for which they are responsible. Vendors have endeavored to satisfy this demand for security by offering security services in a cloud platform, but since these services take many forms and lack transparency with respect to deployed security controls, they have brought market confusion and complicated the selection procedure. This has led to limited reception of cloud-based security services so far. Security as a service is experiencing an exponential development, with Gartner having once predicted the tripling of cloud-based security service usage in many sections by 2013.

Various security vendors are currently leveraging cloud-based models to convey security solutions. This shift has happened for a variety of reasons including more economies of scale and streamlined delivery mechanisms. Clients are increasingly faced with assessing security solutions that do not run on premises. Clients need to understand the unique, various, and pervasive nature of cloud conveyed security offerings so that they are in a position to assess the offerings and to know if the offerings will meet their needs [7].

Despite the impressive array of advantages provided by cloud security services like dynamic scalability, virtually unlimited assets, and larger economies of scale that exist with lower or no expense of ownership, there are concerns regarding security in the cloud environment. Some security concerns are about consistence, multi-tenancy, and merchant lock-in. While these are being referred to as inhibitors to the migration of security into the cloud, these same issues exist with traditional information centers.

Security in the cloud environment is commonly based on the concern that absence of visibility into the security controls implemented implies systems aren't locked down as far as they are in traditional information centers, and that the personnel lack the best possible accreditations and background checks. SECaaS providers perceive the fragility of the relationship and regularly go to amazing lengths to ensure that their area is locked down as much as possible. They often run record checks on their work force that rival even the hardest government background checks and they run them frequently. Physical and staff security is one of the highest priorities of a SECaaS provider.

Consistence has been raised as a concern given the worldwide regulatory environment. SECaaS providers have also recognized this and have gone to great lengths to demonstrate their capacity to not only meet but exceed this necessity or to ensure that it is incorporated into a user's network. An SECaaS provider ought to be aware of the geographical and regional directions that affect the services and their clients, and these directions can be engineered into the offerings and service implementations. The most judicious SECaaS providers frequently enlist mediation and law services to preemptively resolve the regulatory needs of the clients with the territorial regulatory requirements of a jurisdiction. While deploying SECaaS in a very regulated industry or environment, concurrence on the metrics defining the service level required to accomplish regulatory objectives should be arranged in parallel with the SLA records defining service [8].

As with any cloud service, multi-tenancy presents concerns of data spillage between virtual instances. While clients are concerned about this, the SECaaS providers are also highly concerned in light of the hostile nature of modern business. As a result, an experienced offering may take vital precautions to ensure data is very compartmentalized and any data that is shared is anonymized to ensure the identity and source. This similarly applies to the data being observed by the SECaaS providers and to the information held by them such as log and review data from the clients' systems (*both cloud and non-cloud*) that they monitor [9].

Another approach to the litigiousness of multi-tenant environments is expanded analytics coupled with semantic preparing. Resource descriptors and connected jurimetrics, a process through which legal thinking is interpreted as high level ideas and expressed in a machine-readable format, might be employed proactively to determine any legal ambiguity regarding a common resource.

When utilizing a SECaaS merchant, an enterprise places some, numerous or all security logging, consistence, and reporting into the custody of a service provider that may sometimes have exclusive standards. In the event that an enterprise looks for a new provider, they have to concern themselves with an orderly transition and somehow find a way for the current information and log files to be deciphered correctly and in a forensically sound way. It is essential to note that other than multi-tenancy, each of these worries is not *cloud unique* but are issues faced by both in-house models and outsourcing models. Consequently, non-proprietary unified security controls, like those proposed by the Cloud Security Alliance Cloud Controls Matrix, are expected to help enterprises and merchants benefit from the SECaaS domain.

5.6.2   Advantages of Implementing Security as a Service

The potential strategic benefits of utilizing centralized security services are well known by technical specialists who witness the everyday efficiencies gained. Just as distributed computing offers many favorable circumstances to both providers and clients, cloud SECaaS offers many critical benefits due to a number of variables, including aggregation of knowledge, expansive actionable intelligence, and having a full supplement of security experts on hand at all times, to name a few. Organizations that are actively involved in the centralization and institutionalization of security best practices ordinarily gain significant medium- and long-term cost savings and focused benefits over their adversaries in the market because of the efficiencies gained. Security conveyed as a service enables the clients of security services to measure every vendor by a solitary security standard to have a better understanding of what they are obtaining [10].

Competitive Advantages: Organizations that employ third party security service administration gain an aggressive edge over their competitors due to early access to information supportive in understanding the risk proposition of a given IT system. Moreover, through the use of a centralized security infrastructure, clients are better able to stem the incorporation of undesirable content. Organizations that use a third party to report details on regulatory compliance and measure compulsory predicates the inherited legal and contractual obligations connected to identities and data, might avoid costly litigation and fines that their rivals are vulnerable to. Once comprehensive security services are adopted and executed, providers reap the competitive benefits of having the ability to assure their customers that they meet security best practice. Customers making use of those services have the advantage of being able to point to security providers as a part of their consistence framework and to third party assurance providers for confirmation of the achievement of service level agreement commitments.

Enhanced Vendor-Client Relationship: There are many obvious benefits of security as a service. Transparency provided by a third party confirmation service enables clients to understand exactly what they are getting, which facilitates comparison of merchant services and holds the merchant to clear and agreed upon standards. Migration services enable the relocation of data and services from one merchant to another. By leveraging migration services, clients and providers are better enabled to apply market pressures on their tertiary suppliers, improving the value for the companies that expend the services and securing the supply chain.

Assorted Qualities of Existing Security as a Service Offering: Security as a service (SECaaS) is more than an outsourcing framework for security administration; it is a crucial component in secure business versatility and continuity. As a business strength control, SECaaS offers more benefits. Due to the flexible model of services delivered through the Cloud, clients need only pay for the amount they need, such as the quantity of workstations to be ensured, and not for the supporting infrastructure and staffing to support the different security services. A security focused provider offers more prominent security expertise than is normally available within an organization. At last, outsourcing administrative tasks, like log management, can save time and money, allowing an association to devote more assets to its center skills. Gartner had predicted that cloud-based security controls for informing applications like anti-malware and anti-spam programs would create 60 percent of the revenue in that company sector by 2013. The sectors of Cloud SECaaS that will likely interest almost all clients and security professionals are:

1. Identity services and access management services

2. Network security

3. Data loss prevention (DLP)

4. Email security

5. Web security

6. Encryption

7. Security assessments

8. Intrusion management, detection and prevention (IDS/IPS)

9. Business continuity and disaster recovery

10. Security information and event management (SIEM)

5.6.3   Identity, Entitlement, and Access Management Services

Identity-as-a-service (IDaaS) is a nonexclusive term that covers one or many of the services which may contain an identity ecosystem, like policy enforcement points (PEP-as-a-service), policy access points (PAP-as-a-service), and policy decision points (PDP-as-a-service), services that furnish entities with identity, services that give attributes and services that give notoriety.

All these identity services are provided as a solitary stand-alone service, as a mix-and-match service from many providers, or today most likely a hybrid solution of public and private, conventional IAM, and cloud services. These identity services ought to provide controls for identities, access, and benefits management. Identity services ought to include people, procedures, and systems that are used to oversee access to enterprise assets by assuring that the identity of an entity is checked, then granting the right level of access in view of this assured identity. Review logs of activities, such as effective and failed authentication and access endeavors, should be managed by the application/answer or the SIEM service. Identity, access management and entitlement services are a protective and preventative specialized control.

Data Loss Prevention: Monitors and protects data at rest, in motion, and in use, both in the cloud service and on premises. DLP services offer security of data for the most part by running as a customer on desktops/servers and enforcing strategies around what activities are authorized for specific data content. Where these differ from broad rules, such as "no ftp" or "no uploads to web page," is the level to which they comprehend data, e.g., the user can indicate no documents with numbers that seem like credit cards can be emailed; anything saved to USB storage is automatically encoded and can only be decoded on another office-owned machine with a correctly installed DLP customer; and only customers with functioning DLP software can open data or files from the file server. Inside the cloud, DLP services might be offered as something that is given as part of the build such that all servers built for that customer get the DLP software installed with a concurred set of of rules deployed. In addition, DLP may focal central ID- or cloud dealers to enforce usage profiles. The ability to influence a service to monitor and control information flows from an enterprise to the various levels in the cloud service supply chain might be used as a preventative control for transborder transport, and consequent loss, of regulated data data, i.e., PII-143. This DLP offering is a preventative technical control.

Web Security: Web security is real-time assurance offered either on premise through software/appliance installation or via the Cloud by proxying or diverting web traffic to the cloud provider. This gives an added layer of assurance on top of other protection, like anti-malware software, to keep malware from entering the enterprise through activities such as web browser. Policy rules around sorts of web access and the time period when this is permitted can also be enforced through these technologies. Application approval management can be used to provide an additional level of granular and relevant security authorization for web applications. Web security is a protective, investigative, and reactive technical control.

Email Security: Email security should provide management over inbound and outbound email, protecting the association from phishing, malignant attachments, implementing corporate polices such as adequate use and spam prevention, and providing business progression options. Moreover, the solution should offer policy-based encryption of emails as well as incorporating different email server solutions. Digital signatures enabling distinguishing proof and non-repudiation are also features of various email security solutions. The email security offering is a defensive, detective, and reactive technical control.

Security Assessment: Security assessments are third-party or client-driven audits of cloud services or appraisals of on-premises frameworks via cloud provided arrangements based on industry guidelines. Traditional security evaluations for infrastructure, applications and consistence audits are well defined and bolstered by multiple standards, i.e., NIST, ISO, and CIS144. A moderately mature toolset exists, and various tools have been executed using the SECaaS delivery model. In the SECaaS delivery model, supporters get the typical advantages of this cloud-computing variant versatility, negligible setup time, low organization overhead, and pay-per-use with low beginning investments.

While not the focus of this endeavor, additional challenges emerge when these tools are used to review cloud environments. Multiple associations, including the CSA, have been working on guidelines to help organizations comprehend the additional challenges:

1. Virtualization consciousness of the tool, as often as necessary for IaaS platform evaluating

2. Support for common web structures in PaaS applications.

3. Compliance controls for IaaS, PaaS, and SaaS platforms.

4. Automated occurrence and breach notification tools for upkeep of cloud supply chain integrity.

5. Standardized polls for XaaS environments, that help address:

    (a) What should be tested in a cloud domain?

    (b) How does one assure data disengagement in a multi-tenant environment?

    (c) What ought to appear in a commonplace infrastructure vulnerability report?

    (d) Is it adequate to use results provided by a cloud service provider?

Intrusion Detection/Prevention (IDS/IPS): Intrusion detection/prevention frameworks monitor behavior designs using rule-based, heuristic, or behavioral models to distinguish anomalies in activity which are current risks to the enterprise. Network IDS/IPS systems have become widely used over the past decade as a result of their to give a granular view of what is happening within an organization network. The IDS/IPS monitors system traffic and compares the action to a baseline via rule-based engine or factual analysis. IDSes are typically conveyed in a passive mode to inactively monitor sensitive segments of a customer's network whereas the IPS is designed to play an active role in the defense of the customer's network. In a traditional framework, this could include demilitarized zones (DMZs) divided by firewalls or routers where corporate web servers search or monitor connections to an internal database. Inside the cloud, IDS systems regularly focus on virtual system and cross-hypervisor activity where facilitated attacks can disturb multiple tenants and create framework chaos. Intrusion detection systems are analytical technical controls, and intrusion prevention systems are investigative, defensive, and reactive technical controls.

Security Information & Event Management (SIEM): The SIEM framework collects (via push or pull mechanisms) log and event information from virtual and real systems, applications, and systems. This information is then connected and analyzed to give real-time reporting and cautioning on information or events which may require mediation or other types of responses. The logs are ordinarily collected and filed in a manner that prevents altering to enable their use as confirmation in any investigations or authentic reporting. The SIEM SECaaS offering is a detective specialized control but can be designed to be a protective and responsive technical control.

Encryption: Encryption is the process of jumbling/encoding data using cryptographic algorithms, the result of which is encrypted data (referred to as decoded text). Only the planned recipient or system that is in control of the correct key can decode the cipher text. Encryption for muddling systems regularly consists of one or more algorithms in which it is computationally difficult to break one or more keys; and the framework, processes, and methods to manage encryption, decryption, and keys. Each part is effectively useless without the other, e.g., the best algorithm is easy to break if an unauthorized person can access the keys due to weak procedures. In the case of one-way cryptographic functions, a digest or hash is created instead. One-way cryptographic processes include hashing, digital signatures, certificate generation and restoration, and key exchanges. These systems normally consist of one or more algorithms that are easy to replicate but very resistant to phony, along with the processes and procedures to handle them. Encryption technique when outsourced to a SECaaS provider is classed as a protective and analyst technical control.

Business Continuity and Disaster Recovery: Business continuity and disaster recovery are the measures designed and enforced to ensure operational flexibility in the event of any service interruptions. They provide adaptable and reliable failover and DR solutions for needed services in the event of a service intrusion, whether natural or artificial. For instance, in the event of a disaster situation at one location, machines at different locations may shield applications in that location. This Security as a Service offering is a responsive, protective, and detective technical control.

Network Security: Network security consists of security services that limit or allocate access and that disperse, monitor, log, and protect the fundamental resource services. Structurally, network security provides services that location security controls entirely at the network or those controls particularly addressed at the individual system of each fundamental resource. In cloud/virtual network and hybrid network, network security is liable to be provided by virtual devices alongside customary physical devices. Tight integration with the hypervisor to ensure full visibility of all traffic on the virtual network layer is key. These network security offerings include detective, protective, and reactive technical controls.

Permissions:

1. Implementers may use pattern recognition of client activities.

2. Implementers may use secure legal intervention of security metrics for SLA146 expectation management.

3. Implementers may use provided trusted channels for infiltration testing.

Recommendations:

1. Implementers should guarantee secure communication channels between occupant and consumer.

2. Providers should supply computerized secure and continuous notification all through the supply chain on a need-to-know basis.

3. Providers should supply secured logging of inside operations for compliance of service-level agreement.

4. Clients should request addition of unauthorized party audit and SLA intervention services.

5. All users should enable continuous monitoring of all interfaces through institutionalized security interfaces, i.e., SCAP (NIST), CYBEX (ITU-T), or RID & IODEF (IETF).

Identity-as-a-Service Requirements:

- Provide cloud clients provisioning/deprovisioning of accounts (of both cloud and on-reason applications and assets).

- Provide cloud clients authentication (*different forms and factors*).

- Provide cloud clients identity life cycle management.

- Provide cloud clients directory services.

- Provide cloud clients directory synchronization (*multi-horizontal as required*).

- Provide cloud clients federated SSO.

- Provide cloud clients web SSO (granular access implementation & session management which are different from united SSO).

Web Services SECaaS Requirements: Providers of web SECaaS services must:

- Provide cloud clients with web monitoring and sifting.

- Provide cloud clients with malware, spyware, and "botnet" analysis and blocking.

- Provide cloud clients with phishing website blocker.

- Provide cloud customers with instant messaging scanning.

- Provide cloud clients with email security.

- Provide cloud clients with bandwidth management/traffic control.

- Provide cloud clients with data loss prevention.

- Provide cloud clients with fraud prevention.

- Provide cloud clients with web access control.

- Provide cloud clients with backup.

- Provide cloud clients with SSL (decoding/hand off).

- Provide cloud clients with usage policy requirement.

- Provide cloud clients with vulnerability management.

- Provide cloud clients with web intelligence reporting.

Email SECaaS Requirements:

- Provide cloud clients with exact filtering to block spam and phishing.

- Provide cloud clients with deep protection against viruses and spyware before they enter the organization perimeter.

- Provide cloud clients with adaptable policies to define granular mail flow and encryption.

- Provide cloud clients with rich, intuitive reports and correlate ongoing reporting.

- Provide cloud clients with deep content scanning to enforce policies.

- Provide cloud clients with the option to encode some/all emails based on policy.

- Provide cloud clients with integration ability to various email server solutions.

Security Assessment SECaaS Requirements:

- Provide cloud clients with detailed governance processes and measurements (implementers should define, report and process, by which approaches are set and decisions are made).

- Provide an automated solution for informing members about their immediate supply chain in the event of a rupture or security incident; executed by providers of security assessments and governance offerings.

- Provide cloud clients with proper risk management (implementers should define, record, and process to ensure that important business procedures and behaviors remain within the tolerance associated with those policies and decisions).

- Provide cloud clients with details of consistence (implementers should define and record process-of-adherence to policies and decisions).

- Provide cloud clients with policies that can be derived from internal directives, methods, and requirements or external laws, directions, standards and assertions.

- Provide cloud clients with technical consistence audits (computerized auditing of setup settings in devices, OSes, databases, and applications).

- Provide cloud clients with application security appraisals (automated auditing of custom applications).

- Provide cloud clients with vulnerability assessments automated testing of network devices, PCs, and applications for known vulnerabilities and configuration issues; offered by providers of security assessments and governance services.

Intrusion Detection SECaaS Requirements:

- Provide cloud clients with identification of interruptions and policy violations.

- Provide cloud clients with automatic or manual remediation activities.

- Provide cloud clients with coverage for workloads, virtualization layer (VMM/Hypervisor) management plane.

- Provide cloud clients with deep packet investigation using one or more of the following techniques: signature, statistical, behavioral, and heuristic.

- Provide cloud clients with system call monitoring.

SIEM SECaaS Requirements:

- Provide cloud clients with real-time log/event collection, deduplication, standardization, aggregation and visualization.

- Provide cloud clients with forensics support.

- Provide cloud clients with consistence reporting and support.

- Provide cloud clients with IR support.

- Provide cloud clients with irregularity detection not limited to email.

- Provide cloud clients with detailed reporting.

▪ Provide cloud clients with adaptable data retention periods and adaptable policy management.

Encryption SECaaS Requirements:

▪ Provide cloud clients with security of data in transit.

▪ Provide cloud clients with security of data at rest.

▪ Provide cloud clients with key and policy management.

▪ Provide cloud clients with protection of stored data.

Business Continuity and Disaster Recovery Requirements:

▪ Provide cloud clients with flexible infrastructure.

▪ Provide cloud clients with secure backup.

▪ Provide cloud clients with monitored operations.

▪ Provide cloud clients with third-party service connectivity.

Network Security SECaaS Requirements:

▪ Provide cloud clients with details of data threats.

▪ Provide cloud clients with details of access control threats.

▪ Provide cloud clients with access and authentication controls.

▪ Provide cloud clients with security gateways (SOA/API, firewalls, WAF).

▪ Provide cloud clients with security products (IDS/IPS, file integrity monitoring, server tier firewall, DLP, anti-virus, and anti-spam).

5.7   Conclusion

Aside from ancient data security controls (like access controls or encryption), there are two other steps to help operate unapproved data moving to cloud services: Monitor for large internal data migrations with FAM and DAM and monitor for data moving to the Cloud with URL filters and data loss prevention. This chapter provided an overview of detecting and preventing data migrations to the Cloud, protecting data moving to the Cloud, application security, virtualization, VM guest hardening, security as a service, identity as service requirements, web services SECaaS requirements, email SECaaS requirements, security assessment SECaaS requirements, intrusion detection SECaaS requirements, SIEM SECaaS requirements, encryption SECaaS requirements, business continuity and disaster recovery requirements and network security SECaaS requirements.

REFERENCES

1. Rybina, K., Patni, A., & Schill, A. (2014). Analysing the Migration Time of Live Migration of Multiple Virtual Machines. *In CLOSER* (pp. 590-597).

2. Sahni, S., & Varma, V. (2012). A hybrid approach to live migration of virtual machines. In Cloud Computing in Emerging Markets (CCEM), 2012 IEEE International Conference (pp. 1-5). IEEE.

3. Soriga, S. G., & Barbulescu, M. (2013). A comparison of the performance and scalability of Xen and KVM hypervisors. In Networking in Education and Research, 2013 RoEduNet International Conference 12th Edition (pp. 1-6). IEEE.

4. Stress-ng: http://kernel.ubuntu.com/ cking/stress-ng/. Accessed: 2017-08-16.

5. Tao, X., & Alei, L. (2014). Small file access optimization based on GlusterFS. In Cloud Computing and Internet of Things (CCIOT), 2014 International Conference (pp. 101-104). IEEE.

6. Wu, Y., & Zhao, M. (2011). Performance modeling of virtual machine live migration. In Cloud Computing (CLOUD), 2011 IEEE International Conference (pp. 492-499). IEEE.

7. Mansour, I. E. A., Cooper, K., & Bouchachia, H. (2016). Effective Live Cloud Migration. In Future Internet of Things and Cloud (FiCloud), 2016 IEEE 4th International Conference (pp. 334-339). IEEE.

8. Hamad, H. M., & AlQazzaz, A. B. (2016). Secure Live Virtual Machine Migration by Proposed Security Center. *IUG Journal of Natural Studies*, 24(1).

9. Lakshmipriya, B., Sri, R. L., & Balaji, N. (2016). A novel approach for performance and security enhancement during live migration. *Indian Journal of Science and Technology*, 9(4).

10. Devine, W. M., Gottimukkala, S., Huynh, L. T., Joseph, D., Law, M. S., & Overby Jr, L. H. (2017). U.S. Patent No. 9,715,401. Washington, DC: U.S. Patent and Trademark Office.

CHAPTER 6

DYNAMIC LOAD BALANCING BASED ON LIVE MIGRATION

Abstract

Load balancing or scheduling is the science of finding a mapping between jobs to physical resources. Common goals of load balancing include maximizing throughput, minimizing response time, maximizing resource utilization, minimizing execution time, and/or minimizing communication time. The decision-making agent decides when load balancing will occur and which tasks will be moved. In distributed dynamic scheduling, load information is not shared globally. All processors take part in deciding when load-balancing occurs and which tasks will be migrated. This chapter gives an overview of different techniques of load balancing, load rebalancing, and a policy engine to implement dynamic load balancing algorithm, some load balancing algorithms and VMware Distributed Resource Scheduler.

Keywords: Load balancing algorithm, scheduling policies, resource load balancing, load balancing techniques, VMware.

6.1   Introduction

Load balancing is an important part of cloud computing which ensures the high performance of the available resources. Load balancing or scheduling is the science of finding a mapping between jobs to physical resources. In other words, we can say it addresses the problem of deciding which job should be allocated to which particular physical resource.

6.2   Classification of Load Balancing Techniques

Load balancing is essentially a resource management problem (see Figure 6.1). Stated simply, load balancing knows how to divide work between available machines in a way that achieves performance goals. Common goals of load balancing include maximizing throughput, minimizing response time, maximizing resource utilization, minimizing execution time, and/or minimizing communication time.

Load balancing techniques can be broadly classifying as static and dynamic load balancing [1, 2]. In static load balancing, the mapping of jobs to resources is not allowed to change after the load balancing has been done. Static algorithms are appropriate for systems with low variations in load. On the other hand, dynamic load balancing will change the mapping of jobs to resources at any point, but there may be a cost associated with the changes. There are two main types of dynamic load balancing algorithms: preemptive and non-preemptive. In a preemptive algorithm, the mapping of jobs to physical resources may change while a job is running. In contrast, with non-preemptive algorithms, once a job has started the physical resources assigned to that job cannot change.

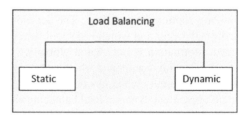

Figure 6.1   Types of load balancing approaches.

System designers should know the system's specific load balancing goals before choosing an algorithm. Load balancing is also a scheduling problem. The OS on each processor performs local scheduling. Local scheduling involves deciding which processes should run at a given moment. Global scheduling, on the other hand, is the process of deciding where a given process should run. Global scheduling may be performed by a central authority or it can be distributed among all of the processors.

6.2.1 Static and Dynamic Scheduling

Static scheduling [2] assigns tasks to processors before execution begins. Tasks will not change processors while the system is executing any given task. One challenge of static scheduling is predicting the execution behavior of a system. Another challenge of static scheduling is partitioning tasks to processors in a way that maximizes resource utilization and minimizes communication time. But the greatest obstacle related to static scheduling, however, is that finding the optimal solution is NP-complete. Because of this, much of the research done for static scheduling has involved developing heuristics. One common heuristic in static scheduling is to give priority to long tasks. In addition to the limitation of being NP-complete, it is also challenging to estimate task execution times before a task runs. This is difficult because the run-time behavior of a task is often accented by things that cannot be predicted beforehand, such as conditional constructs or network congestion. Dynamic scheduling redistributes tasks during execution. The redistribution typically moves tasks from heavily loaded processors to lightly loaded processors. A dynamic scheduling algorithm typically has three parts.

1. *Information Policy:* This explains how much information is available to the decision-making components.

2. *Transfer Policy:* This determines when tasks will be redistributed.

3. *Placement Policy:* This decides where a task will be placed.

A dynamic scheduling algorithm can be centralized or distributed. In centralized dynamic scheduling, all information is sent to a single decision-making agent. The decision-making agent decides when load balancing will occur and which tasks will be moved. In distributed dynamic scheduling, load information is not shared globally. All processors take part in deciding when load balancing occurs and which tasks will be migrated.

When compared with static scheduling, one major advantage of dynamic scheduling is that the run-time behavior of the system does not need to be known in advance. Dynamic scheduling algorithms are very good at maximizing utilization of all resources. Unfortunately, dynamic scheduling has runtime overhead associated with gathering information and transferring tasks to different processors. If the runtime overhead is greater than the extra work achieved by moving tasks from heavily loaded to lightly loaded processors, the dynamic load balancing may have slow execution.

6.2.2 Load Rebalancing

Load rebalancing [3] is a more specialized version of the load balancing problem. In load rebalancing, given a suboptimal assignment of jobs to processors, we are interested in reducing the load on the heaviest loaded processor. This is accomplished by migrating jobs from the heaviest loaded processor to other processors. The rebalancing problem given an assignment of the n jobs to m processors, and a positive integer

k, relocates no more than k jobs so as to minimize the maximum load on a processor. More generally, we are given a cost function c_i which is the cost of relocating job i, with the constraint that the total relocation cost be bounded by a specified budget B.

Load rebalancing has some interesting features. In particular, they may be classified into different load rebalancing problems, such as load rebalancing with constraints on which machines a job may be assigned to, or constraints on which jobs may be on the same machine. The theorems are too numerous to list here, but in general the load rebalancing is an NP-hard problem. Some researchers dispute the effectiveness of dynamic load balancing. In particular, Eager *et al.* argued that dynamic load balancing by migrating jobs will never yield major performance benefits compared to balancing load through initial placement of jobs. They argued that only under extreme conditions can migration offer modest performance benefits. However, this point is disputed, and many researchers continue to argue that dynamic load balancing can be effective, even in circumstances that aren't extreme. Also, dynamic load balancing can have many benefits besides performance. For example, when load across a system is low, dynamic load balancing could allow for many VMs to be combined and for hardware to be turned off. This could lead to the system consuming significantly less power, which would probably save money [7].

6.3 Policy Engine

A policy engine is created to implement dynamic load balancing algorithm [4]. Each host will send state information to the policy engine. The policy engine will then make all migration decisions based on the information it receives and the policy that is currently running. By changing the policy used by the policy engine, one can implement different dynamic load balancing algorithms or even migrate for reasons other than load balancing. For example, the policy engine could be used to migrate VMs when hardware fails.

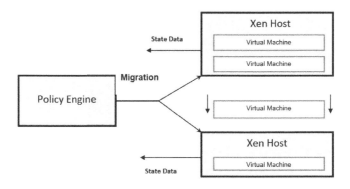

Figure 6.2   Relationship between policy engine and the Xen hosts.

The relationship between the host machines running Xen and the policy engine is shown in Figure 6.2. There are two host machines running the Xen VM monitor. Each of the hosts is sending state data to the policy engine. The policy engine will tell the Xen hosts when a VM should migrate to a new host depending on the state of the hosts and the policy that is being executed. In Figure 6.2, one VM is currently being moved to a new host. In the rest of this chapter, we will discuss our policy engine in greater detail.

The Specifics of Policy Engine: A policy engine is a software program which executes commands based on a set of rules known as a policy. The policy engine makes decisions about when to migrate VMs between hosts. Using a policy engine, a user can automatically migrate VMs to new hosts in a variety of including when hardware fails, to balance load, to place VMs on certain hosts in ways that might optimize performance, or to move VMs that should not be turned off from a host that is being shut down.

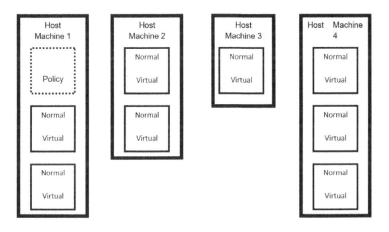

Figure 6.3   For our prototype, the policy engine runs inside of a VM separate from everything else.

The policy engine running inside of a VM [5] using a linux kernel, queries each host for information that is relevant to the policy which is running. Relevant information could include, but is not limited to, CPU usage, memory usage, and the state of the operating system. This information is relayed through a simple web service running on each Xen host to the policy engine. Based on the information the hosts report, the policy engine will act within the parameters of its policy to decide when a VM should migrate. The policy engine will also determine which host will accept the migrating VMs. We configured this policy engine to dynamically load balance VMs based on CPU thresholds [8].

For more details about the dynamic load balancing algorithm we used for our policy, see Figure 6.3 for an example system. Here we have four hosts, with the policy engine running on host machine 1. Please note that the policy engine is running as a normal VM. From an external perspective it looks like any other VM. In fact, the policy engine could even move itself to a different host like any other VM. In Figure 6.4 we see the communication links between the policy engine and the host machines. Notice that the policy engine communicates with all of the hosts. The policy engine will periodically query the hosts for information. Based on the reported information, the policy engine will instruct hosts to migrate VMs.

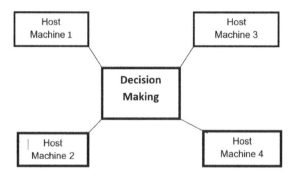

Figure 6.4   The prototype policy engine communicates with all hosts to decide when VMs should be migrated and to initiate migration when necessary.

6.4   Load Balancing Algorithm

The algorithm we implemented inside our policy engine is a modified version of the Central Scheduler Load Balancing (CSLB) algorithm developed [4]. We selected the CSLB algorithm because it met our requirement of being published in an academic venue while also being easy to understand and implement. Also, because the CSLB uses a central node that makes all load balancing decisions, it fits our current implementation of our policy engine better than a distributed scheduling load balancing algorithm. The differences between our algorithm and the algorithm presented by Lan and Yu will be discussed after the introduction of CSLB algorithm [9].

The CSLB Algorithm: We will describe the CSLB algorithm using the five phases of dynamic load balancing algorithms introduced by Watts and Taylor. One critical difference between the work of Watts and Taylor and our work is that Watts and Taylor were working with processes; they were not working with VMs. These phases are load evaluation, profitability determination, work transfer vector calculation, task selection, and task migration.

Load Evaluation: As its name implies, the CSLB is a central scheduling algorithm; all load information is sent to a central node. In the CSLB algorithm, the information to evaluate the work load can either be sent at a set interval or when load information changes substantially. The CSLB algorithm also includes two global thresholds: one light threshold and one heavy threshold [6]. These thresholds change based on the average CPU load of the nodes. The central scheduler computes the thresholds and broadcasts them to the other nodes. Each node determines load by using a heuristic to estimate how much time is needed to complete all of the jobs in its buffer. Each node puts itself into one of three groups based on the two thresholds and their load. Each node will then inform the central scheduler which group it is a part of. Figure 6.5 illustrates how nodes divide themselves into groups. Darker colors represent heavier loads. Based on the two thresholds created by the central scheduler, three groups are created. One group is for lightly loaded nodes, one group is for moderately loaded nodes, and the final group is for heavily loaded nodes.

Profitability Determination: Migration will be considered profitable if there is at least one host in the heavily loaded group and at least one host in the lightly loaded group.

Work Transfer Vector Calculation: Lan and Yu do not describe how to calculate the ideal amount of work to transfer in their work about the CSLB algorithm.

Task Selection: The CSLB also does not describe how to decide which tasks to migrate.

Task Migration: The CSLB does not describe how the jobs are actually transferred.

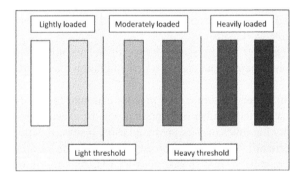

Figure 6.5   Distribution of nodes in groups based on load thresholds.

6.5 Resource Load Balancing

Dynamic live migration of VMs can be used to maximize the utilization of system resources in virtualization clusters by constantly balancing server loads, i.e., moving VMs from overloaded physical hosts to those hosts that are underutilized. Such load balancing can either be done manually by an administrator, or automatically by a load balancer integrated with virtualization infrastructure manager. In this section, we will discuss various requirements that are put on such dynamic load balancers [10].

6.5.1 Server Load Metric

In order to tell which cluster node is overloaded and which one is underutilized, physical server load needs to be quantified first. A common approach is to measure the relative utilization of its resources (*e.g., CPU time, memory utilization, network, disk I/O traffic and other performance counters*). A server load metric is then defined as a weighted sum of these resource utilizations, where weights denote relative importance of the performance counter. Some balancers even use SLA-based metrics; for example, server priority level or number of transactions executed per second.

6.5.2 System Imbalance Metric

A system imbalance metric can measure the workload imbalance across the entire cluster. If it is lower than a specified threshold, the system is considered to be balanced. One of the ways the overall system imbalance metric can be defined is the coefficient of variation of individual server loads [11, 12].

6.5.3 Other Key Parameters

Imbalance Threshold: If the threshold is too high, the system will stay imbalanced. If too low, balanced state may never be achieved and thus migrations would never stop, even with stable workloads.

Balancing Frequency: The balancing frequency defines how often the balancer evaluates performance metrics and creates a new migration plan. Typical frequency is 5 minutes.

Live Migration Time: The migration process can take up to several minutes, meaning that only a limited number of migrations can be executed in the balancing period. Future migration times may be predicted using historical data.

Migration Overhead: The migration process itself consumes a significant amount of system resources, mainly memory and network I/O. As a result, the decrease in performance caused by frequent migrations can overwhelm the benefits of balancing the system.

Level of Automation: Load balancers can often work in two modes: manual and automatic. In manual mode, administrator has to approve every proposed migration before it is executed.

Initial Placement: Common feature of load balancers is initial placement of a VM to the least utilized host when the VM is powered on or resumed from suspension. The same algorithm as for load balancing can be used.

Affinity Rules: Load balancers may support affinity rules that can be used to solve some issues which may arise when VMs are freely migrated between nodes. Some common business rules are:

- *VM-VM Affinity:* A VM-VM affinity rule specifies whether selected individual VMs must run on the same host. A typical scenario would be tying a web server and the database server it intensively communicates with together to eliminate network latency.

- *VM-VM Anti-Affinity:* A VM-VM anti-affinity rule specifies whether selected individual VMs must be kept on separate hosts. This rule might be used to separate primary and secondary DNS servers. In that case, if a problem occurs with one host, not all DNS servers would be placed at risk.

- *VM-Host Affinity:* A VM-Host affinity rule specifies on which hosts a VM can run. As some software vendors still tie their software to physical computers, by forcing the VMs running the software in question to run on specific servers, licensing compliance can be ensured. This type of rule can also be used when a VM utilizes a physical resource that is available only on specific hosts.

Power Management: With green IT initiatives gaining in popularity, some load balancing solutions have introduced power management features. When VMs in a cluster need fewer resources, such as during nights and weekends, some load balancers can consolidate workloads onto fewer servers and power off the rest to reduce power and cooling costs. When VM resource requirements increase, powered-down hosts are brought back online to ensure service levels are met.

6.6   Load Balancers in Virtual Infrastructure Management Software

According to the latest server virtualization market research conducted by Gartner, the major competitors in the market are VMware and Microsoft [5]. Thus, we will focus on their respective solutions in the next sections. Although both of these companies offer free server virtualization solutions, load balancers are only available in their paid editions. Each company has a different name for this feature (*or set of features*):

1. VMware Distributed Resource Scheduler (DRS) and Distributed Power Management (DPM)

2. Microsoft Performance and Resource Optimization (PRO)

   To our knowledge, OpenNebula is the only open source, virtual infrastructure manager in production level of development that has at least some limited load balancing capabilities.

6.7   VMware Distributed Resource Scheduler

VMware vCenter Server (*virtualization infrastructure management software*) with VMware vSphere Enterprise license, is considered to be the leading commercially available load balancing solution for virtualization clusters. VMware DRS dynamically balances computing capacity across the cluster and allocates available resources among the VMs based on predefined rules. When a VM experiences an increased load, VMware DRS automatically allocates additional resources by redistributing VMs among the physical servers in the cluster [13, 14]. VMware DRS continuously collects resource usage information from servers and VMs, and periodically generates recommendations to optimize VM allocation. These recommendations can be executed automatically or manually by performing live migration of VMs through VMware VMotion. Both VM-Host and VM-VM affinity and anti-affinity rules are supported by DRS and can be used to fulfill some special performance, availability and licensing requirements. A feature called **VMware Distributed Power Management (DPM)** can also reduce energy consumption in the datacenter by consolidating workloads and powering off power consuming servers.

6.7.1   OpenNebula

OpenNebula[1] is an open source (see Figure 6.6), virtual infrastructure manager that deploys virtualized services on both a local pool of resources and external IaaS clouds [6]. It automates VM setup (*preparing disk images, setting up networking, and so on*) regardless of the underlying virtualization layer (Xen, KVM, or VMware are currently supported) or external cloud (EC2 or ElasticHosts are currently supported) [15].

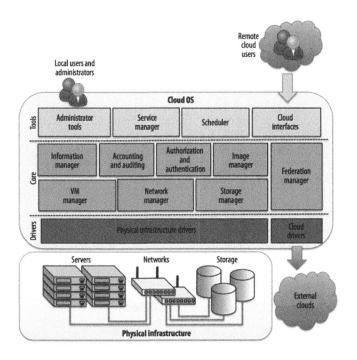

Figure 6.6   OpenNebula architecture.

[1]https://opennebula.org/

6.7.2 Scheduling Policies

The Scheduler module is in charge of the assignment between pending VMs and known Hosts. It is designed in a generic way, so it is highly modifiable and can be replaced by third-party developments. OpenNebula comes with a matchmaking scheduler that implements the Rank Scheduling Policy for initial placement. The goal of this policy is to prioritize those resources more suitable for the VM. The matchmaking algorithm works as follows:

1. First those hosts that do not meet the VM requirements and do not have enough resources (*available CPU and memory*) to run the VM are filtered out.

2. The Rank expression is evaluated using the information gathered by the monitor drivers.

3. Those resources with a higher rank are used first to allocate VMs.

Several placement heuristics can be implemented by choosing a Rank expression. As each VM has its own Rank and so its own policy, different policies can be applied to different instance types:

- *Packing Policy:* The target is to minimize the number of cluster nodes in use. Those nodes with more VMs running are used first to reduce VM fragmentation.

- *Striping Policy:* The target is to maximize the resources available to VMs in a node. Those nodes with fewer VMs running are used first to spread the VMs in the cluster nodes.

- *Load-Aware Policy* The target is to maximize the resources available to VMs in a node. Those nodes with freer CPU are used first.

6.8 Conclusion

The objective of load balancing is to improve the throughput of the system. This chapter gave an overview of different techniques of load balancing, load rebalancing, and a policy engine to implement dynamic load balancing algorithm, some load balancing algorithms and VMware Distributed Resource Scheduler.

REFERENCES

1. Dobale, M. R. G., & Sonar, R. P. (2015). Load balancing in cloud. *International Journal of Engineering Research and General Science*, 3(3), 160-167.

2. Xu, M., Tian, W., & Buyya, R. (2017). A survey on load balancing algorithms for virtual machines placement in cloud computing. *Concurrency and Computation: Practice and Experience*, 29(12).

3. Devi, D. C., & Uthariaraj, V. R. (2016). Load balancing in cloud computing environment using Improved Weighted Round Robin Algorithm for nonpreemptive dependent tasks. *The Scientific World Journal*, 2016.

4. Lan, Y., & Yu, T. (1995). A dynamic central scheduler load balancing mechanism. In Computers and Communications, 1995., Conference Proceedings of the 1995 IEEE Fourteenth Annual International Phoenix Conference (pp. 734-740). IEEE.

5. Mark Hinkle (2010). Eleven Open Source Cloud Computing Projects to Watch. *Socialized Software*.

6. Sempolinski, P., & Thain, D. (2010). A comparison and critique of eucalyptus, opennebula and nimbus. In Cloud Computing Technology and Science (CloudCom), 2010 IEEE Second International Conference (pp. 417-426). IEEE.

7. Dave, A., Patel, B., & Bhatt, G. (2016, October). Load balancing in cloud computing using optimization techniques: A study. In Communication and Electronics Systems (ICCES), International Conference (pp. 1-6). IEEE.

8. Tiwari, P. K., & Joshi, S. (2016, December). Dynamic weighted virtual machine live migration mechanism to manages load balancing in cloud computing. In Computational Intelligence and Computing Research (ICCIC), 2016 IEEE International Conference (pp. 1-5). IEEE.

9. Liu, C. (2016). A Load Balancing Aware Virtual Machine Live Migration Algorithm. In Proceedings of theInternational Conference on Sensors, Measurement and Intelligent Materials (pp. 370-373).

10. Xu, M., Tian, W., & Buyya, R. (2016). A Survey on Load Balancing Algorithms for VM Placement in Cloud Computing. arXiv preprint arXiv:1607.06269.

11. Zhang, M., Wang, S., Huang, G., Li, Y., Zhang, S., & Qian, Z. (2016). Dynamic Load Balancing for Physical Servers in Virtualized Environment. In Parallel and Distributed Computing, Applications and Technologies (PDCAT), 2016 17th International Conference (pp. 227-232). IEEE.

12. Tiwari, P. K., & Joshi, S. (2016). A review on load balancing of virtual machine resources in cloud computing. In Proceedings of First International Conference on Information and Communication Technology for Intelligent Systems: Volume 2 (pp. 369-378). Springer International Publishing.

13. Xu, M., Tian, W., & Buyya, R. (2017). A survey on load balancing algorithms for virtual machines placement in cloud computing. *Concurrency and Computation: Practice and Experience*, 29(12).

14. Javadi, S. A., & Gandhi, A. (2017, July). DIAL: Reducing Tail Latencies for Cloud Applications via Dynamic Interference-aware Load Balancing. In Autonomic Computing (ICAC), 2017 IEEE International Conference on (pp. 135-144). IEEE.

15. Shen, H. (2017). RIAL: Resource intensity aware load balancing in clouds. *IEEE Transactions on Cloud Computing*.

CHAPTER 7

LIVE MIGRATION IN CLOUD DATA CENTER

Abstract

The cost of housing, running and cooling data centers continues to rise, while the cost of commodity hardware, such as consumer-level network routers and switches, continues to drop. Data centers operators have not been blind to this, and have adapted multi-rooted fat tree topologies to make use of cheap, commodity Ethernet switches that can provide equal or better bandwidth performance than hierarchical topologies using expensive high-end switches. This chapter discusses how resource virtualization, through VMM, is now commonplace in data centers, and how VMM can be used to improve system-side performance for VMs, or how load can be better balanced across the network through strategic VMM. However, all the VMM works in this chapter have not addressed the fundamental problem of actively targeting and removing congestion from oversubscribed core links within data center networks.

Keywords: Dynamic frequency, voltage scaling, VMS, cloud data centers, powering down.

7.1 Definition of Data Center

The backbone of any data center is its data network [1]. Without this, no machine is able to communicate with any other machine, or the outside world (see Figure 7.1). As data centers are densely packed with servers, the cost of providing a network between all servers is a major initial outlay for operators in terms of networking equipment required. To limit the outlay required for putting a network infrastructure in place, a compromise often has to be reached between performance and cost, such as oversubscribing the network at its core links.

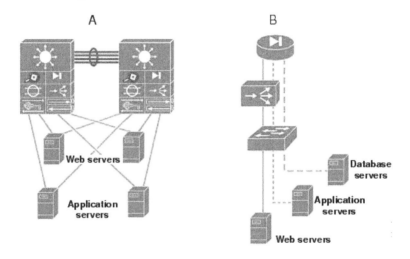

Figure 7.1 Data center architecture.

Due to the highly interconnected nature of data centers, several scalable mesh architectures have been designed to provide networks of high capacity with great fault tolerance. DCell is a scalable and fault-tolerant mesh network that moves all packet routing duties to servers, and relies upon its own routing protocol. BCube is another fault-tolerant mesh network architecture designed for use in sealed shipping containers. As components fail over time, the network within the shipping container exhibits graceful performance degradation. BCube makes use of commodity switches for packet forwarding, but doesn't yet scale above a single shipping container, making it unsuitable for current data center environments. While mesh networks can provide scalable performance bounds as the networks grow, the wiring schemes for mesh networks are often complex, which can make future maintenance and fault-finding a nontrivial task. The high redundancy of links in mesh networks that happens to allow for good fault tolerance also increases the infrastructure setup cost due to the volume of networking hardware required.

The more commonly used alternative to mesh networks in the data center is multitiered tree networks. The root of the tree, which is the core of the network, has switches or routers that provide a path between any two points within a data center.

From the root, the network branches out to the edge, or leaf, interconnects that link individual servers into the network. In a multi-rooted tree, there are often two or more tiers of routers providing several levels of aggregation, or locality, within which shorter paths may be taken, without the need for all packets to pass through the core of the network. Multi-tiered trees are also often multi-rooted trees, providing redundant paths between any two points in the network, while still requiring less wiring and less network hardware than mesh networks.

The most often used architecture in data centers [2] is a slight variation of a multi-tiered tree, known as a fat tree, which is based upon communication architecture used to interconnect processors for parallel computation. Instead of having links of equal capacity within every layer of the tree, bandwidth capacity is increased as links move away from edges and get closer to the core, or root, of the tree. Having increased capacity as we move towards the core of the tree can ensure that intra-data center traffic that may have to traverse higher-level links has enough capacity for flows between many servers to occur without significant congestion.

The costs of housing, running and cooling data centers continues to rise, while the cost of commodity hardware, such as consumer-level network routers and switches, continues to drop. Data center operators have not been blind to this, and have adapted multi-rooted fat tree topologies to make use of cheap, commodity Ethernet switches that can provide equal or better bandwidth performance than hierarchical topologies using expensive high-end switches. A typical configuration for a fat tree network is to provide 1 Gbps links to each server, and 1 Gbps links from each top of rack switch to aggregation switches. Further layers up to the core then provide links of 10 Gbps, increasing capacity for traffic which may have to traverse the core of the network. Amazon is known to use such architecture.

Tree-like networks are typically oversubscribed from ratios of 1:2.5 to 1:8, which can result in serious congestion hotspots in core links. VL2 has been developed in order to achieve uniform traffic distribution and avoid traffic hot spots by scaling out the network. Rather than make use of hierarchical trees, VL2 advocates scaling the network out horizontally, providing more interconnects between aggregate routers, and more routes for packets to traverse. A traffic study found data center traffic patterns to change quickly and be highly unpredictable. In order to fully utilize their architecture with those findings, they made use of valiant load balancing, which makes use of the increased number of available paths through the network by having switches randomly forward new flows across symmetric paths.

While some data center architecture works attempt to expand upon existing network topology designs, PortLand attempts to improve existing fat tree-style topologies. Port Land is a forwarding and routing protocol designed to make the operation and management of a dynamic network, such as a cloud data center network, where VMs may continually join and leave the network in a more straightforward manner. It consists of a central store of network configuration information and location discovery, as well as the ability to migrate a VM transparently without breaking connectivity to the rest of the hosts within the network. The transparent VMM is achieved by forcing switches to invalidate routing paths and update hosts communicating with that VM, and forwarding packets already in transit to the new location of the migrated VM. PortLand merely adapts existing architectures to provide a plug-and-play infrastructure, rather than attempting to improve performance in any serious way. This is revealed through the evaluation, which measured the number of ARP messages required for communication with the central network manager component as the number of hosts grows, rather than evaluating the protocol under varying application traffic loads.

Multi-rooted tree architectures are currently the most used architecture for data center networks but they have problems with high oversubscription ratios. While studies such as VL2 have further adapted multi-rooted tree architectures, they still do not completely overcome the oversubscription issue, requiring other, more targeted action to be taken.

7.2 Data Center Traffic Characteristics

A server within a rack will also either talk to almost all other servers within a rack [3], or fewer than 25%, and will either not talk to any server outside the rack, or talk to $1-10\%$ of them. In terms of actual numbers, the median communication for a server is two servers within a rack and four servers outside its rack. In terms of congestion, 86% of links experience congestion lasting over 10 seconds, and 15% experience congestion lasting over 100 seconds, with 90% of congestion events lasting between 1 to 2 seconds. Flow duration is less than 10 seconds for 80% of flows, with 0.1% of flows lasting for more than 200 seconds, and most data is transferred in flows lasting up to 25 seconds, rather than in the long-lived flows. Overall, it has been revealed that very few machines in the data center actually communicate the traffic changes quite quickly with many short-lived flows, and even flow inter-arrivals are bursty.

A study of SNMP data from 19 production data centers has also been undertaken. The findings are that, in tree-like topologies, the core links are the most heavily loaded, with edge links (within racks) being the least loaded. The average packet size is around 850 bytes, with peaks around 40 bytes and 1500 bytes, and 40% of links are unused, with the actual set of links continuously changing. The observation is also made that packets arrive in bursty ON/OFF fashion, which is consistent with the general findings of other studies revealing bursty and unpredictable traffic loads.

A more in-depth study of traffic properties has been provided. SNMP statistics from 10 data centers were used. The results of the study are that many data centers have a diverse range of applications transmitting data across the network, such as LDAP, HTTP, MapReduce and other custom applications. For private data centers, the flow inter-arrival times are less than 1 ms for 80% of flows, with 80% of the flows also smaller than 10 KB and 80% also lasting less than 11 seconds. Packet sizes are also grouped around either 200 bytes and 1400 bytes and packet arrivals exhibited ON/OFF behavior, with the core of the network having the most congested links, 25% of which are congested at any time, similar to the findings. With regard to communication patterns, 75% of traffic is found to be confined within racks.

The data center traffic studies discussed in this section have all revealed that the majority of data center traffic is composed of short flows lasting only a few seconds, with flow inter-arrival times of less than 1 ms for the majority of flows, and packets with bursty inter-arrival rates. The core links of the network are the most congested in data centers, even though 75% of traffic is kept within racks. All these facts can be summarized to conclude that data center traffic changes rapidly and is bursty and unpredictable by nature, with highly congested core links.

7.3   Traffic Engineering for Data Centers

In order to alleviate some of the congestion that can occur with highly unpredictable intra-data center traffic [4], several control loop schemes have been devised. The majority of control loops available nowadays are for scheduling the routing of individual flows to avoid or limit, congested paths. Multi-rooted tree architectures provide at least two identical paths of equal cost between any two points in the network. To take advantage of this redundancy equal-cost multi-path (ECMP) routing was developed. In ECMP, a hash is taken over packet header fields that identifies a flow, and this hash is used by routers to determine the next hop a packet should take. By splitting a network and using a hash as a key to routing, different hashes will be assigned to different paths, limiting the number of flows sharing a path. A benefit of the hashing scheme is that TCP flows will not be disrupted or re-routed during their lifetime. However, ECMP only splits by flow hashes, and does not take into account the size of flows. Therefore, two or more large flows could end up causing congestion on a single path. Similarly, hashing collisions can occur, which can result in two large flows sharing the same path.

Valiant load balancing (VLB), used in VL2, is a similar scheme to ECMP. However, rather than computing a hash on a flow, flows are bounced off randomly assigned intermediate routers. While the approach may more easily balance flow s, as it uses pseudo-random flow assignments rather than hash-based assignments, it is not any more intuitive than ECMP. By not targeting the problem of unpredictable traffic, and merely randomizing the paths for flow s, link congestion can still occur.

While the scheme discussed above makes unintuitive decisions about routing flows in the data center, there has been a move towards scheme that dynamically adapt to the actual traffic characteristics. It is a flow scheduling system designed to provide high bisection bandwidth on fat tree networks. Built upon PortLand and ECMP, it uses adaptive scheduling to identify large flows that have been in existence for some length of time. After identifying large flows, it uses simulated annealing to schedule paths for flows to achieve close-to-optimal bisection bandwidth. Their evaluations found that a simple first-fit approach for assigning large flows beats ECMP, and their simulated annealing approach beat both ECMP and the first-fit approach. However, as they did not have access to data center traffic traces, they evaluated their algorithms based upon synthetic traffic patterns designed to stress the network, rather than attempting to generate synthetic traffic patterns using reported data center traffic characteristics.

It use of short-term predictability to schedule flows for data centers. ECMP and Hedera both achieve $15 - 20\%$ below the optimal routing on a canonical tree topol-

ogy, with VL2 being 20% below optimal with real data center traces. While studies
have shown data center traffic to be bursty and unpredictable at periods of 150 seconds or more, the authors of MicroTE state that 60% of top-of-rack to top-of-rack
traffic is predictable on the short timescales of between 1.6 and 2.6 seconds, on average, in cloud data centers [5]. The cause of this is said to be during the reduce
step in MapReduce clients transfer the results of calculations back to a master node
in a different rack. MicroTE is implemented using the OpenFlow protocol that is
based on a centralized controller for all switches within a network. When a new flow
arrives at a switch, it checks its flow table for a rule. If no rule exists for that flow,
it contacts a single central OpenFlow controller that then installs the appropriate
rule in a switch. In MicroTE, servers send their average traffic matrix to the central
OpenFlow controller at a periodicity of 2 seconds, where aggregate top-of-rack to
top-of-rack matrices are calculated. Predictable traffic flows are then packed onto
paths and the remaining unpredictable flows are placed using a weighted form of
ECMP, based upon remaining bandwidth on available paths after predictable flows
have been assigned. By rerunning the data center traces, it is shown that MicroTE
achieves slightly better performance than ECMP for predictable traffic. However, for
traffic that is unpredictable, MicroTE actually performs worse than ECMP. An evaluation of the scalability of MicroTE reveals that the network overhead for control
and flow installation messages is 4 MB and 50 MB, respectively, for a data center
of 10,000 servers, and new network paths can be computed and installed in under 1
second. While MicroTE does rely on some predictability, it provides minimal improvement over ECMP and can provide poorer flow scheduling than ECMP when
there is no predictability, and also has a greater network overhead than ECMP, making it unsuitable for data centers where traffic really is unpredictable and not based
upon MapReduce operations.

Another flow scheduler is DeTail. It tackles variable packet latency and long flow
completion time tails in data centers for deadlines in serving web pages. Link layer
flow control (LLFC) is the primary mechanism used to allow switches to monitor
their buffer occupancy and inform switches preceding it on a path, using Ethernet
pause frames, to delay packet transmissions to reduce packet losses and retransmissions that result in longer flow completion times. Individual packets are routed
through lightly loaded ports in switches using packet-level adaptive load balancing
(ALB). As TCP interprets packet reordering as packet loss, reordering buffers are
implemented at end hosts. Finally, DeTail uses flow priorities for deadline-sensitive
flows by employing drain byte counters for each egress queue. Simulations and
testbed experiments show that DeTail is able to achieve shorter flow completion times
than flow control and priority queues alone under a variety of data center workloads,
such as bursty and mixed traffic. Unlike ECMP and VLB, DeTail adapts to traffic in
the network and schedules individual packets based on congestion, rather than performing unbalanced pseudo-random scheduling. However, DeTail pushes extra logic
to the switches and end hosts, rather than tackling the problem of placement of hosts
within the network infrastructure to achieve efficient communication.

7.4   Energy Efficiency in Cloud Data Centers

Potential Power Consuming Units in Cloud Data Centers: To improve energy efficiency in the cloud [6], it is important to study the power in typical data centers and to understand how power is distributed. In fact, more than half of the electrical power is feeding the IT loads. According to the EPA's report to congress on server and data center energy, servers consume 80% of the total IT load and 40% of total data center power consumption. The rest of power is consumed by other devices like transformers, distribution wiring, air conditioners, pumps, and lighting.

The power consumption of cooling equipment is important but it is proportional to the IT power consumption. Technologies like free cooling that are used by big companies (*e.g., Google, Facebook, eBay*), are interesting for reducing the power consumption of cooling. These approaches lower the air temperature in data centers by using naturally cool air or water instead of mechanical refrigeration. As a result, the electrical power needed for cooling is enormously decreased. Savings can even reach 100% in the case of zero refrigeration, which is possible in many climates.

7.5   Major Cause of Energy Waste

As explained in the last section, servers are the main power consumers in cloud data centers. The key reasons for this huge consumption are the following:

- *Low Server Utilization:* As data centers are growing in size, the number of servers is continuously increasing. Most data center servers are underused. According to a Natural Resources Defense Council (NRDC) report, average server utilization remained static between 12% and 18% from 2006 and 2012, while servers drew between 60% and 90% of peak power. Consolidating virtual servers on a smaller number of hosts allows running the same applications with much lower power consumption. By increasing server utilization, the number of required servers and overall energy use will be greatly reduced.

- *Low Idle Power Waste:* Data center servers sit idly and ado not process useful work about $85 - 95\%$ of the time. An idle server consumes about 70% of its peak power even if it is not used. This waste of idle power is considered as a major cause of energy inefficiency. Hence, idle servers in data centers could be turned o to reduce energy consumption.

7.5.1   Lack of a Standardized Metric of Server Energy Efficiency

To insure energy efficiency optimizations, it is important to use energy efficiency metrics for servers to sort them according to their energy efficiency and to enable scheduling algorithms to make decisions and to select the best resources to maximize energy efficiency. Even though some metrics focusing on IT efficiency have appeared in recent years, they do not provide a simple benchmark that can drive the optimization of energy efficiency.

7.5.2 Energy Efficient Solutions Are Still Not Widely Adopted

As stated in the NRDC report, many big Cloud farms do a great job on energy efficiency, but represent less than 5% of the global data centers' energy use. The other 95% small, medium, corporate and multi-tenant operations are much less efficient on average. Hence, more energy efficiency best practices should be adopted and used especially for small- and medium-sized data centers that are typically very inefficient and consume about half of the amount of power consumed by all data centers.

7.6 Power Measurement and Modeling in Cloud

Before dealing with power and energy measurement and modeling [7], it is important to understand the power and energy relationship and to present their units of measure. Power consumption indicates the rate at which a machine can perform its work and can be found by multiplying voltage and current while electrical energy is the amount of power used over a period of time. The standard metric unit of power is the watt (W) and the energy unit is watt-hour (Wh). Power and energy can be defined as shown in Eq. (7.1) and Eq. (7.2), where P is power consumption, I is current, V is voltage, E is energy and T is a time interval:

$$P = IV \tag{7.1}$$

$$E = PT \tag{7.2}$$

To quantify power and energy consumption in Cloud, we distinguish between measurement techniques and power and energy estimation models. The first one directly measures actual power consumption via instant monitoring tools. Power metering models estimate the power consumption of servers and VMs using hardware-provided or OS-provided metrics.

7.7 Power Measurement Techniques

Power direct measurement in Cloud can be achieved in data centers that embed monitoring capabilities and probes such as smart power distribution units (PDUs). This section introduces several measurement methods to obtain information about the power consumption of servers and VMs.

7.7.1 Power Measurement for Servers

The obvious way to get accurate information about energy consumption of servers is to directly measure it. However, this requires extra hardware to be installed in the hosts, and the need to add intelligent monitoring capabilities in the data center and to deal with huge amounts of data. Green open cloud (GOC) is an example of energy monitoring and measurement framework that relies on energy sensors to monitor the electricity consumed by Cloud resources. It collects statistics of the power usage in real time and embeds electrical sensors that provide dynamic measurements of energy consumption and an energy data collector.

7.7.2 Power Measurement for VMS

Even if power consumption of servers can be measured in real time, power consumption of VMs cannot be measured by any sensor and cannot be connected to a hardware measurement device. Some effort was put into measuring VM power consumption. The VM power consumption is computed by retrieving the idle power from the power consumption of the server when it hosts the VM, which is impractical and not very accurate. Alternative solutions based on extending a power monitoring adaptor between the server driver modules and the hypervisor are proposed. However, these solutions measure the total power consumed by the virtualization layer and don't provide per VM power usage.

7.7.3 Power and Energy Estimation Models

As most servers in modern data centers are not equipped with power measurement devices and as VM power cannot be measured by sensors, models that estimate the power and energy consumption as well as VMM power cost are becoming more and more attractive for power metering. This section presents a general overview of power estimation models and tools in Cloud and introduces data center energy efficiency metrics.

7.7.4 Power and Energy Modeling for Servers

Power consumption models for servers have been extensively studied in the literature and vary from complex to simple. As the CPU of a server consumes the most important amount of power and as the relationship between power and CPU utilization is linear, CPU-based linear models represent a lightweight and a simple way to estimate servers' power usage. Simple utilization-based power models for servers are proposed. They assume that CPU (Figure 7.2) is the only factor in their power models and present an approximation for total power against CPU utilization (U).

$$P = P_{idle} + U(P_{Peak}P_{idle}) \qquad (7.3)$$

P is total power consumption, P_{Peak} is peak power consumption, P_{idle} is idle power consumption, and U is CPU utilization (a fraction between 0 and 1).

More complex power models enter into further details and present deeper analysis of power consumption. More parameters like network access rate, hard disk access rate and memory access rate are considered and implicated [8, 9].

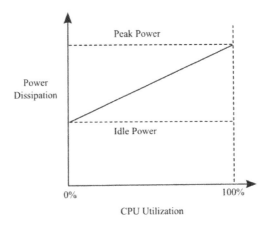

Figure 7.2 Server power model based on CPU utilization.

7.7.5 Power Modeling for VMs

Estimating the power of VMs is important to better organize and schedule them in a way that minimizes the data center energy consumption. Like the estimation models used for servers, CPU utilization could also be used to calculate the power consumption of the CPU by a VM. Models rely on information such as the resource utilization (CPU and memory) and/or information provided by performance monitoring counters (PMCs), also known as hardware performance counters (HPCs). Based on the idea of combining PMC and CPU utilization, the authors herein present a VM power metering approach and VM power estimation software called Joulemeter. This latter has the ability to accurately infer the power consumption without adding any additional hardware or software instrumentation [10].

7.7.6 Power Modeling for VM Migration

Virtual machine live migration (VMLM) consists of moving VM between physical hosts without service interruption. This mechanism allows VM consolidation to achieve better energy efficiency; however, it also brings additional power consumption and its cost in terms of energy is not negligible. Energy costs of migration have not been considered when migrating VMs. Key points for efficient VM consolidation are how to estimate the energy consumption of each VMM and how to make migration decisions. To investigate the energy cost of VMM and to model it, the energy overhead of live migration depends essentially on the amount of memory used by the VM and on the available network bandwidth. It increases with an increasing VM size and decreases with an increasing network bandwidth. A lightweight mathematical model is used to estimate the energy cost of VMLM. The model is derived through linear regression and the relationship between the energy cost of migration, the network bandwidth and the VM size is expressed in Eq. (7.4) where s represents VMs size, b represents the network bandwidth and A, B and C represent constant values.

$$E_{mig} = A + Bs + Cb \qquad (7.4)$$

7.7.7   Energy Efficiency Metrics

In addition to power models, improving energy efficiency in cloud data centers requires metrics that reflect data centers and servers' efficiency and provide the necessary information for high level management and scheduling decisions. Some metrics of energy efficiency have been proposed for data centers. *The Green Grid* defined two data centers efficiency metrics: power usage effectiveness (PUE) and data center efficiency (DCE).

PUE is defined as the total power consumed by the data center divided by the power used by the IT equipment, as shown in Eq. (7.5):

$$PUE = \frac{TotalFacilityPower}{ITEquipmentPower} \qquad (7.5)$$

DCE is the indicator ratio of IT data center energy efficiency and is defined as the reciprocal of PUE (Eq. 7.6).

$$DCE = \frac{1}{PUE} = \frac{ITEquipmentPower}{TotalFacilityPower} \qquad (7.6)$$

These two metrics measure only the proportion of power used by IT equipment and can be used to compare data center efficiency. Energy efficiency metrics for servers that could be used to sort them according to their efficiency and to enable scheduling algorithms to make decisions have not been widely investigated. Performance per watt (PPW) has become a popular metric, as it can be used to measure and rank the energy efficiency of servers. It can be defined as the rate of transactions or computations that can be delivered by a computer for every watt of power consumed. Formally the PPW is defined by Intel as: *"The term performance-per-watt is a measure of the energy efficiency of computer architecture or computer hardware. It can be represented as the rate of transactions or computations or a certain performance score that can be delivered by a computer for every watt of power consumed"*. This metric provides scores and rank servers no matter their size or structure. The higher the performance per watt, the more energy efficient the server is [11, 12].

7.8   Power Saving Policies in Cloud

The main power saving strategies in cloud data centers are dynamic frequency voltage scaling (DVFS), servers powering down and VM consolidation.

7.8.1 Dynamic Frequency and Voltage Scaling

Dynamic frequency and voltage scaling (DVFS) is a power management tool that aims to reduce the power consumption of servers when the load is low. DVFS, also known as CPU throttling, dynamically scales the voltage and frequency of the CPU at runtime. For example, Linux kernel allows for DVFS that can be activated in different policies: Performance, Power Save, User Space, Conservative, and On Demand. Each policy has a governor that decides whether the frequency must be updated or not. As this method decreases the number of instructions the processor executes in running a program, the program takes a longer time and the performance is reduced. DVFS is also too dependent on hardware and is not controllable according to the changing needs, and its resulting power savings are low compared to other methods. Even if DVFS aims at reducing power consumption, it just acts at server level. As a completely idle server still consumes up to 70% of power, DVFS power savings remain narrow. These reasons have led to the appearance of other data center level solutions that consolidate workloads onto fewer servers and switch or put in lower power mode the idle hosts [13].

7.8.2 Powering Down

Important reduction in energy consumption can be achieved by powering down or switching off servers when they are not in use. As many servers in the data center are idle most of the time, they could be powered down or put into sleep mode in the periods of time when they are not used and then powered up if needed. This dynamic capacity provisioning or dynamic shutdown problem is challenging as it requires careful planning to select servers to power down and different factors must be considered. On/Off approaches have been proposed to dynamically turn on and off data center servers, thus minimizing the energy use. Although its complexity, this technique is efficient and can achieve significant reduction in power consumption [14, 15].

7.8.3 Energy-Aware Consolidation

A key technique of power saving in cloud data centers is workload consolidation onto a smaller number of servers. This approach aims to reduce the high consumption of energy by selecting the most energy efficient servers. Dynamic optimization and further workload consolidation into an even fewer number of servers can be performed thanks to VM live migration. It is an essential mechanism that dynamically moves VMs to different hosts without rebooting the operating system inside the VM.

7.9 Conclusion

In this chapter, data center network architectures and various network control mechanisms were introduced. Discussed in the chapter was how resource virtualization, through VMM, is now commonplace in data centers, and how VMM can be used to improve system-side performance for VMs, or how load can be better balanced across the network through strategic VMM. However, all the VMM works in this chapter have not addressed the fundamental problem of actively targeting and removing congestion from oversubscribed core links within data center networks.

REFERENCES

1. Pike Research 2010, Cloud computing to reduce global data center energy expenditures by 38% in 2020, 2010, (accessed on 21/01/2013). [Online]. Available: http://www.pikeresearch.com/newsroom/ cloud-computing-to-reduce-global-data-center-energy-expenditures-by-38-in-2020.

2. Pinheiro, E., Bianchini, R., Carrera, E. V., & Heath, T. (2001). Load balancing and unbalancing for power and performance in cluster-based systems. In Workshop on compilers and operating systems for low power (Vol. 180, pp. 182-195).

3. Plaxton, C. G., Sun, Y., Tiwari, M., & Vin, H. (2006). Reconfigurable resource scheduling. In Proceedings of the eighteenth annual ACM symposium on Parallelism in algorithms and architectures (pp. 93-102). ACM.

4. Rackspace, US Inc. 2012, Rackspace hosting reports second quarter 2012 results, 2012, (accessed on 06/11/2012). [Online]. Available: http://ir.rackspace.com/phoenix.zhtml?c=221673&p=irol-newsArticle&ID=1723357

5. Raghavendra, R., Ranganathan, P., Talwar, V., Wang, Z., & Zhu, X. (2008, March). No power struggles: Coordinated multi-level power management for the data center. *In ACM SIGARCH Computer Architecture News* (Vol. 36, No. 1, pp. 48-59). ACM.

6. Rajkumar, R., Juvva, K., Molano, A., & Oikawa, S. (1997). Resource kernels: A resource-centric approach to real-time and multimedia systems. In Multimedia Computing and Networking 1998 (Vol. 3310, pp. 150-165). International Society for Optics and Photonics.

7. Ranganathan, P., Leech, P., Irwin, D., & Chase, J. (2006). Ensemble-level power management for dense blade servers. In ACM SIGARCH Computer Architecture News (Vol. 34, No. 2, pp. 66-77). IEEE Computer Society.

8. Bi, J., Yuan, H., Tan, W., Zhou, M., Fan, Y., Zhang, J., & Li, J. (2017). Application-aware dynamic fine-grained resource provisioning in a virtualized cloud data center. *IEEE Transactions on Automation Science and Engineering*, 14(2), 1172-1184.

9. Khosravi, A., Nadjaran Toosi, A., & Buyya, R. (2017). Online virtual machine migration for renewable energy usage maximization in geographically distributed cloud data centers. *Concurrency and Computation: Practice and Experience*.

10. Zhang, W., Qi, Q., & Deng, J. (2017). Building Intelligent Transportation Cloud Data Center Based on SOA. *International Journal of Ambient Computing and Intelligence (IJACI)*, 8(2), 1-11.

11. Tarafdar, N., Lin, T., Fukuda, E., Bannazadeh, H., Leon-Garcia, A., & Chow, P. (2017). Enabling Flexible Network FPGA Clusters in a Heterogeneous Cloud Data Center. In Proceedings of the 2017 ACM/SIGDA International Symposium on Field-Programmable Gate Arrays (pp. 237-246). ACM.

12. Dalvandi, A., Gurusamy, M., & Chua, K. C. (2017). Application scheduling, placement, and routing for power efficiency in cloud data centers. *IEEE Transactions on Parallel and Distributed Systems*, 28(4), 947-960.

13. Havet, A., Schiavoni, V., Felber, P., Colmant, M., Rouvoy, R., & Fetzer, C. (2017). Gen-Pack: A generational scheduler for cloud data centers. In Cloud Engineering (IC2E), 2017 IEEE International Conference on (pp. 95-104). IEEE.

14. Yuan, B., Zou, D., Jin, H., Yu, S., & Yang, L. T. (2017). HostWatcher: Protecting hosts in cloud data centers through software-defined networking. *Future Generation Computer Systems*. DOI: 10.1016/j.future.2017.04.023

15. Zheng, K., Wang, L., Yang, B., Sun, Y., & Uhlig, S. (2017). Lazyctrl: A scalable hybrid network control plane design for cloud data centers. *IEEE Transactions on Parallel and Distributed Systems*, 28(1), 115-127. DOI: 10.1109/TPDS.2016.2558512

CHAPTER 8

TRUSTED VM-VTPM LIVE MIGRATION PROTOCOL IN CLOUDS

Abstract

Several applications are available to provide integration of a trusted platform module (TPM) hardware with other systems as well as provide a wider functionality based on the capabilities of the TPM. This chapter introduces a platform-agnostic trusted launch protocol for a GVMI. GVMIs are VM images that do not differ from the vendor-supplied VM images (*colloquially known as vanilla software*). They are made available by IaaS providers for clients that intend to use an instance of a VM image that was not subject to any modifications, such as patches or injected software. The protocol described in this chapter allows a client that requests a GVMI to ensure that it is run on a trusted platform.

Keywords: Trusted platform module, trusted computing, operation, applications, extensions.

8.1 Trusted Computing

The Trusted Computing Group (TCG)[1] consortium has developed specifications for the TPM, a hardware component that is a cornerstone of trusted computing (see Figure 8.1). Trusted computing is a concept developed and promoted by the TCG and has at its core the ability to verify and enforce a certain consistent behavior using hardware means. Furthermore, the TPM [1] can be used to allow external parties to ensure that a certain host bearing the TPM is booted into a trusted state. That is performed by verifying the set of digests (*called measurements*) of the loaded software, successively produced throughout the boot process of the device. The measurements are stored in a protected storage built into the TPM chip and are therefore resistant to software attacks, although vulnerable to hardware tampering.

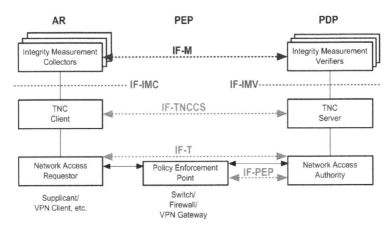

Figure 8.1   Trusted computing standards.

8.2 TPM Operations

Using the above-described components, the TPM provides a set of standard unsociable functionality predefined by the hardware vendor according to the TPM specification. Several functions that are important in the scope of this chapter are: The integrity measurement function which enables the TPM to collect the measurement digests of the operational state of the system. Such measurement digests are stored in the PCRs and all subsequent digests are stored by extending the hash according to the formula

$$PCR[n+1] = SHA - 1(PCR[n]||MeasuredData) \qquad (8.1)$$

---

[1]https://trustedcomputinggroup.org/

The PCR values [2] are discarded and rewritten on each system reboot. The TPM provides Integrity reporting functionality in order to report and attest to the authenticity of the stored PCR values for external attestation purposes. This is done by digitally signing the integrity reports based on the PCR values with an AIK generated and stored in the TPM. As an endpoint of communication, the TPM provides a set of operations for secure message exchange based on the use of asymmetric cryptography, with the keys being generated and managed by the TPM. The four operations provided by the TPM are described below:

- *Binding:* TPM offers protection of the message by means of asymmetric cryptography using encryption keys generated and maintained by the TPM. Thus, a message encrypted using a particular TPM's public key is decryptable only by using the private key of the same TPM.

- *Signing:* The functionality is implemented according to the same principles of asymmetric encryption described.

- *Sealing:* A special case of the binding functionality, where the encrypted messages produced through binding are only decryptable in a certain platform state to which the message is sealed. This ensures that an encrypted message can only be decrypted by a platform which is in a certain prescribed state.

- *Sealed Signing:* It offers the possibility to verify that the platform producing the signature is in a certain specific configuration. The verification is based on the measurements from a set of predetermined PCRs that are evaluated to determine whether the platform has the required configuration.

Having covered several essential points of the TPM specification [3], we visit the state of the art with regard to the support for trusted computing technology from the main server and PC manufacturers, namely Intel and Advanced Micro Devices (colloquially known as AMD). Intel has implemented support for the TPM through the Trusted Execution Technology (TXT), which includes a set of hardware enhancements that allow the creation of multiple separate execution environments. A recent contribution towards trusted computing from Intel is the OpenAttestation software development kit. AMD has developed AMD Presidio", a technology similar to Intel's TXT. However, AMD Presidio only offers rudimentary support for TPM.

8.3   TPM Applications and Extensions

Several applications are available to provide integration of the TPM hardware with other systems as well as provide a wider functionality based on the capabilities of the TPM [4]. Starting with the lowest level, the following hierarchy of TPM applications is available:

- *TrouSerS:* a trusted computing software stack developed by IBM and released under the common public license, supported on i386 GNU/Linux. Several *nix distributions are supported such as SUSE, Fedora Core and RHEL however, functionality for specific releases requires ongoing testing.

- *Linux-IMA:* first introduced in the Linux Kernel version 2.6.30, Integrity Measurement Architecture (IMA) maintains a runtime measurement list and an aggregate ingrate value over the list (if anchored to a TPM). Linux-IMA may or may not be enabled by default on specific distributions.

- *Grub-IMA:* An enhancement of the Linux boot loader supporting TCG-compliant platforms enabled with TPM versions 1.1 and 1.2. The GRUB-IMA patch supports GRUB version 0.97 available for RHEL/Cent OS, Fedora Core and Ubuntu.

- *OpenPTS:* Open Platform Trust Services is a software stack that allows the verification of integrity of TPM-enabled platforms as well as their conformance to certain specific trust models. Open PTS relies on TrouSerS, Linux-IMA and GRUB-IMA for data collection.

- *Intel OpenAttestation SDK:* In April 2012 Intel has launched the OpenAttestation project, a software development kit that enables creation of cloud management tools with the capability to establish host integrity information. This functionality is supported by the TPM attestation procedure, based on the measurement values stored in the TPM's PCRs.

8.4   TPM Use Cases

The trusted computing group defines four initial use cases for the trusted platform module in the TCG specification architecture overview: TPM can be used to reduce the risk to information assets and to facilitate risk management by offering additional protection to the credentials used to verify and assert the integrity and authenticity of data. This is achieved by using the TPM to store keys, hash values and other secrets in protected hardware storage. Restricted access data is thus protected from software attacks and can only be obtained through hardware tampering. As a facilitator of asset management, TPM can be used as part of the functionality to assert the ownership of the platform while also allowing certain third parties to have access to the data protected by the TPM.

TPM chips could also be used in the context of e-commerce transactions in order to maintain the context of a secure and verified transaction throughout future transactions without the need for repeated verification of the client's and vendor's integrity. In the context of security monitoring and emergency response, the TPM provides the capability to correctly report or verify the state of the system. This can be used to e.g., identify the systems that require an update or to identify compromised systems. An example of a commercial product built on top of the trusted platform module is Microsoft's BitLocker or HP's Protect Tools. BitLocker is full disk encryption functionality available with certain versions of the Microsoft Windows operating system, which allows protecting data from unauthorized inspection. HP Protect Tools is a tool for security management implemented using HP proprietary technology, which uses the trusted platform module for key management.

While the use cases defined by the TCG are broadly defined to encompass multiple applications of the TPM, the current chapter creates a new special use case for the TPM and trusted computing by placing them in the context of cloud computing. Hence, we consider a new use case for TPM components in commodity hardware.

8.5 State of the Art in Public Cloud Computing Security

8.5.1 Cloud Management Interface

One of the fulfilled promises of cloud computing is the reduction of the upfront hardware purchase and setup costs. Thus, the client running VM does not need to bear the overhead of managing of the location and the hardware aspects [5] of the server that is being used. Instead, a web administration console is the single interaction point between the cloud service provider and the image administrator. The web administration console offers a wide range of administrative controls, such as creating instances, generating SSH keys for the instances, starting and stopping VMs, as well as commissioning other cloud services. In this situation, the authentication framework employed by the cloud provider is the only safeguard between malicious actors and the control of a cloud user's account. The web accessibility of the administrative console makes it vulnerable both due to the sheer accessibility and to its potential susceptibility to web-based attacks such as cross-site scripting, phishing attacks, DNS cache poisoning, session hijacking, etc.

Attack: An analysis of both novel signature wrapping attacks and cross-site scripting vulnerabilities in order to gain control of the Amazon EC2 and S3 services. Cross-site scripting attacks are based on exploiting the relationship between a web client and a server considered trusted, which makes it possible to execute an injected script on the client side with the server's privileges. The authors define three factors facilitating the wide distribution of XSS vulnerabilities, namely predominance of web applications that display untrusted input, availability of an unsafe default for passing untrusted input to the client in most web application programming languages, and the availability of multiple, often browser-specific ways of invoking the JavaScript interpreter.

In the case of signature wrapping attacks, the authors used the meaningful and informative SOAP message responses to check the possibility of the signature wrapping attack. Using a single eavesdropped Monitor Instances SOAP request, the authors were able to start new VM instances, stop any running instances or create new images and gateways in a victim's cloud environment. The authors remark that the use of SSL/TLS is not a solution to signature wrapping attacks, since signed SOAP messages can be traced by other means. In the case of the identified cross-site scripting (XSS) vulnerability, the authors used a download link vulnerability in the Amazon store website in order to gain control over the cloud management interface.

Counter Measures: Below is a selection of the countermeasures research lines with respect to signature wrapping attacks examined by the authors of the attack. The selection includes: Validating each message against an appropriate security policy; however, the countermeasures were considered ineffective; XML schema validation, which can detect SOAP messages modified by a signature wrapping attack; however, this operation carries a significant performance hit and is not performed by the standard web frameworks.

Providing and signing additional information on the structure of the SOAP request has also been suggested; however, this approach can also be circumvented using the extensible and flexible structure of SOAP. The countermeasure suggested by the authors themselves is a stronger isolation between the signature verification functionality and the business logic of the application.

8.5.2 Challenges in Securing the Virtualized Environment

A significant body of research [6] has been carried out in the area of secure VMs and particularly confidentiality of VMs in untrusted environments. Below is an overview of publications which explore the possibility to secure the integrity of the VM and its environment.

Focus on VM Isolation: Kong attempts to secure the VM in a XEN virtualization environment where `Dom0` is susceptible to both internal and external attacks (i.e., is generally unadjustable). Five components of the architecture are considered: During the system boot phase the author examines the challenge of building a trusted computing base from the platform power to BIOS to the boot loader and finally the hypervisor. In order to tackle that, the author proposes enhancing the BIOS with a core root of trust for measurement" (CRTM) that will be first component to be loaded.

Direct memory access is used with inputoutput memory management units (IOMMUs) in order to isolate the devices and only allow access to certain memory ranges assigned to each VM; a virtual TPM is instantiated and placed in a specialized domain `Dom0` U and further executes the role of the TPM for other `Dom0` X.

The guest VM boot process uses a custom protocol which relies on asymmetric cryptography in order to ensure the VM is instantiated in a trusted environment; In the process of saving and restoring the image the authors adopt a per page encryption method" to encrypt the instance before it's handed over to `Dom0`.

Minimizing the TCB: As minimizing and sealing the attack surface is one of the basic principles of application security, several of the examined approaches aim to solve this by reducing the trusted computing base. The issue is based on the assumption that in a virtualized environment the management OS should not be trusted. The authors propose the architecture with a reduced TAB which excludes the management OS and ensures a secure runtime environment for the guest VM. In the proposed solution `Dom0` is able to manage the domains without knowing their contents, with the architecture providing a secure runtime environment, network interface, and secondary storage for a guest VM.

The authors consider the scenarios when a Dom0 can subvert the VM to insert root kits or other external code, to undermine the integrity of the new VM execution environment by setting up wrong initial page tables, corrupt the new VM execution environment, and maintain foreign mappings of the new VM memory area in order to read the memory area during the VM runtime.

The solution considers several steps for executing the proposed solution: During the domain building and shutdown a malicious Dom0 could potentially subvert the launched VM in a number of ways. In order to mitigate this the authors propose to modify the hypervisor to perform foreign mapping cleaning, to check that none of the pages allocated to the new VM are pointing to Dom. In addition to that an integrity check for the new VM kernel and the CPU context is performed during the Dom0 hypercall to the supervisor to check the integrity of the VM before launching.

With regard to the domain runtime the authors analyze the types of hyper calls used within the communication between Dom0 and Dom0 U and specifically consider the hyper calls that are harmful to the privacy and security of Dom0 U but necessary for its management. The suggested solution includes pushing hyper calls related to memory and CPU calls into the hypervisor. Similar to some previous solutions, the proposed architecture involves a significant overhead, which is, however, considered by the authors acceptable since the tasks incurring the overhead are not performed continuously.

A more radical step towards the minimization of the TAB is taken for a virtualization architecture that does not assume the presence of a hypervisor, except for the VM creation and boot stages. Instead of relying on the hypervisor for arbitration of resources between VMs, the task is performed by mechanisms built into the hardware (e.g., hardware paging mechanisms for memory isolation, or virtualization capabilities in some hardware devices [like NICs]). The key ideas of the proposed NoHype architecture are preallocating memory and cores, using only virtualized I/O devices, short-circuiting the system discovery process and avoiding indirection. A prototype implementing the proposed architecture based on Xen 4.0, Linux 2.6.35.4 and commodity Intel hardware offers a 1% performance improvement compared to the use of a Xen hypervisor, except for GCC benchmarks. It is important to note, however, that the use of a hypervisor is not fully excluded in the architecture proposed by Szefer. While security risks can potentially be decreased by reducing the role of the hypervisor to VM creation and boot, the authors do not mention how a compromised hypervisor can be prevented from performing malicious actions and compromise the integrity of the VM during the stages when it is employed.

8.5.3   The Trust in TPM

Multiple research projects aiming to secure the VMs in a cloud environment [7] which heavily rely on the TCG TPM can be found, as well as the more recent ones. All of the above use the TPM component in order to provide a reliable root of trust that could be used to either bootstrap the rest of the software stack on a TPM-enabled machine or obtain certain guarantees regarding the integrity or the policy compliance of the target host when migrating a VM instance to a different host.

A reliable and trustable TPM indeed offers a wide range of capabilities to enhance the security of virtualization environments in particular, and cloud computing environments in general. Current solutions were examined with regard to provisioning of a root of trust. The authors distinguish four types of solutions, namely, general-purpose devices with significant resistance to physical tampering, general-purpose devices without significant physical defenses, special-purpose minimal devices, and research solutions that attempt to instantiate a root of trust without custom hardware support. IBM 4758 is an example of a full-blown general purpose tamper-resistant and tamper-responding cryptographic co-processor, which includes capabilities to respond to hardware tampering in several ways, e.g., erasing the data or disabling the device. TPM on the other hand, is a general-purpose device without significant physical defenses, and has been designed to be secure only against software attacks. TPM provides sealed protected storage, rather than tamper-responding protected storage. Thus, a TPM physically accessible by an adversary without physical audit capabilities on the client side cannot be trusted. Alas, one of the core driving forces behind today's rapid development of cloud computing is the reduction of the hardware maintenance overhead by purchasing computation storage capabilities from cloud providers who maintain the hardware infrastructure and hence have full access to the servers, including the TPM. That opens the door to a number of additional potential vulnerabilities. The above-named hardware attacks have been discussed earlier and are out of the scope of this chapter. Instead, we will focus on some attacks against the TPM in general and the Intel Trusted Execution Technology (which relies on the TPM).

In a cuckoo attack, malware on the user's machine forwards the calls intended for the local TPM to a remote attacker who feeds the messages to a TPM controlled by an adversary. The physical control of the machine allows violation of the security of the TPM (Red Hat 2013) via hardware attacks and thus controls all communication between the verifier and the local TPM. In this scenario, the attacker will be able to access all of the answers the local TPM is expecting by the TPMs manufacturer confirming that the TPM is genuine and is used to endorse the public key of the TPM. However, it only endorses the fact that the public key belongs to some genuine TPM and not the specific TPM. A potential solution would be to corroborate the public key provided by the TPM with the public key provided by the manufacturer; however, this raises issues regarding secure distribution of TPM public keys by the manufacturers. There are vulnerabilities in the design of Intel's Trusted Execution Technology, which is Intel's response to the trusted computing trend. The attack that allows subverting the Xen hypervisor is based on two vulnerabilities identified in the System Management Mode, which on x86x86 64 architectures [8] is more privileged than ring 0 mode and a hardware hypervisor (VT/AMD-v). While the specific bugs described in the chapter are likely to be patched by the chipset manufacturer, a number of questions are raised regarding the security considerations of the TXT architecture.

8.5.4 Challenges

A review of research challenges within cloud computing reveals a whole spectrum of issues, from the hardware TPM security to the higher level aspects of IaaS and PaaS cloud computing security. Recent chapters on research trends within cloud computing security include Chen and Katz's assessment of security challenges that are specific to cloud computing security, security challenges in IaaS cloud computing and a broader assessment of the state of the art and research challenges within cloud computing by Zhang *et al.*

Auditability: The currently unsolved and increasingly important issue of mutual auditability is emphasized. It suggest that the remote attestation capabilities enabled by the TPM could be used for attestation on single machines; however, they are not due to the dynamic migration of VMs between machines in the cloud environment. This is addressed by the solution proposed by Santos *et al.*, in which a fixed set of attested trusted machines within the cloud could be extended to enable auditability even in the event of VM migration within the cloud.

Periodic probing of certain functions, or licenses presents special case of auditability and is specifically relevant for specialized clouds, e.g., telecommunication services clouds. Aspects of this task could be addressed by applying some principles of the VM introspection-based architecture for intrusion detection described. In this case the VMM-based intrusion detection component described in and could be reconfigured to periodically take a set of VM probes that have been agreed upon by both the cloud host and client. This could complement TCG-oriented solutions aimed at ensuring trusted virtualized environments.

Reducing the Trusted Computing Base: As mentioned above, several authors have researched the possibility of improving the security of virtualized environments by reducing the trusted computing base. Reduction of the trusted computing base is likely to reduce the potential for software vulnerabilities as more of the functions currently performed by the hypervisor could potentially be implemented increasingly closer to the mechanisms provided by the underlying hardware. While reduced functionality and some performance hits might arise as potential challenges on the way, some solutions could be used for specialized clouds with less strict performance or functionality requirements yet higher security demands.

New Approaches for Avoiding Cross-VM Attacks: As preventing cross-CM attacks in the case of VMs placed on the same physical machine is difficult, they cannot be executed other than by placing the VMs on different physical servers. Despite the drastically increasing costs in case of such a solution, it might be applicable to certain types of specialized clouds. The question in this case is how placement on different physical machines could be leveraged to implement additional mechanisms to enhance the security of such a virtualized environment.

Minimizing Impact Compromised TPM Private Keys: While discussing hardware revocation the authors consider only the case when the private key of a specific TPM chipset has been compromised. We do mention that the compromise of the manufacturer's signing key would have much more serious consequences without providing any further solutions. Given the wide acceptance of TPM modules and the large number of research projects heavily relying on TPM on one hand and the recent cases of root CA breaches on the other hand, an exposure of a manufacturer's signing keys cannot be excluded. Given the difficulties of revoking certificates embedded in the TPM chips, it is necessary to explore the available options that could be used in the event of manufacturer signing keys exposure.

8.6   Launch and Migration of Virtual Machines

8.6.1   Trusted Virtual Machines and Virtual Machine Managers

Santos *et al.* propose a design of a trusted cloud computing platform (TCCP) that ensures VMs are running on a secure hardware and software stack with a remote and untrusted host. The platform is comprised of three trusted components, namely a trusted VM monitor, trusted coordinator (TC) and an external trusted entity (ETE) and an untrusted cloud manager. The TCCP allows a client to reliably and remotely attest the platform at the cloud provider's location to verify that it is running trusted VMM implementation and thus make sure that the computation running in a guest VM is secure.

The usual attestation process involves compiling a measurement list (ML) that contains an array of hashes of the software stack involved in the boot sequence. The ML is securely stored in the machine's TPM and can be subsequently used for remote attestation using a protocol based on asymmetric encryption using the TPMs private/public key pair. However, this attestation mechanism does not guarantee that the measurement list obtained by the remote party corresponds to the actual configuration of the host where the VM has been running.

To circumvent that, Joshua Reich *et al.* propose an enhanced attestation process where a trusted coordinator (TC) stores the list of attested hosts that run a TVMM [9] and which can securely run the client's VMs. Each of the trusted hosts maintains in their memory a trusted key (TK) that is used for identification, each time the client instantiates a VM on the trusted host. Finally, the TC is hosted by an external trusted entity which is out of the reach of the cloud provider and hence cannot be tampered with (here the authors make a parallel to the root CAs found in the public key infrastructure [PKI] model)

Darrell Reimer *et al.* [10] presents a good initial set of ideas for secure VM launch and migration, in particular the use of an external trusted entity. However, a significant drawback of this solution is the fact that the TK resides in the memory of the trusted hosts, which leaves the solution vulnerable to cold boot attacks, where the key can be extracted from memory. Furthermore, the authors require that the ETE maintains information about all of the hosts deployed on the IaaS platform, but do not mention any mechanisms for anonymzing this information, making it valuable to potential attackers and unacceptable for a public cloud service provider. Finally, the paper does not mention any mechanism for revocation of the TK, nor any considerations for the regeneration of TKs outside of host reboot.

8.6.2   Seeding Clouds with Trust Anchors

A decentralized approach to integrity attestation is adopted by Schiffman *et al.* [11]. The primary concerns addressed by this approach are the limited transparency of cloud computing platforms and the limits to scalability imposed by third party integrity attestation mechanisms, as described. Thus, the role of a third-party host attestation component is fulfilled by a proposed "cloud verifier" (CV). The authors in [12] examine a trusted cloud architecture where the integrity of the cloud hosts (termed "network controller") is verified by the IaaS client through the CV, which resides in the application domain of the IaaS platform provider. Integrity verification is performed based on the measurements produced by the TPM component of the CV host. Thus, in the first step of the protocol the client verifies the integrity of the CV in order to include the CV into its trust perimeter, if the integrity level of the CV is considered satisfactory. In the second step of the protocol, the CV sends attestation requests from the node controllers (NC) where the client's VM will be launched, thus extending the trust chain to the NC. Next, the NC verifies the integrity of the VM image, which is countersigned by the CV and returned to the client, which evaluates the VM image integrity data and allows or disallows the VM launch on the NC.

While the idea of increasing the transparency of the cloud computing platform for the client is indeed supported by the industry, the authors in [10, 11, 12, 13] do not clarify how the introduction of an additional integrity attestation component in the architecture of the IaaS platform has any positive effect on the transparency of the cloud platform. Furthermore, the proposed protocol increases the complexity model for the IaaS client in two aspects. First is the necessity to evaluate the integrity attestation reports of the CV and NC. Second is introduction of additional steps in the trusted VM launch, where the client has to take actions based on the data returned from the CV. This requires either human interaction or a fairly complex integrity attestation evaluation component (or a combination thereof) on the client side, something which will not contribute to a wide-scale adoption of the solution [10, 11, 14, 15].

8.6.3   Securely Launching Virtual Machines on Trustworthy Platforms in a Public Cloud

The case of trusted VM launch in public IaaS platforms has been examined. The section explores the scenario when a client employs VM images provisioned through a procurement server by an IaaS provider and focuses exclusively on the launch stage of the CM life cycle in an IaaS platform. Trusted computing base (TAB) up to the level of Management VM (known as Dom0 in the Xen VMM model) relies on the use of TPM hardware for key generation and platform integrity. In order to ensure that the VM instance requested by the client is launched on a host with variable integrity, the client encrypts the VM image (along with all the injected data) with a symmetric key which is sealed to a particular configuration of the host (reflected through the values in the PCRs in the TPM deployed on the host). To do that, the client must connect to the cloud service provider's network through an IPSec tunnel and negotiate a host that satisfies the client's security requirements. As a result, the client receives the means to directly communicate with the destination host (where the VM instance will be deployed), as well as TPM-signed data certifying the integrity of the host. Furthermore, prior to that the client must attest the destination host platforms which are presented as trusted by the cloud service provider, and generate an asymmetric bind key that can be used to decrypt the VM image provided by the client. As a result, the VM image is only accessible by the host when in a certain trustable state. The protocol satisfies requirements regarding authentication, confidentiality, integrity, non-repudiation and replay protection.

A model has been proposed which is suitable in the case of trusted VM launch scenarios for enterprise clients. It requires that the VM image is prepackaged and encrypted by the client prior to the IaaS launch. However, a plausible scenario like the launch of a generic VM image made available by the IaaS provider is not covered in the proposed model. Furthermore, we believe that in order to decrease the number of barriers in the adoption of a trusted cloud computing model, as few actions as possible should be required from the client side. Likewise, direct communication between the client and the destination host as well as significant changes to the existing VM launch protocol implementations in cloud computing platforms hamper the implementation of such a protocol and should be avoided. A more lightweight approach needs to be adopted in terms of required user actions and requirements towards the launched VM image and the cloud computing platform [11].

8.7   Trusted VM Launch and Migration Protocol

This section introduces a platform-agnostic trusted launch protocol for a GVMI. GVMIs are virtual machine images that do not differ from the vendor-supplied VM images (colloquially known as vanilla software). They are made available by the IaaS providers for clients that intend to use an instance of a VM image that was not subject to any modifications, such as patches or injected software. The protocol described in this section allows a client that requests a GVMI to ensure that it is run on a trusted platform. The concept of GVMI is also explained in further details below.

Attacker Model: The use case for a trusted VM launch in public clouds assumes that several parties are involved, such as the following:

Malicious IaaS Provider: The domain of the IaaS provider is generally considered to be untrusted. That includes the deployment of the cloud management platform, as well as the hardware and software configuration of the physical machines supporting the IaaS infrastructure. The untrusted domain also includes the communication between servers that are part of the IaaS platform, as well as the generic VMs made available by the IaaS provider (although it is assumed that they are identical the ones supplied by the vendor). However, this attacker model considers that the physical security of the hardware and the integrity of the TPM are ensured. This is important in order to be able to rely on the security model of the Trusted Computing Group (TCG), since the TCG model is not designed to withstand physical attack. This assumption builds on the fact that the TPM is tamper-evident and a visual inspection would be enough to discover a hardware attack [12].

Other Actors: The client is a user of cloud computing services and intends to launch or use a VM. The client can be both technically skilled (e.g., capable of assessing the security of platform configurations based on values from the measurement list, etc.) and a non-expert that requires access to a generic VM instance launched and running on a trusted platform. The trusted third party (TTP) is, as the name implies, trusted by both the client and the CSP. The breaching of certificate authorities in 2011 emphasized the drawbacks of centralized security models and their susceptibility to attacks. The more complex the operations performed by the TTP, the higher the probability of it having exploitable vulnerabilities. It is therefore important to keep the implementation of the TTP as simple as possible. The main task of the TTP is to attest the configuration of the nodes that will host the generic VMs and asses their security profile according to some predefined policies. Within the current trust model, TTPs could be implemented on the client side, as long as the IaaS provider agrees to that and the client has the capability to set up and operate an attestation and evaluation engine [13].

Generic Virtual Machine Images: A peculiar aspect of GVMIs is that they by definition cannot posses any variable properties that could distinguish two different instances launched using a GVMI. That is, all of the GVMI of a particular distribution offered by the vendor are binary identical. This property of GVMI makes it difficult for an IaaS client to verify that the VM instance it interacts with runs on a particular hardware or software stack, since as mentioned above, the VM instance launched from a GVMI does not possess any unique properties. In the case of trusted launch of a generic VM, it is essential for the client to be able to ensure both the integrity of the underlying platform and of the VM image supplied by the IaaS provider. The fact that all GVMIs are identical can be used in the context of a secure launch protocol in order to verify that a generic VM image has been launched on a trusted platform [14].

Specific Attacker Model: The situation when a non-expert user requires the launch of a VM on a secure platform implies a recommendation that such VMs should generally not be used for business-critical operations. However, since this generic VM will be part of the security perimeter of a larger organization, it is important to provide a security level that is as high as the setup allows. Hence, the following attacker actions are likely in this situation: The IaaS provider ignores the request for launching the VM on a trusted platform and launches the VM on a generic platform. This situation is addressed by requirement $R1$ and $R4$. The IaaS provider launches a VM on a trusted platform, but alters the generic VM (e.g., by injecting forged SSL certificates) in order to intercept the communication between the client and the VM to obtain valuable information (addressed by requirement $R3$). Revisiting requirement $R2$, in the following trusted launch protocol, obtaining a correct response to a challenge from the client to the VM (the object of the challenge being a secret nonce which is sealed by the TTP on the destination node after it has been attested) is sufficient proof that the VM is launched on a trusted platform [15].

8.8   Conclusion

The TPM can be used to allow external parties to ensure that a certain host bearing the TPM is booted into a trusted state. That is performed by verifying the set of digests (called measurements) of the loaded software, successively produced throughout the boot process of the device. The measurements are stored in a protected storage built into the TPM chip and are therefore resistant to software attacks, although vulnerable to hardware tampering. This chapter introduced a platform-agnostic trusted launch protocol for a GVMI. GVMIs are VM images that do not differ from the vendor-supplied VM images (*colloquially known as vanilla software*). They are made available by the IaaS providers for clients that intend to use an instance of a VM image that was not subject to any modifications, such as patches or injected software. The protocol described in this chapter allows a client that requests a GVMI to ensure that it is run on a trusted platform.

REFERENCES

1. Potter, S., & Nieh, J. (2005). Autopod: Unscheduled system updates with zero data loss. In Autonomic Computing, 2005. ICAC 2005. Proceedings. Second International Conference (pp. 367-368). IEEE.

2. Prevelakis, V., & Spinellis, D. (2001). Sandboxing Applications. In USENIX Annual Technical Conference, FREENIX Track (pp. 119-126).

3. PT-GRID Project 2012. Modellierung und Simulation von plasma technologischen Anwendungen im Grid. http://www.pt-grid.de/.

4. Quigley, D., Sipek, J., Wright, C. P., & Zadok, E. (2006). Unionfs: User-and community-oriented development of a unification filesystem. In Proceedings of the 2006 Linux Symposium (Vol. 2, pp. 349-362).

5. Quinlan, S., & Dorward, S. (2002). Venti: A New Approach to Archival Storage. In FAST (Vol. 2, pp. 89-101).

6. Michael O. Rabin (1981). Fingerprinting by Random Polynomials. Center for Research in Computing Technology, Aiken Computation Laboratory, Harvard University.

7. Razavi, K., & Kielmann, T. (2013). Scalable virtual machine deployment using VM image caches. In Proceedings of the International Conference on High Performance Computing, Networking, Storage and Analysis (p. 65). ACM.

8. Red Hat 2013, Inc. Software Management Guide. http://docs.fedoraproject. org/en-US/Fedora/18/html/System_Administrators_Guide.

9. Reich, J., Laadan, O., Brosh, E., Sherman, A., Misra, V., Nieh, J., & Rubenstein, D. (2012). VMTorrent: scalable P2P virtual machine streaming. In CoNEXT (Vol. 12, pp. 289-300).

10. Reimer, D., Thomas, A., Ammons, G., Mummert, T., Alpern, B., & Bala, V. (2008). Opening black boxes: Using semantic information to combat virtual machine image sprawl. In Proceedings of the fourth ACM SIGPLAN/SIGOPS international conference on Virtual execution environments (pp. 111-120). ACM.

11. Hou, C., Huang, C., Dai, H., Ding, Y., He, L., & Ji, M. (2016). Enabling User-Policy-Confined VM Migration in Trusted Cloud Computing. In Foundations and Applications of Self* Systems, IEEE International Workshops (pp. 66-71). IEEE.

12. Mahfouz, A. M., Rahman, M. L., & Shiva, S. G. Secure Live Virtual Machine Migration through Runtime Monitors.

13. Gu, J., Hua, Z., Xia, Y., Chen, H., Zang, B., Guan, H., & Li, J. (2017). Secure Live Migration of SGX Enclaves on Untrusted Cloud. In Dependable Systems and Networks (DSN), 2017 47th Annual IEEE/IFIP International Conference (pp. 225-236). IEEE.

14. Wu, T., Yang, Q., & He, Y. (2017). A secure and rapid response architecture for virtual machine migration from an untrusted hypervisor to a trusted one. *Frontiers of Computer Science*, 11(5), 821-835.

15. Zhang, X., Wang, Z., Zhi, Y., & Yuan, H. (2017). A Model of Trusted Connection Architecture. In MATEC Web of Conferences (Vol. 100, p. 02064). EDP Sciences.

CHAPTER 9

LIGHTWEIGHT LIVE MIGRATION

Abstract

High availability is increasingly important in today's data centers, cloud, and cluster computing environments. A highly available service is one that is continuously operational for a long period of time. Any downtime experienced by clients of the service may result in significant revenue loss and customer loyalty. Replication is a classical approach for achieving high availability through redundancy; once a failure occurs to a service (*e.g., failure of hosting node*), a replica of the service takes over. Whole-system replication is one of the most traditional instantiations. This chapter presents a set of techniques that provide high availability through VMLM, their implementation in the Xen hypervisor and the Linux operating system kernel.

Keywords: Virtual cluster, check pointing, disk migrations, resumption, FGBI.

9.1   Introduction

Once the primary machine fails, the running applications are taken over by a backup machine. However, whole-system replication is usually unattractive for deployment due to several limitations. For example, maintaining consistent states of the replicas may require application-level modifications (*e.g., to orchestrate state updates*), often using third-party software and sometimes specialized hardware, increasing costs. Furthermore, since the applications directly run on the OS and therefore are not isolated from each other, it may cause security vulnerabilities, especially in cloud environments, where applications are almost always second/third-party and therefore UN trusted. Additionally, such systems often require complex customized configurations, which increase maintenance costs.

Virtualization overcomes these limitations by introducing a layer of abstraction above the OS; the VM. Since applications now run on the guest VM [1], whole-system replication can be implemented easily and efficiently by simply saving a copy of the whole VM running on the system, which avoids any application modifications. Also, as a guest VM is totally hardware independent, no additional hardware expenses are incurred. Due to the VM's ability to encapsulate the state of the running system, different types of OSes and multiple applications hosted on each of those OSes can run concurrently on the same machine, which enables consolidation, reducing costs. Moreover, VM monitors or hypervisors increase security; a VM monitor isolates concurrently running OSes and applications from each other. Therefore, malicious applications cannot impact other applications running on another OS, although they are all running on the same machine.

Besides these benefits, as a VM and its hosted applications are separated from the physical resources, another appealing feature of a VM is the flexibility to manage the workload in a dynamic way. If one physical machine is heavily loaded and a running VM suffers performance degradation due to resource competition, the VM can be easily migrated to another less loaded machine with available resources. During that migration, the applications on the source VM are still running [2], and if they are network applications, their clients do not observe any disruption. This application- and client-transparent migration process is called *"live migration"* and is supported by most state-of-the-art practice virtualization systems. For small size systems, live migration can be done manually (*e.g., by a system administrator*). In a large-scale system such as a cloud environment, it is done automatically.

9.2   VM Checkpointing

To provide benefits such as high availability and dynamic resource allocation, a useful feature of virtualization is the possibility of saving and restoring an entire VM through transparent checkpointing (see Figure 9.1). Modern virtualization systems provide a basic checkpointing and resumption mechanism to save the running state of an active VM to a checkpoint file, and also, to resume a VM [3] from the checkpoint file to the correct suspended state. Unlike application-level checkpointing, VM-level checkpointing usually involves recording the virtual CPU's state, the current state of all emulated hardware devices, and the contents of the running VM's memory. VM-level check pointing is typically a time consuming process due to potentially large VM memory sizes (*sometimes, it is impractical as the memory size may be up to several gigabytes*). Therefore, for solo VM checkpointing, often a lightweight methodology is adopted, which doesn't generate a large checkpoint file.

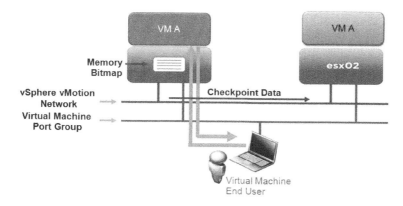

Figure 9.1   VM Checkpointing.

Downtime is the key factor for estimating the high availability of a system, since any long downtime experience for clients may result in loss of client loyalty and thus revenue loss. The VM run on primary host and its memory state is checkpointed and transferred to the backup host. When the VM fails, the backup host will take over and roll-back each VM to its previous checkpointed state. Under the primary-backup model, there are two types of downtime:

1. The time from when the primary host crashes until the VM resumes from the last checkpointed state on the backup host and starts to handle client requests;

2. The time from when the VM pauses on the primary host (to save for the check-point) until it resumes.

9.2.1 Checkpointing Virtual Cluster

The checkpointing size also affects the scalability of providing high availability when checkpointing multiple VMs together. A virtual cluster (VC) generalizes the VM concept [4] for distributed applications and systems. A VC is a set of multiple VMs deployed on different physical machines but managed as a single entity. A VC can be created to provide computation, software, data access, or storage services to individual users, who do not require knowledge of the physical location or configuration of the system. End users typically submit their applications, often distributed, to a VC, and the environment transparently hosts those applications on the underlying set of VMs. VCs are gaining increasing attention in the PaaS and IaaS paradigms in the cloud computing domain.

In a VC, since multiple VMs are distributed as computing nodes across different machines; the failure of one VM can affect the states of other related VMs, and may sometimes cause them to also fail. For example, assume that we have two VMs, V Ma and V Mb, running in a VC. Say, V Mb sends some messages to V Ma and then fails. These messages may be correctly received by V Ma and may change the state of V Ma. Thus, when V Mb is rolled-back to its latest correct check-pointed state, V Ma must also be rolled-back to a checkpointed state before the messages are received from V Mb. In other words, all the VMs (i.e., the entire VC) must be checkpointed at globally consistent states.

9.2.2   VM Resumption

In effective VM-level suspension and checkpointing [5], the hypervisor must be able to quickly resume the VM from a checkpointed state. Clients of network applications and other users are more inclined to suspend an idle VM if the latency magnitudes for resumption are in the order of seconds rather than minutes. The ability to quickly restore from a saved checkpointed image can also enable many other useful features, including fast relocation of VM, quick crash recovery, testing, and debugging. Traditional VM resumption approaches can be classified into two solution categories. The first solution is to restore everything that is saved in the checkpoint, and then start VM execution. As the VM memory size dominates the checkpoint size, this solution works well for small memory sizes (*e.g., MBs*). However, VM resumption time significantly increases (*e.g., 10s of seconds*) when memory size becomes large (*e.g., GBs*). Time is taken by native Xen's save and restore mechanisms as a function of memory size. We observe that Xen's save/restore times are in the order of multi-digit seconds when the memory size approaches 1 GB.

In order to start the VM as quickly as possible, an alternate approach is to restore only the CPU and device states that are necessary to boot a VM, and then restore the memory data saved in the checkpoint file after the VM starts. In this way, the VM can start very quickly. Since the VM is still running when restoring the memory data, its performance would not be influenced by the VM memory size. However, with this approach, immediately after the VM starts, performance degrades due to cascading page faults, because there is no memory page loaded to use. Therefore, to further reduce the downtime, a checkpointed VM must be resumed quickly, while avoiding performance degradation after the VM starts.

9.2.3   Migration without Hypervisor

Most VMMs provide a hypervisor-based migration solution. However, relying on hypervisor [6] in the migration has several disadvantages that have recently received significant attention. The main problem is that the hypervisor plays a key role throughout the entire migration process, and takes care of many system "chores" from the start to the end of the migration. This central role of the hypervisor has increasingly become the source of several major security concerns. One concern is that if the hypervisor is attacked successfully by a malicious party, the attacker can easily inspect memory, expose confidential information, or even modify the software running in the VM. Note that an investigation of such security problems is outside the scope of this chapter. However, the potential security problems caused by the hypervisor motivate us to explore VMLM mechanisms that do not involve the hypervisor during the migration.

In an attempt to resolve these issues, a live migration mechanism without the hypervisor is needed. Besides addressing the security issues, the solution should also cover use case scenarios that arise from common VM practice. One representative scenario is a data center setting, which offers an isolated VM for each user. In such a setting, a fully customized VM is usually created for each user, with custom environment and applications. In this scenario, there are several reasons why an administrator might decide to migrate the VMs, such as for load balancing and fault-tolerance purposes. In that case, what are the metrics that must be considered in providing high-availability service?

As discussed before, the downtime experienced by the user, i.e., the time interval during which the user cannot access the system, is clearly one important metric. Downtime must be as short as possible. Most hypervisor-based migration mechanisms provide minimal downtime. In addition to downtime, another important metric is the total waiting time to complete the migration, as it affects the release of resources on both source and target hosts. For example, for load balancing, energy-saving policies, hardware upgrades, etc., a running host must often be shut down. In such cases, all active VMs must be migrated to other hosts and resumed on the target machines before resources can be released on the source and target machines.

9.2.4   Adaptive Live Migration to Improve Load Balancing

The virtualized networked environment [7], where multiple physical machines running VMs are interconnected via fast networking technologies, is able to increasingly provide on-demand computational services and high availability. One of its most interesting features is that the pool of available resources (CPU, virtual memory, secondary storage, etc.) can be shared between all the machines through the available interconnections. It is observed that many resources, however, are actually unused for a considerable amount of the operational time. Therefore, load balancing is of great interest in order to avoid situations where some machines are overloaded while others are idle or uderused.

Traditionally, there are several ways to achieve load balancing in networked systems. One straightforward solution is static load balancing, which assigns applications to machines at the beginning. The efficiency of this strategy depends on the accuracy of the prior load prediction. A dynamic load balancing strategy can be exploited by migrating application processes at runtime among the different machines. A dynamic strategy is more efficient than limiting the applications to run on the machines where they were first assigned. However, it is usually complex to implement a process migration mechanism, because applications are often tightly bound to the host OS as well as the underlying platform. Moreover, some types of processes may depend on shared memory for communication, which suffers from the problem of residual dependencies and causes further complications. The limitations of process migration are overcome through VMLM. Unlike process migration, VM live migration transfers the virtual CPU state, the emulated devices' state, and the guest OS memory data, which eliminates OS or platform dependencies. Also, VMLM has several potential advantages for load balancing. A VM that hosts different applications on a heavily loaded machine can be migrated to a VMM on another machine that is idle, in order to exploit the availability of all the resources. Moreover, in contrast to stop-and-resume VMM, VMLM natively ensures minimal downtime and minimally interrupts the VM users' interaction. Therefore, a good load balancing strategy should also provide minimal downtime for users.

9.2.5   VM Disk Migrations

In contrast to live migration in local area networks (LANs), VMM in wide area networks (WANs) poses additional challenges. When migrating a VM [8] in a LAN, the storage of both the source and target machines are usually shared by network-attached storage (NAS) or storage area network (SAN) media. Therefore, most data that needs to be transferred in LAN-based migration is derived from the runtime memory state of the VM. However, when migrating a VM in a WAN, besides the memory state, all the disk data, including the I/O device state and the file system, must also be migrated, because they are not shared in both source and target machines. The disk data, in particular for I/O intensive applications, is usually very large. Hence, LAN-based migration techniques that only migrate memory data (which is usually in the order of GBs) may not be suitable when applied to VM migration in WANs.

A straightforward approach to do this explored in the past is to suspend the VM on the source machine, transfer its memory and local disk data (as a self-contained image file) over the network to the target machine, and resume the VM by reloading the memory and the file system. However, such stop-and-resume mechanisms suffer long downtime. In order to reduce the large amount of disk data that has to be transmitted, several optimization techniques have also been introduced, e.g., data compression during migration and content-based comparison among memory and disk data. However, these optimizations introduce either memory or computational overheads. Thus, it is necessary to develop new methods for migrating VMs and their potentially large file systems with minimal downtime and acceptable overhead.

To achieve fast VMLM in WANs, the large amount of disk data that needs to be transferred across the WAN must be reduced. Traditional LAN-based migration efforts (including our previous work) use the checkpointing/resumption methodology to migrate memory data. Moreover, they also use an incremental checkpointing solution to reduce the updated memory data that need to be transferred during each migration epoch. The incremental checkpointing technique can also be used for disk migration to reduce downtime, but the large data in memory and disk combined can still result in unacceptable total migration time. Therefore, a fast disk migration mechanism is needed.

9.3 Enhanced VM Live Migration

Remus is now part of the official Xen repository [9]. It achieves high availability by maintaining an up-to-date copy of a running VM on the backup host, which automatically activates if the primary host fails. Remus copies over dirty data after memory update, and uses the memory page as the granularity for copying. However, the dirty data tracking method is not efficient. Thus, the goal of this chapter is to further reduce the size of the memory transferred from the primary to the backup host, by introducing a fine-grained mechanism.

To do this, three memory state synchronization techniques are used to achieve high availability in systems such as Remus: dirty-block tracking, speculative state transferring and active backup. The first technology is similar to the proposed method, however, it incurs additional memory associated overhead. For example, when running the Exchange workload in [10] evaluation, the memory overhead is more than 60%. Since main memory is always a scarce resource, the high percentage overhead is a problem.

To solve the memory overhead problems under Xen-based systems, there are several ways to harness memory redundancy in VMs, such as page sharing and patching. Past efforts showed the memory sharing potential in virtualization-based systems. Working set changes were examined, and their results showed that changes in memory were crucial for the migration of VMs from host to host. For a guest VM with 512 MB memory assigned, low loads changed roughly 20 MB, medium loads changed roughly 80 MB, and high loads changed roughly 200 MB. Thus, normal workloads are likely to occur between these extremes. The evaluation in also revealed the amount of memory changes (within minutes) in VMs running different light workloads. None of them changed more than 4 MB of memory within two minutes. The content-based page sharing (CBPS) method also illustrated the sharing potential in memory. CBPS was based on the compare-by-hash technique introduced. As claimed, CBPS was able to identify as much as 42.9% of all pages as sharable and reclaimed 32.9% of the pages from ten instances of Windows NT doing real-world workloads. Nine VMs running Red Hat Linux were able to find 29.2% of sharable pages and reclaimed 18.7%. When reduced to five VMs, the numbers were 10.0% and 7.2%, respectively.

To share memory pages efficiently, recently, the copy-on-write (CoW) sharing mechanism was widely exploited in the Xen VMM. Unlike the sharing of pages within an OS that uses CoW in a traditional way, in virtualization, pages are shared between multiple VMs. Instead of using CoW to share pages in memory, authors use the same idea in a more fine-grained manner, i.e., by sharing among smaller blocks. The Difference Engine project demonstrates the potential memory savings available from leveraging a combination of page sharing, patching, and in-core memory compression. It shows the huge potential of harnessing memory redundancy in VMs.

However, Difference Engine also suffers from complexity problems when using the patching method because it needs additional modifications to Xen.

9.4   VM Checkpointing Mechanisms

Checkpointing is a commonly used approach for achieving high availability [10]. Checkpoints can be taken at different levels of abstraction. Application-level checkpointing is one of the most widely used methods. For example, a file operation wrapper layer was developed with which a copy-on-write file replica is generated while keeping the old data unmodified. Wrap standard file I/O operations buffer file changes between checkpoints. However, these checkpointing tools require modifying the application code, and thus, they are not transparent to applications.

OS-level checkpointing solutions have also been widely studied. For example, Libckpt is an open-source, portable checkpointing tool for UNIX. It mainly focuses on performance optimization, and only supports single-threaded processes. The Zap system decouples protected processes from dependencies to the host operating system. A thin virtualization layer is inserted above the OS to support checkpointing without any application modification. However, these solutions are highly context-specific and often require access to the source code of the OS kernel, which increases OS dependence. In contrast, VPC doesn't require any modification to the guest OS kernel or the application running on the VM.

VM-level checkpointing can be broadly classified into two categories: stop-and-save checkpointing and checkpointing through live migration. In the first category, a VM is completely stopped, its state is saved in persistent storage, and then the VM is resumed. This technique is easy to implement, but incurs a large amount of system downtime during checkpointing. LVMM is designed to avoid such a large amount of downtime. During migration, physical memory pages are sent from the source (primary) host to the destination (backup) host, while the VM continues to run on the source host. Pages modified during replication must be resent to ensure consistency. After a bounded iterative transferring phase, a very short stop-and-copy phase is executed, during which the VM is halted, the remaining memory pages are sent, and the destination hypervisor is signaled to resume the execution of the VM.

Disk-based VM checkpointing has also been studied. For example, efforts such as CEVM create a VM replica on a remote node via live migration. These techniques employ copy-on-write to create a replica image of a VM with low downtime. The VM image is then written to disk in the background or by a separate physical node. However, disk-based VM checkpointing is often costly and unable to keep up with high frequency checkpointing. Remus uses high frequency checkpointing to handle hardware fail-stop failures on a single host with whole-system migration. It does this by maintaining a completely up-to-date copy of a running VM on the backup machine, which automatically activates if the primary machine fails. However, Remus incurs large overhead.

9.5   Lightweight Live Migration for Solo VM

In this section, we first overview the integrated fine-grained block identification (FGBI) design, including some necessary preliminaries about the memory saving potential. We then present the FGBI architecture, explain each component, and discuss the execution flow and other implementation details. Finally, we compare the evaluation results by comparing with related FGBI design work.

Remus and lightweight live migration (LLM) track memory updates by keeping evidence of the dirty pages at each migration epoch. Remus uses the same page size as Xen (for x86, this is 4 KB), which is also the granularity for detecting memory changes. However, this mechanism is not efficient. For instance, no matter what changes an application makes to a memory page, even just modifying a boolean variable, the whole page will still be marked dirty. Thus, instead of one byte, the whole page needs to be transferred at the end of each epoch. Therefore, it is logical to consider tracking the memory update at a finer granularity, like dividing the memory into smaller blocks.

An FGBI mechanism uses memory blocks (*smaller than page sizes*) as the granularity for detecting memory changes. FGBI calculates the hash value for each memory block at the beginning of each migration epoch. Then it uses the same mechanism as Remus to detect dirty pages. However, at the end of each epoch, instead of transferring the whole dirty page, FGBI computes new hash values for each block and compares them with the corresponding old values. Blocks are only modified if their corresponding hash values do not match. Therefore, an FGBI marks such blocks as dirty and replaces the old hash values with the new ones. Afterwards, FGBI only transfers dirty blocks to the backup host.

However, because of using block granularity, FGBI introduces new overhead. If we want to accurately approximate the true dirty region, we need to set the block size as small as possible. For example, to obtain the highest accuracy, the best block size is one bit. That is impractical, because it requires storing an additional bit for each bit in memory, which means that we need to double the main memory. Thus, a smaller block size leads to a greater number of blocks and also requires more memory for storing the hash values. Based on these past efforts illustrating the memory saving potential, we present two supporting techniques: block sharing and hybrid compression. These are discussed in the subsections that follow.

9.5.1   Block Sharing and Hybrid Compression Support

It is observed that while running normal workloads on a guest VM, a large percentage of memory is usually not updated. For this static memory, there is a high probability that pages can be shared and compressed to reduce memory usage, which is known as block sharing. It should be noted that these past efforts use the memory page as the sharing granularity. Thus, they still suffer from the one byte differ, both pages cannot be shared problem. Therefore, consider using a smaller block in FGBI as the sharing granularity to reduce memory overhead.

The Difference Engine project also illustrates the potential savings due to sub-page sharing, both within and across VMs, and achieves savings up to 77%. In order to share memory at the sub-page level, book authors construct patches to represent a page as the difference relative to a reference page. However, this patching method requires selected pages to be accessed infrequently; otherwise the overhead of compression/decompression outweighs the benefits. Their experimental evaluations reveal that patching incurs additional complexity and overhead when running memory-intensive workloads on guest VMs.

Unlike Difference Engine, we use a straightforward sharing technique to reduce the complexity. The goal of the sharing mechanism is to eliminate redundant copies of identical blocks. We share blocks and compare hash values in memory at runtime, by using a hash function to index the contents of every block. If the hash value of a block is found more than once in an epoch, there is a good probability that the current block is identical to the block that gave the same hash value. To ensure that these blocks are identical, they are compared bit by bit. If the blocks are identical, they are reduced to one block. If, later on, the shared block is modified, we need to decide which of the original constituent blocks has been updated and will be transferred through hybrid compression. Compression techniques can be used to significantly improve the performance of live migration. Compressed dirty data takes a shorter amount of time to be transferred through the network. In addition, network traffic due to migration is significantly reduced when there is much less data transferred between primary and backup hosts. Therefore, for dirty blocks in memory, we consider compressing them to reduce the amount of transferred data. Before transmitting a dirty block, we check for its presence in an address-indexed cache of previously transmitted blocks (through pages). If there is a cache hit, the whole page (including this memory block) is XORed with the previous version, and the differences are run-length encoded (RLE). At the end of each migration epoch, we send only the delta from a previous transmission of the same memory block, so as to reduce the amount of migration traffic in each epoch. Since a smaller amount of data is transferred, the total migration time and downtime can both be decreased.

However, in the current migration epoch, there still may remain a significant fraction of blocks that is not present in the cache. In these cases, there are a great number of zero bytes in the memory pages (as in the smaller blocks). For this kind of block, we just scan the whole block and record the information about the offset and value of non-zero bytes. And for all other blocks with weak regularities, a universal algorithm with high compression ratio is appropriate. Here we use a general purpose and very fast compression technique to achieve a higher degree of compression.

9.5.2 Architecture

The FGBI mechanism is integrated with sharing and compression support. In addition to LLM, we add a new component, shown as FGBI, and deploy it at both `Domain 0` and guest VM. For ease of presentation, we divide FGBI into three main components:

- *Dirty Identification:* It uses the hash function to compute the hash value for each block, and identify the new update through the hash comparison at the end of migration epoch. It has three subcomponents:

- *Block Hashing:* It creates a hash value for each memory block;

- *Hash Indexing:* It maintains a hash table based on the hash values generated by the block hashing component. The entry in the content index is the hash value that reflects the content of a given block;

- *Block Comparison:* It compares two blocks to check if they are bitwise identical.

- *Block Sharing Support:* It handles sharing of bitwise-identical blocks.

- *Block Compression:* It compresses all the dirty blocks on the primary side, before transferring them to the backup host. On the backup side, after receiving the compressed blocks, it decompresses them first before using them to resume the VM.

Basically, the Block Hashing component produces hash values for all blocks and delivers them to the Hash Indexing component. The Hash Indexing and Block Comparison components then check the hash table to determine whether there are any duplicate blocks. If so, the Hash Comparison component requests the Block Sharing Support component to update the shared blocks information. At the end of each epoch, the Block Compression component compresses all the dirty blocks (including both shared and not shared).

In this architecture, the components are divided between the privileged VM `Domain 0` and the guest VMs. The VMs contain the Block Sharing Support component, house the Block Sharing Support component in the guest VMs to avoid the overhead of using shadow page tables (SPTs). Each VM also contains a Block Hashing component, which means that it has the responsibility of hashing its address space. The Dirty Identification component is placed in the trusted and privileged `Domain 0`. It receives hash values of the hashed blocks generated by the Block Hashing component in the different VMs.

9.5.3 FGBI Execution Flow

Hashing: At the beginning of each epoch, the Block Hashing components at the different guest VMs compute the hash value for each block.

Storing: FGBI stores and delivers the hash key of the hashed block to the Hash Indexing component.

Index Lookup: It checks the content index for identical keys, to determine whether the block has been seen before. The lookup can have two different outcomes:

- Key Not Seen Before: Add it to the index and proceed to step 6.

- Key Seen Before: An opportunity to share, so request block comparison.

Block Comparison: Two blocks are shared if they are bitwise identical. Meanwhile, it notifies the Block Sharing Support Components on corresponding VMs that they have a block to be shared. If not, there is a hash collision, the blocks are not shared, and proceed to previous steps.

Shared Block Update: If two blocks are bitwise identical, then store the same hash value for both blocks. Unless there is a write update to this shared block, it doesn't need to be compared at the end of the epoch.

Block Compression: Before transferring, compress all the dirty blocks.

Transferring: At the end of the epoch, there are three different outcomes:

- Block Is Not Shared: FGBI computes the hash value again and compares with the corresponding old value. If they don't match, mark this block as dirty, compress and send it to the backup host. Repeat step 1 (which means begin the next migration epoch).

- Block Is Shared but No Write Update: It means that either block is modified during this epoch. Thus, there is no need to compute hash values again for this shared block, and, therefore, there is no need to make comparison, compression, or transfer either. Repeat previous steps.

- Block Is Shared and Write Update Occurs: This means that one or both blocks have been modified during this epoch. Thus, FGBI needs to check which one is modified, and then compress and send the dirty one or both to the backup host. Repeat step 1.

9.6 Lightweight Checkpointing

Since a VC may have hundreds of VMs, to implement a scalable lightweight checkpointing mechanism for the VC, we need to checkpoint/resume each VM with minimum possible overhead. To completely record the state of an individual VM, checkpointing typically involves recording the virtual CPU's state, the current state of all emulated hardware devices, and the contents of the guest VM's memory. Compared with other preserved states, the amount of the guest VM memory which needs to be checkpointed dominates the size of the checkpoint. However, with the rapid growth of memory in VMs (*several gigabytes are not uncommon*), the size of the checkpoint easily becomes a bottleneck. One solution to alleviate this problem is incremental checkpointing, which minimizes the checkpointing overhead by only synchronizing the dirty pages during the latest checkpoint. A page fault-based mechanism is typically used to determine the dirty pages. We first use incremental checkpointing in VPC. We deploy a VPC agent that encapsulates our checkpointing mechanism on every machine. For each VM on a machine, in addition to the memory space assigned to its guest OS, we assign a small amount of additional memory for the agent to use. During system initialization, we save the complete image of each VM's memory on the disk. To differentiate this state from checkpoint, we call this state "non-volatile copy." After the VMs start execution, the VPC agents begin saving the correct state for the VMs. For each VM, at the beginning of a checkpointing interval, all memory pages are set as read-only. Thus, if there is any write to a page, it will trigger a page fault. Since we leverage the shadow-paging feature of Xen, we are able to control whether a page is read-only and to trace whether a page is dirty. When there is a write to a read-only page, a page fault is triggered and reported to the Xen hypervisor, and we save the current state of this page.

When a page fault occurs, this memory page is set as writeable, but VPC doesn't save the modified page immediately, because there may be another new write to the same page in the same interval. Instead, VPC adds the address of the faulting page to the list of changed pages and removes the write protection from the page so that the application can proceed with the write. At the end of each checkpointing interval, the list of changed pages contains all the pages that were modified in the current checkpointing interval. VPC copies the final state of all modified pages to the agent's memory, and resets all pages to read-only again. A VM can then be paused momentarily to save the contents of the changed pages (*which also contributes to the VM's downtime*). In addition, we use a high frequency checkpointing mechanism, which means that each checkpointing interval is set to be very small, and, therefore, the number of updated pages in an interval is small as well. Thus, it is unnecessary to assign a large amount of memory to each VPC agent.

Note that this approach incurs a page fault whenever a read-only page is modified. When running memory-intensive workloads on the guest VM, handling so many page faults affects scalability. On the other hand, according to the principle of locality on memory accesses, recently updated pages tend to be updated again (i.e., spatial locality) in the near future (i.e., temporal locality). In VPC, we set the checkpointing interval to be small (tens to hundreds of milliseconds). So similarly, the dirty pages also follow this principle. Therefore, we use the updated pages in the previous checkpointing interval to predict the pages which will be updated in the upcoming checkpointing interval i.e., by pre-marking the predicted pages as writable at the beginning of the next checkpointing interval. By this improved incremental checkpointing methodology, we reduce the number of page faults.

The page table entry (PTE) mechanism is supported by most current generation processors. For predicting the dirty pages, we leverage one control bit in the PTE: accessed (A) bit. The accessed bit is set to enable or disable write access for a page. Similar to the incremental checkpointing approach, for each VM, at the beginning of a checkpointing interval, all memory pages are set as read-only (accessed bit is cleared as 0). Thus, if there is any write to a page, it will trigger a page fault, and the accessed bit is set to 1. However, unlike our incremental checkpointing approach, after the dirty pages in a checkpointing interval are saved in the checkpoint, we do not clear the accessed bits of these newly updated pages at the end of a checkpointing interval. Instead, the accessed bits of these pages are kept as writeable to allow write during the next interval. At the end of the next interval, we track whether these pages were actually updated or not. If they were not updated, their accessed bits are cleared, which means that the corresponding pages are set as read-only again. The experimental evaluation shows that, this approach further reduces the (solo) VM downtime.

9.6.1   High-Frequency Checkpointing Mechanism

Virtual predict checkpointing (VPC) uses a high frequency checkpointing mechanism. The motivation for this methodology is that, several previous fault injection experiments have shown that most system crashes occur due to transient failures. For example, in the Linux kernel, after an error happens, around 95% of crashes occur within 100 million CPU cycles, which means that, for a 2 GHz processor, the error latency is very small (within 50 ms).

Suppose the error latency is T_e and the checkpointing interval is T_c. Thus, as long as T_e T_c, the probability of an undetected error affecting the checkpoint is small. For example, if more than 95% of the error latency is less than T_e, the possibility of a system failure caused by an undetected error is less than 5%. Therefore, as long as T_c (*application defined*) is no less than T_e (*in this example, it is 50ms*), the checkpoint is rarely affected by an unnoticed error. Thus, this solution is nearly error-free by itself. On the other hand, if the error latency is small, so is the checkpointing interval that choose. A smaller checkpointing interval means a high frequency methodology.

In VPC, for each VM, the state of its nonvolatile copy is always one checkpointing interval behind the current VM's state, except for the initial state. This means that, when a new checkpoint is generated, it is not copied to the nonvolatile copy immediately. Instead, the last checkpoint will be copied to the nonvolatile copy. The reason is that, there is a latency between when an error occurs and when the failure caused by that error is detected.

Since most error latencies are small, in most cases, $t_1t_0 < T_e$. In case A, the latest checkpoint is chp1, and the system needs to roll-back to the state S_1 by resuming from the checkpoint chp1. However, in case B, an error happens at time t_2, and then a new checkpoint chp3 is saved. After the system moves to the state S_3, this error causes a failure at time t_3. Here, we assume that $t_3t_2 < Te$. But, if we choose chp3 as the latest correct checkpoint and roll the system back to the state S_3, after resumption, the system will fail again. We can see that, in this case, the latest checkpoint should be chp2, and when the system crashes, we should roll it back to the state S_2 by resuming from the checkpoint chp2.

VPC is a lightweight checkpointing mechanism, because, for each protected VM, the VPC agent stores only a small fraction of, rather than the entire VM image. For a guest OS occupying hundreds of megabytes of memory, the VPC checkpoint is no more than 20 MB. In contrast, past efforts such as VNsnap duplicates the guest VM memory and uses the entire additional memory as the checkpoint size. In VPC, with a small amount of memory, we can store multiple checkpoints for different VMs running on the same machine. Meanwhile, as discussed, the size of the checkpoint directly influences the VM downtime. This lightweight checkpointing methodology reduces VPC's downtime during the checkpointing interval.

9.6.2   Distributed Checkpoint Algorithm in VPC

9.6.2.1   Communication Consistency in VC   To compose a globally consistent state of all the VMs in the VC, the checkpoint of each VM must be coordinated.

Besides checkpointing each VM's correct state, it is also essential to guarantee the consistency of all communication states within the virtual network. Recording the global state in a distributed system is non-trivial because there is no global memory or clock in a traditional distributed computing environment. So the coordination work must be done in the presence of non-synchronized clocks for a scalable design.

The messages exchanged among the VMs are marked by arrows going from the sender to the receiver. The execution line of the VMs is separated by their corresponding checkpoints. The upper part of each checkpoint corresponds to the state before the checkpoint and the lower part of each checkpoint corresponds to the state after the checkpoint. A global checkpoint (*consistent or not*) is marked as the "*cut*" line, which separates each VM's timeline into two parts. We can label the messages exchanged in the virtual network into three categories: The state of the message's source and the destination are on the same side of the cut line. The source state and the destination state of message m_1 are above the cut line. Similarly, both the source state and the destination state of message m_2 are under the cut line. The message's source state is above the cut line while the destination state is under the cut line, like message m_3. The message's source state is under the cut line while the destination state is above the cut line, like message m_4. For these three types of messages, we can see that a globally consistent cut must ensure the delivery of type (1) and type (2) messages, but must avoid type (3) messages.

9.6.2.2 *Globally Consistent checkpointing Design in VPC*

Several past approaches require FIFO channels to implement globally consistent check-pointing. There are several limitations in these approaches such as the high overheads of capturing in-transit Ethernet frames and VM coordination before checkpointing. Therefore, in VPC design, we modify a distributed checkpointing algorithm for non-FIFO channels. Mattern's algorithm relies on vector clocks, and uses a single initiator process. At the beginning, a global snapshot is planned to be recorded at a future vector times. The initiator broadcasts these times and waits for acknowledgments from all the recipients. When a process receives the broadcast, it remembers the value s and acknowledges the initiator.

After receiving all acknowledgments, the initiator increases its vector clock to s and broadcasts a dummy message. On the receiver's side, it takes a local snapshot, sends it to the initiator, and increases its clock to a value larger than s. Finally, the algorithm uses a termination detection scheme for non-FIFO channels to decide whether to terminate the algorithm.

We develop a variant of this classic algorithm as the basis of our lightweight checkpointing mechanism. As illustrated before, type (3) messages are unwanted, because they are not recorded in any source VM's checkpoints, but they are already recorded in some checkpoints of a destination VM. In VPC, there is always a correct state for a VM, recorded as the non-volatile copy in the disk. The state of the non-volatile copy is one checkpointing interval behind the current VM's state, because we copy the last checkpoint to the nonvolatile copy only when we get a new checkpoint. Therefore, before a checkpoint is committed by saving to nonvolatile copy, we buffer all the outgoing messages in the VM during the corresponding checkpointing interval. Thus, type (3) messages are never generated, because the buffered messages are unblocked only after saving their information by copying the checkpoint to the nonvolatile copy. The algorithm works under the assumption that the buffering messages will not be lost or duplicated.

In VPC, there are multiple VMs running on different machines connected within the network. One of the machines is chosen to deploy the VPC Initiator, while the protected VMs run on the primary machines. The Initiator can be running on a VM which is dedicated to the checkpointing service. It doesn't need to be deployed on the privileged guest system like the `Domain 0` in Xen. When VPC starts to record the globally consistent checkpoint, the Initiator broadcasts the checkpointing request and waits for acknowledgments from all the recipients. Upon receiving a checkpointing request, each VM checks the latest recorded non-volatile copy (not the in-memory checkpoint), marks this nonvolatile copy as part of the global checkpoint, and sends a "success" acknowledgment back to the Initiator. The algorithm terminates when the Initiator receives the acknowledgments from all the VMs. For example, if the Initiator sends a request (marked as r_n) to checkpoint the entire VC, a VM named VM_1 in the VC will record a nonvolatile copy named vm_1 global r_n. All of the nonvolatile copies from every VM compose a globally consistent checkpoint for the entire VC. Besides, if the VPC Initiator sends the checkpointing request at a user-specified frequency, the correct state of the entire VC is recorded periodically.

9.7   Storage-Adaptive Live Migration

Besides the previous discussion that addresses how to reduce the transmitted data resident in both memory and disk storage, we propose to further reduce the network traffic generated by the migration when disks are implemented by different storage options. Our mechanism is based on Xen, which supports many different storage options, each of which has its own benefits and limitations. They can be separated into two categories: file based and device based. Compared to device-based storage, file-based storage has the advantage of being simple, easy to move, mountable from the host OS with minimal effort, and easy to manage. It used to be slow, but with the advent of `blktap` driver, the speed is no longer a problem. The `blktap2` driver provides disk I/O interface on user-level. Using its associated libraries, `blktap2` allows virtual block devices presented to VMs to be implemented in user space and to be backed by different formats, e.g., raw image. Compared with device-based storage, the key benefit of `blktap2` is that it makes it easy and fast to manipulate. `Blktap2` currently supports different disk formats, including:

1. Raw images which can be deployed on both partitions and in image files.

2. Fast sharable RAM disk between VMs. Note that this format requires modification of the guest kernel, in order to be supported by cluster-based file system.

3. VHD, which involves snapshots and sparse images.

4. `Qcow2`, which also involves snapshots and sparse images.

In the preliminary experiments, however, we found that a general disk migration mechanism does not work well in all cases; for example, when dealing with raw format, a straightforward encoding method actually incurs shorter downtime due to the there are many unused chunks in raw image file. Therefore, we finally implemented a storage-adaptive migration mechanism which could apply different migration methods based on the types of the disk formats.

Using an adaptive live migration mechanism for both raw and Qcow2 formats, a raw image is simple to create and can be manipulated using standard Linux tools. It can also be mounted directly via the loopback device. With a strictly local installation, raw image is probably the best choice because it is easy to manipulate. After a raw image is created, when a tool needs to copy it, the tool will need to read the logical size of the image. That is, if you create a 10 GB image with only 1 GB of actual data, the copy operation will need to read 10 GB of data. Because the content of a raw image is sparse, i.e., a great percentage of the image file does not contain real data, we propose to use run-length encoding (RLE) to compress all the dirty chunks on the source host before transmitting to the target host. Note that we initialized the full raw image at 0 in order to take advantage of RLE.

On the other hand, a Qcow2 image has a smaller file size, so it can be efficiently copied over the network. It requires special tools to manipulate and can only be mounted using the qemu-nbd server. However, Qcow2 provides a key advantage over raw disk images: the format only stores data that has been written to the image. The practical impact is that the logical size of the file is the same as the physical size. Following the same example as above, a 10 GB Qcow2 image with only 1 GB of data would only require reading/writing 1 GB of data when copying the image. Therefore, there are no free chunks, and it does not hamper correctness because no assumptions on the contents of free chunks can be made. Moreover, Qcow2 supports copy-on-write so that the image only represents the latest changes. If there are several memory pages in the page cache which update the same disk chunk, the VM restoration needs to follow the same order as each memory page that is transmitted to the target host. We apply zlib-based compression to compress the data before transmission. The final mechanism is summarized as follows:

1. In the first migration epoch, on the source host, all the memory pages of the selected VM are transmitted to the target host while the VM is still running.

2. Still on the source host, all the disk data of the selected VM are also transmitted to the target host while the VM is still running. For different disk formats, these data are handled in the corresponding way (RLE, zlib-based compression) before transmission.

3. For subsequent migration epochs, at the end of each migration epoch, the mechanism checks the dirty bitmap to determine which memory pages have been updated in this epoch. Then only the newly updated pages are transmitted. The VM continues to run on the source host during these epochs.

4. For those dirty pages with corresponding PFN existing in the pfn to sec map, they are scheduled to be flushed to disk in the near future but this activity may

not occur in this migration epoch. Because these pages are already transmitted to the target host, there is no need to transmit the corresponding disk data again, even if its status is marked as dirty.

5. For all of the disk chunks which are updated more than threshold times, the mechanism marks each chunk as dirty and avoids transmitting it to the target during the subsequent migration epoch. Instead, these chunks are only transmitted in the last migration epoch.

6. When the pre-copy phase is no longer beneficial, the VM is stopped on the source node, the remaining data (newly updated memory pages and disk chunks, CPU registers and device states, etc.) is transmitted to the target node, and the VM is prepared to resume on the target host.

9.8 Conclusion

This chapter presented a set of techniques that provide high availability through VMLM, their implementation in the Xen hypervisor and the Linux OS kernel, and experimental studies conducted using a variety of benchmarks and production applications. The techniques include: a novel fine-grained block identification mechanism called FGBI; a lightweight, globally consistent checkpointing mechanism called VPC; a fast VM resumption mechanism called VM resume; a guest OS kernel-based live migration technique that does not involve the hypervisor for VM migration called HSG-LM; an efficient live migration-based load balancing strategy called DC balance; and a fast and storage-adaptive migration mechanism called FDM.

REFERENCES

1. Armbrust, M., Fox, A., Griffith, R., Joseph, A. D., Katz, R., Konwinski, A., ... & Zaharia, M. (2010). A view of cloud computing. *Communications of the ACM*, 53(4), 50-58.

2. Menon, A., Santos, J. R., Turner, Y., Janakiraman, G. J., & Zwaenepoel, W. (2005, June). Diagnosing performance overheads in the xen virtual machine environment. In Proceedings of the 1st ACM/USENIX international conference on Virtual execution environments (pp. 13-23). ACM.

3. Dhingra, M., Lakshmi, J., & Nandy, S. K. (2012, September). Resource usage monitoring in clouds. In Grid Computing (GRID), 2012 ACM/IEEE 13th International Conference on (pp. 184-191). IEEE.

4. Lakshmi, J. (2010). *System Virtualization in the Multi-core Era-a QoS Perspective*. Dissertation., Supercomputer Education and Research Centre., Indian Institute of Science., Bangalore.

5. Popek, G. J., & Goldberg, R. P. (1974). Formal requirements for virtualizable third generation architectures. *Communications of the ACM*, 17(7), 412-421.

6. Bobroff, N., Kochut, A., & Beaty, K. (2007). Dynamic placement of virtual machines for managing sla violations. In Integrated Network Management, 2007. IM'07. 10th IFIP/IEEE International Symposium (pp. 119-128). IEEE.

7. Mishra, M., Das, A., Kulkarni, P., & Sahoo, A. (2012). Dynamic resource management using virtual machine migrations. *IEEE Communications Magazine*, 50(9).

8. Gupta, R., Bose, S. K., Sundarrajan, S., Chebiyam, M., & Chakrabarti, A. (2008, July). A two stage heuristic algorithm for solving the server consolidation problem with item-item and bin-item incompatibility constraints. In Services Computing, 2008. SCC'08. IEEE International Conference (Vol. 2, pp. 39-46). IEEE.

9. Agrawal, S., Bose, S. K., & Sundarrajan, S. (2009). Grouping genetic algorithm for solving the serverconsolidation problem with conflicts. In Proceedings of the first ACM/SIGEVO Summit on Genetic and Evolutionary Computation (pp. 1-8). ACM.

10. Kannan, R., Karpinski, M., & Prmel, H. J. (2004). Approximation Algorithms for NP-Hard Problems. *Oberwolfach Reports*, 1(3), 1461-1540.

CHAPTER 10

VIRTUAL MACHINE MOBILITY WITH SELF-MIGRATION

Abstract

This chapter discusses different mobility systems, from fine-grained object mobility systems and programming languages, to operating systems that support process migration, to coarse-grained VMM systems. A common factor in all of these systems is that they use some form of checkpointing mechanism in order to consistently migrate the program state between physical machines. Systems supporting transparent mobility often strive to make a location change transparent not only to the program being migrated, but also to external observers. Software which is not purely batch-oriented, e.g., software interacting with human users or software which is part of a distributed system, needs to respond to requests in a timely manner, as external peers often interpret a prolonged silence as a sign of a crash or disconnect.

Keywords: Object mobility, self-migration, migration freeze time, device drivers, coarse-grained mobility models.

10.1   Checkpoints and Mobility

A checkpoint is a snapshot of all application states [1], potentially with the exception of a soft state that can be recreated on demand. A checkpoint c of a process p is consistent at the time tc, if and only if any input event e to p happening before tc is recorded in c, and no event happening after t is recorded in c. It is often desirable to move long-running computations between processors or, in a cluster system, between different hosts altogether, and a checkpointing facility is often the main ingredient of such mobility systems. A checkpoint is captured at the source host, transmitted to the destination host, and resumed there. Checkpoints can be taken of individual processes, or of an entire operating system. A process-level checkpoint will often fail to capture all relevant states, such as, state in open files or shared memory segments, whereas a system-wide checkpoint will be able to capture all local states. Distributed state is less trivial to capture, but the failure modes that can arise from the loss of distributed state is better understood than for a single-process checkpoint. Whereas few application programs can handle the sudden loss of an open file or state kept in a shared memory segment, most OS network stacks will be able to cope with the loss of a few network packets.

Even though complete checkpoints require more storage than application-specific data formats, they can still be useful. The main advantages are that a system-wide checkpoint is able to capture the state of multiple independent threads and processes, and that checkpointing can be provided as a global and application-transparent feature. Checkpoints are useful in coarse-grained mobility systems, where a group of processes are moved as a whole.

One application of checkpointing is *hibernation*, the ability to store a checkpoint of a running system on stable storage. Many laptop computers have a *suspend-to-disk* feature, where either the BIOS or the operating system has the ability to checkpoint itself to disk or nonvolatile memory, to allow the user to continue work at some next volume. Here, we are concerned mainly with the use of checkpoints for mobility, and consider the wider issues of distributed checkpoint correctness to be out of the scope of this work. This functionality is weaker than what a persistent system provides, but because the computer is turned off immediately after the checkpoint, also simpler to implement. All relevant in-memory states become part of the checkpoint, and because state-on-disk state remains constant as long as the system is off, it will remain checkpoint-consistent. Because the likeness of the system is no longer a concern, most parts of it can be suspended during the checkpoint, simplifying the checkpoint implementation.

10.2   Manual and Seamless Mobility

Mobility systems aim to increase the flexibility of computing installations [2] and to reduce the need for manual configuration. When data, objects, processes, or VMs, become mobile, it is possible to grow or shrink the installation simply by adding or removing hardware. Though not many advanced mobility systems have been successful and seen widespread use, simple forms of manual mobility are present every-where from the simple act of moving a hard-drive full of system binaries to a new machine, to a cell phone downloading and running Java applets off a wireless con-nection. Naturally we do not consider these scenarios as genuine mobility systems, and the main reason is that they involve explicit shutdown, saving, or restoration stages. In other words, they are not examples of seamless mobility systems. A seam-less mobility system is one in which mobility is transparent, whether to a user, to objects, or to a set of processes, and where no explicit steps are taken to externalize program state.

10.3   Fine-and Coarse-Grained Mobility Models

As described in the following sections, mobility [3] can be achieved at several levels of granularity and both manually and transparently. We describe the granularity levels, and some of the more well-known implementations.

10.3.1   Data and Object Mobility

A simple yet limited way of achieving mobility is to rely on each application cor-rectly externalizing its state to a form from which the state of the program may later be recreated. Data mobility is achieved by moving the externalized data between machines. If the externalized state utilizes an efficient format, data mobility is also likely to incur lower transmission costs than full checkpoint mobility. In the many cases where data mobility is possible, e.g., when the mobile program expects and supports it, data mobility is therefore likely to be more effective.

An object mobility system is one with objects shown as circles and dependencies as arrows. Fine-grained objects can be moved between hosts, by the mobility kernel. Communication between the objects is transparently forwarded over the network. The next step up from data mobility is object mobility. In programming language terms, an object encapsulates code and data as a single unit, and object mobility can be achieved by moving serialized objects between hosts. If all inter-object communi-cation happens through object method invocations, remote method invocation (RMI) may be used for transparently forwarding calls to a remote object. In RMI and object mobility systems, a global registry is often used for keeping track of object locations, or forwarding addresses are installed afterwards to help locate moved objects. If an object is live, i.e., one or more threads are executing inside the object, and thus keep parts of the object state in CPU registers or the stack, mobility becomes more com-plicated [4], as this state must be written back to the object activation record before the object can be safely moved to another host. Some systems wait for object in-vocations to reach certain safe points of execution, before mobility is allowed. RMI and object mobility systems are often implemented as part of programming language runtimes, e.g., the Eden and Emerald kernels or the Java VM. Thus, they function independently of the underlying operating system. A small number of objects are distributed across two hosts, with object mobility provided as a transparent service by a mobility kernel.

10.3.2   Process Migration

Object mobility is fine-grained. A whole program may contain hundreds or thousands of objects, and each of these can roam freely between hosts. At the other end of the spectrum we find more coarse-grained techniques, namely process migration and VMM. Like object mobility, process migration moves program state and data together as a single unit. Process migration systems view each process as an opaque object, and are often implemented as a feature of the underlying operating system. The advantages are that coarse-grained VMs can be moved between hosts, all object and process dependencies are captured as part of the VM checkpoint, and there is no need to forward communication. Other advantages of this approach of this approach is that any process may be a candidate for migration, independently of implementation language, and that existing operating system mechanisms may be used for safely preempting and migrating processes, without having to worry about critical sections or safe points. Migration thus happens transparently to the process.

In contrast to object systems [5], the interfaces that processes communicate through are more complex, and this can cause problems or prevent migration. For example, UNIX single-copy semantics stipulate that all writes to a file are immediately visible to readers of that file, and this causes problems when some readers have been transparently migrated to a remote host. Because migration is transparent, processes will not expect file system semantics to change to a weaker form of consistency, causing process failure or incorrect execution. Some types of processes may depend on shared memory for communication, causing further complications. Process migration systems suffer from the problem of residual dependencies. This problem occurs when a process leaves behind open files or other states in the operating system on the originating host. Both systems attempt to solve this problem by leaving a proxy processes on the originating host, handling access to local resources on behalf of the migrated process. This solution is problematic for two reasons: performance and stability. If all access to a resource has to go via the network, execution may be slowed, and by relying on resources on the originating host, the vulnerability of the migrated process to a machine crash is increased, because the process will fail if just one of the two involved hosts crashes. Examples of operating systems supporting process migration include Distributed, Sprite and MOSIX.

10.4   Migration Freeze Time

Systems supporting transparent [6] mobility often strive to make a location change transparent not only to the program being migrated, but also to external observers. Software which is not purely batch-oriented, e.g., software interacting with human users or software which is part of a distributed system, needs to respond to requests in a timely manner, as external peers often interpret a prolonged silence as a sign of a crash or disconnect. Thus, a system which communicates with the outside world is often subject to soft real-time demands, and this aspect needs to be taken into account by mobility systems. Simple stop the world schemes for obtaining and migrating system checkpoints are therefore inadequate for many uses, and iterative algorithms with better real-time characteristics are often preferable, because they shorten the freeze time during which the migrated program is unresponsive. Below, we describe three popular approaches to migration, and the measures that they take to reduce migration freeze times:

- *Stop-and-Copy:* The task is stopped, and memory as well as task state information is transferred to the new host, where the state is restored and the task resumed. This scheme is the simplest scheme, and transfers all data only once. The task is unresponsive during the entire copy.

- *Lazy Copy:* In lazy-copy migration, the migrating task is stopped and kernel and CPU task state is transferred to the new host, where the task is resumed immediately, inside an empty address space. When the task page faults, the faulting page is fetched from the old host before the task is allowed to continue. The task is only unresponsive for the short amount of time taken to transfer task state to the new host, but performance of the task running at the new host suffers initially, since every page-fault must be resolved across the network. Pages that are not referenced can optionally be transmitted in the background, to avoid leaving a residual dependency trail on the original machine. One problem with lazy migration is that a failure of the network or the source or destination host during migration, will result in irrecoverable failure of the migrating task because no hosts possess a current and complete version of the entire task state.

- *Pre-Copy*: In pre-copy migration, the task is left running at the source machine and all memory owned by the task is mapped read-only and copied to the new host. When the still running task attempts to modify one of its pages, a page fault is raised, and the page marked as dirty. The page is then mapped read-write to the task, which continues running. After the initial transfer, a subset of the pages will be dirty, and these are again mapped read-only and copied to the new host. This goes on until the dirty subset is sufficiently small, after which the task is suspended at the originating host, the remaining dirty pages copied across, and the task is resumed on the new host. The downtime of the task is reduced to the time taken to copy the last set of dirty pages to the new host, but a number of pages will be copied more than once.

10.5 Device Drivers

Device drivers pose a special challenge for OS designers [7], because they need unrestricted hardware access, while at the same time being user-installable and upgradeable. VM monitors frequently provide idealized abstractions through which guest operating systems can get hardware access, but at the lowest level the VMM still must implement a set of device drivers for the actual hardware present in the machine. Furthermore, applications depend on drivers for correct execution, and drivers may contain state that is hard or impossible to extract if the driver needs restarting, or the application wishes to migrate to alternative hardware. Our work has not dealt with device drivers primarily, but how device drivers are implemented and where in a system they are located, has a profound effect on how the remainder of the system can be implemented. The purpose of this section is to provide the reader with background for the discussion and design choices with regards to device access presented in subsequent chapters.

10.5.1   Design Space

Software that is unable to communicate with the outside world is of limited use. A system for on-demand computing, such as the one we are trying to build, needs to provide applications with multiplexed peripheral access, e.g., to the network for communication with the end user or with jobs on other nodes, and to disk storage for saving interim results or staging input data for future use. The device driver interface that the base software provides influences how application software is written, and should be defined in a way that does not unduly limit future development or access to new and smarter peripherals. The actual placement of device drivers influences the amount of privileged and trusted code, and may also impact performance to a great extent.

The design space is defined by parameters such as whether to expose a high-level (e.g., the UNIX socket API) interface or a low-level one (e.g., raw Ethernet frames). At the lowest level, it is also possible to allow applications to access peripheral hardware directly, in the style of an Exokernel. High-level models are often easier to multiplex, because the multiplexing layer has a better understanding of the workload and more freedom to adapt the workload (for example, by reordering disk requests or batching network packets) to the current situation. On the other hand, low-level models provide the application with more flexibility, such as the ability to upgrade a transport protocol without changing the underlying layers.

10.5.2   In-Kernel Device Drivers

In contrast to processes that execute within a protection boundary, device drivers in the majority of deployed systems are frequently allowed unhindered access to the OS address space and resources. There are a number of motivations for such a tightly coupled design:

- *Performance:* During execution, the driver needs to interact with the OS to allocate resources, to influence scheduling, or to communicate with shared subsystems, such as the TCP/IP stack of file system. This is simpler to achieve when the driver resides within and has full access to the OS address space.

- *Application Memory Access:* The majority of devices employ DMA to operate asynchronously from the CPU(s). If, say, an application queues a write request for the disk driver, the driver will need to pin the data for the request in system memory, until the request has been completed. Pinning of memory is simpler to achieve with tight coupling between driver and OS, and essential to performance.

- *No Driver API:* Defining a programming interface (or API) for driver access is hard, because future hardware developments cannot always be predicted. For example, a driver API for an Ethernet controller designed 10 years ago would include the ability to send and listen for Ethernet frames, but would likely be missing interfaces to TCP-offload mechanisms currently present on many controllers. A driver residing with the OS will be able to access arbitrary OS interfaces, in this case TCP/IP stack internals, and as a result novel hardware features will be easier to support.

- *The DMA Problem:* The final point is that few systems at this point provide a hardware indirection layer (or IO-MMU) for device direct memory access. In other words, there is no way a malicious or badly programmed device may be prevented from accessing arbitrary memory-regions. Thus, with current hardware, most driver encapsulation schemes may still fail in some conditions, and are vulnerable to malicious drivers. It is thus arguable whether the overhead introduced by device driver encapsulation techniques is at all justifiable in systems without an IO-MMU. Fortunately, IO-MMUs are on the horizon, e.g., AMD's Pacifica hardware contains a device exclusion vector (DEV), a bitmap that decides which memory pages can be accessed by devices.

This tight coupling is of course problematic if the driver contains bugs, or if the driver installation API is used as a vehicle for installing trojans or spyware into an otherwise trusted kernel. Various micro-kernel systems have advocated a loose coupling model, with device drivers being treated more like processes. One of the earliest designs with this characteristic was the RC 4000 nucleus, where special internal processes were used for dealing with access to peripheral hardware. The RC 4000 did not sport hardware memory protection, and thus protection-wise, processes and drivers were equivalent. More recent designs, such as the L4 microkernel, permitted processes (tasks in L4 terminology) to receive hardware interrupts formatted as IPC messages, and access to memory mapped I/O registers and I/O port space could be controlled using virtual memory access grants. The Nooks system attempted to retrofit driver isolation into an existing Linux operating system, by allowing device drivers to execute in the normal virtual address ranges, but with access permissions set more restrictively than normal. Neither of these systems attempted to deal with the DMA problem, and while still able to contain many accidental types of faults, were not able to withstand attacks from directly malicious device drivers. Furthermore, the cost of making changes to virtual address spaces by context switching often added quite large execution overheads, because drivers, which normally run for very short times before returning control to the operating system of controlling user application, often are unable to amortize large switching costs.

10.5.3　Use of VMs for Driver Isolation

Similar to microkernels, it has been suggested that VMs [8] could provide a solution to the problem of device driver isolation. Indeed, by providing idealized, API abstraction to guest VMs, VMMs are often used as compatibility layers between experimental or legacy operating systems and hardware for which these possess no driver implementations.

This approach also has downsides. VMs containing full operating systems are much more coarse-grained abstractions than traditional driver modules, so there is a large memory overhead. Because the driver VM will be a black box, the user may find it harder to configure and troubleshoot than a traditional system. Finally, this approach only solves the problem for classes of hardware for which an emulation protocol has been defined. In a traditional driver model, support for whole new classes of hardware can be added directly, whereas in the driver-VM model a communications protocol for the new class must be added to both the application and the driver VM.

10.5.4　Context Switching Overhead

Regarding supporting segment architecture, the cost of address space switches can be reduced by using segmentation instead of paging hardware for isolation. When switching between virtual address space, the contents of the TLB need to be flushed, and the performance degradation resulting from the subsequent slew of TLB misses is a larger factor in the total cost of a context switch. If the virtual address spaces are small enough to make several of them fit inside the maximum addressable range, another option is to enforce isolation with segments. This change required modifications to the Xen VMM, to the driver and guest Linux kernels, and to the user-space applications running in the driver VM. Specifically:

1. When performing a VM *world switch*, Xen would check if the old and new VM would both fit in the virtual address space at the same time, and in that case skip the TLB flush.

2. The driver VM was relinked to fit into a very small address space, just below the Xen VMM at the top of memory.

3. All user-space applications running in the driver VM had to be relinked to run in a small address space, above guest kernels, but below driver VMs. In practice this was achieved by using the BusyBox v1 multi-call binary to provide most of the user-space functionality for the driver VM.

4. The guest Linux kernel was modified to use a slightly smaller portion of virtual memory, to make room for the driver VM and its user-space.

5. The user-space applications running in the guest VMs were not modified. The system was thus still able to host unmodified guest applications.

We measured an 8% improvement in TCP bandwidth between a guest VM and a remote host, with throughput increased from 574 MBps to 620 MBps, using the iperf bandwidth measurement tool. We conjecture that real-world applications that overlap computation and communication, would see larger performance improvements. On 32-bit platforms, this technique is applicable only when driver VM applications can be re-linked and have very modest virtual address space requirements. One such scenario is the Evil Man on-demand computing platform.

10.5.5   Restarting Device Drivers

In traditional systems, drivers are not allowed to fail. Failure of a driver often leads to corruption of memory and CPU state, and in most cases the only way out is a system-wide reset. If drivers are encapsulated and allowed to fail, the consequences of failure must be taken into consideration. The Nooks project implemented a best-effort safety mechanism for drivers, but though the system is able to recover from many types of driver failure, many applications relying on correct driver functioning are not. The problem is twofold; drivers may fail in byzantine ways and feed invalid data to applications, and even if drivers are fail-stop, they are likely to contain state that must be recreated after a driver restart.

The shadow driver tracks state changing commands, so that they can be replayed to the real driver if it ever crashes and needs to restart. The problem of byzantine driver failure is not addressed by Nooks, but is nevertheless quite interesting and challenging. Detection of a byzantine driver may be non-trivial if the driver never fail-stops, but perhaps knowledge of the hardware class can be exploited, e.g., an Ethernet driver should return frames in a certain format and with a valid checksum, and most network applications are programmed to survive garbage-in. The situation is worse for hardware, such as, disk drives that are expected to behave predictably and return previously stored data unscathed. Many applications will likely crash on byzantine input files, and the only transparent solution to these problems would be the use of a lightweight checkpointing mechanism, to allow the application to roll back to safe state after the failure of a driver.

10.5.6   External Device State

The problem of restoring or retrieving external state in drivers [8] or in the peripheral hardware itself, is not only related to driver crash recovery. External state also poses a big challenge to systems attempting to implement mobility, e.g., process and VM migration systems. In a VM system supporting mobility, it is important that all state relevant to the functioning of a VM either resides within the VM, or is simple to extract from the VMM or host environment. Ideally, the host/VMM should keep no state at all, as this will allow it to be policy-free with regards to the amount of state it is possible to store outside the VM. Naturally, some if this state is trusted, and cannot be safely stored in the VM without additional validity checking being performed before it is used. This would be the case for a permission table describing areas on disks to which the VM has access, or the integer value describing the

VM's memory allowance, and for the list of pages the VM is allowed to map. One possible solution would be to introduce a caching model, where all state in kept in the VM is sealed using encryption, and with the VMM caching relevant parts of this information after verifying that is has not been tampered with. As part of this work, we implemented a 3D graphics display system, called Blink, for VMs. Blink is an example of how a driver layer can be constructed to be restorable, and to support migration and checkpointing of client applications.

10.5.7 Type Safe Languages

Device driver safety may also be addressed by writing drivers in type-safe languages. Safe-language kernel extensions have been proposed, e.g., the device monitors of Concurrent Pascal and in the SPIN and Exokernel operating systems. In Exokernel, applications download code such as packet filters into the kernel, where it is compiled into native code and checked for misbehavior before letting it execute. In SPIN, and in more recent systems such as Singularity, the compiler is trusted to produce code that abides by the type-safety rules of the implementation language. Provided that the compiler is correctly implemented, safe-language extensions can safely execute inside the OS kernel. So far, driver developers seem to prefer unsafe language such as C or C++ for driver development, and the type safety is only a partial solution, as it does not address the DMA problem described above. Finally, there is a tension between creating a trustworthy compiler, i.e., one that is simple enough to be thoroughly audited, and one that produces well-optimized code.

10.5.8 Software Fault Isolation

For device drivers that cannot be rewritten in type-safe languages, an alternative is to use a software fault isolation (SFI) or sandboxing technique. Such techniques rely on a combination of software and hardware protection, but the core idea is the use of inlined reference monitors (IRM) embedded in the program instruction stream. The IRM-code monitors program state at runtime, and throws a software exception if the security policy is violated. IRMs are typically installed during compilation, and their presence is verified before the program runs. In contrast to type-safe languages, this division of concerns removes the necessity for trusting the compiler, and only requires that the verifier is trusted. Early SFI systems made very strong assumptions about the underlying instruction set architecture (ISA), e.g., about the alignment of instructions, and as such were only applicable to certain RISC architectures. Also, they were mostly targeted at user-space extensions, and could not always prevent sandboxed code from getting the CPU into a irrecoverable state by use of certain privileged instructions. The recent XFI project extends SFI to also work on CISC platforms. XFI addresses the complexities of the x86 ISA, e.g., the ability to jump to the middle of an instruction, by only allowing a subset of the instruction set to pass the verifier, and by enforcing control flow integrity (CFI). CFI enforcement means that all computed jumps (e.g., return instructions and jumps through pointer tables) are restricted to a predetermined set of addresses. With the CFI guarantee in place, it is possible to reason about the possible flows through a program, and thus to verify the presence of an IRM policy.

10.6   Self-Migration

Based on the experiences with the NomadBIOS hosted migration system, it find that it was possible to migrate running operating system VMs across a network, with very short freeze times, but that adding this functionality to the VMM inflated the size of the trusted computing base. These observations led leads to design the self-migration algorithm, which has comparable performance, but does not inflate the trusted computing base.

10.6.1   Hosted Migration

The first implementation of hosted VMM was the NomadBIOS system. Nomad-BIOS was a prototype host environment for running several adapted Linux instances concurrently and with the ability to migrate these between hosts without disrupting service (now commonly referred to as *live migration*.) NomadBIOS ran on top of the L4 microkernel, multiplexing physical resources for a number of concurrently running guest operating system instances. It contained a TCP/IP stack for accepting incoming migrations, and for migrating guest operating systems elsewhere. Nomad-BIOS ran incoming guest operating systems as new L4 tasks inside their own address spaces, and provided them with backing memory and filtered Ethernet access. An adapted version of L4 Linux 2.2, called Nomad Linux, binarily compatible with native Linux, was used as guest OS. All guest memory was paged by NomadBIOS, so it was simple to snapshot the memory state of a guest OS and migrate it to another host, though quite a lot of cooperation from the guest was needed when extracting all thread control block state from the underlying L4 microkernel. To reduce downtime, NomadBIOS used pre-copy migration, Pre-copy migration is not covered in chapter 11, keeping the guest OS running at the originating host while migrating, tracking changes to its address space and sending updates containing the changes to the original image over a number of iterations. The size of the updates would typically shrink down to a hundred kilobytes or less. As a further optimization, a gratuitous ARP packet was then broadcast to the local Ethernet, to inform local peers about the move to a new interface on a new host. Nomad Linux running under NomadBIOS was benchmarked against Linux 2.2 running under VMware Workstation 3.2 and against a native Linux 2.2 kernel where relevant. Performance was generally on par with VMware for CPU-bound tasks, and scalability when hosting multiple guests markedly better.

Problems with Hosted Migration: As described above, hosted migration requires extensions to the VMM and other parts of the trusted software installation on the machine. Whether or not this is a concern depends on the way the system is deployed and used. For example, VMware recommends using a separate, trusted network for migrations, and naturally this reduces the risk of an attack on the migration service. Also, the ability to relocate a VM without its knowledge or cooperation may be practical in some scenarios. The focus of the work is grid or utility computing, and often we cannot trust neither the network nor the applications we are hosting on behalf of customers. In addition, we should try to stay as flexible as possible, and to refrain from providing policies where mechanisms would suffice. We therefore try to avoid implementing functionality in the trusted parts of the system, where its presence may be exploited by an attacker, and where it can only be changed through a system-wide software upgrade [9].

The experiences from developing NomadBIOS led to the design of a new system, based on the self-migration algorithm. The self-migration implementation is based on the Xen VM monitor (or hypervisor) which divides a commodity Intel PC into several virtual domains, while maintaining near-native performance. Xen originally lacked comfortable abstractions common to other microkernels, such as the paging-via-IPC mechanism and recursive address spaces of L4, and did not provide any clean way of letting a guest OS delegate paging responsibilities to an external domain. However, this is required when implementing host-driven live-migration as otherwise there is no way of tracking changed pages from the outside. While the Xen team was working to add such functionality, we decided to pursue another approach: In-line with the end-to-end argument [9, 10].

Security: By placing migration functionality within the unprivileged guest OS, the footprint and the chance of programming errors of the trusted computing base is reduced. For instance, the guest will use its own TCP stack, and the trusted base needs only provide a filtered network abstraction.

Accounting and Performance: The network and CPU cost of performing the migration is attributed to the guest OS, rather than to the host environment, which simplifies resource accounting. This has the added benefit of motivating the guest to aid migration, by not scheduling uncooperative processes, or by flushing buffer caches prior to migration.

Flexibility: By implementing migration inside the guest OS, the choices of network protocols and security features are ultimately left to whoever configures the guest OS instance, removing the need for a network-wide standard, although a common bootstrapping protocol will have to be agreed upon.

Portability: Because migration happens without hypervisor involvement, this approach is less dependent on the semantics of the hypervisor, and can be ported across different hypervisors and microkernels, and perhaps even to the bare hardware.

Support for Direct I/O: When vitalizing the CPU, current VMMs come close to having native performance. The performance of network and disk I/O is more of a problem, especially in hosted VMMs such as Xen and VMware Workstation, where a context switch is required when servicing interrupts. One possible solution is the use of special hardware that can be safely controlled directly by the unprivileged VM, without involving the VMM or a host OS. Unfortunately this model works badly with hosted migration, because the state of the guest VM may change without the VMMs knowledge, through direct device DMA. Self-migration, on the other hand, is not in conflict with direct I/O mechanisms. The main drawbacks of self-migration are the following:

- *Implementation Effort for Each Guest OS:* Self-migration has to be re-implemented for each type of guest OS. While implementing self-migration in Linux proved relatively simple, this may not generalize to other systems. Also, developments in the guest OS may result in incompatibilities, and will require ongoing maintenance.

- *Only Works for Para-virtualized Guests:* Self-migration requires that each guest OS is extended with new functionality. In cases where this is not possible, such as when not having access to the source code of the guest OS, self-migration will not work. In some cases, it may be possible to extend the OS by installing a self-migration driver as a binary kernel module. Because we are targeting on-demand, high-performance computing, we have mostly been focusing on open source operating systems such as Linux. Linux is popular in these settings because of its low cost, and because it can be customized easily. When running each workload in a separate VM, the licensing costs of a commercial OS could also become a serious issue. Self-migration may be less applicable in other situations, where the ability to host proprietary operating systems, such, Microsoft Windows is of higher importance.

10.6.2 Self-Migration Prerequisites

Apart from the somewhat vague statement that this works in a virtual machine, it is worth considering the exact prerequisites of self-migration, e.g., to find out which technique would be applicable in other process models, such as the one found in UNIX systems [10]. The following prerequisites have been identified:

1. The ability to trap and handle page faults.

2. The ability to log all peripheral-induced changes to memory state (DMA).

3. The ability to write-protect all virtual memory mappings, atomically.

4. Some way of externalizing checkpoint state, e.g., to a disk or network device.

In UNIX-like systems, it is possible to write-protect memory using the `mmap()` system calls, and possible to handle page faults with a signal handler. Simple forms of I/O, e.g., using `open()` and `read()`, can also be intercepted and logged. More problematic are features such as shared memory, where an external process may change memory state without notification, and shared files where one-copy semantics mandate that the results of a write are immediately visible to all readers of the file. Finally, the need for atomic write-protection of all virtual memory is problematic in a UNIX-like OS, as this would entail having the ability to stop scheduling of program threads while walking the address space and protecting memory. An alternative here would be a system call for revoking all writable memory mappings in a single operation, as is present in the L4 microkernel. Various attempts have been made at freezing process state in UNIX systems, without kernel extensions.

The common solution is to somehow force a process core dump, and to later restore that into a running process again. The problem here, as with traditional process migration, is that a UNIX process is likely to make use of, e.g., the file system or shared memory, and so large amounts of residual dependencies are likely to exist. Self-migration can be implemented with relatively simple support from the hosting platform, and in theory should not even require a VM, but could be made to run directly on the native hardware.

10.7   Conclusion

There are still many open problems relating to device drivers. Existing systems trade driver safety for performance and ease of development, and device drivers are a major source of system instability. Attempts have been made to improve the situation, hardware protection techniques, e.g., microkernels and Nooks, and through software-enforced isolation. Commodity systems do not enforce addressing restrictions on device DMA, limiting the effectiveness of the described techniques. Finally, if applications are to survive a driver crash, the OS or driver protection mechanism must have a way of recreating lost hardware state on driver re-initialization.

REFERENCES

1. Panigrahy, R., Talwar, K., Uyeda, L., & Wieder, U. (2011). Heuristics for vector bin packing. *Research*. Microsoft.com.

2. Wood, T., Shenoy, P. J., Venkataramani, A., & Yousif, M. S. (2007). Black-box and Gray-box Strategies for Virtual Machine Migration. *In NSDI* (Vol. 7, pp. 17-17).

3. Mishra, M., & Sahoo, A. (2011). On theory of vm placement: Anomalies in existing methodologies and their mitigation using a novel vector based approach. In Cloud Computing (CLOUD), 2011 IEEE International Conference (pp. 275-282). IEEE.

4. Wu, Y., Tang, M., & Fraser, W. (2012). A simulated annealing algorithm for energy efficient virtual machine placement. In Systems, Man, and Cybernetics (SMC), 2012 IEEE International Conference on (pp. 1245-1250). IEEE.

5. Lee, G., Tolia, N., Ranganathan, P., & Katz, R. H. (2010). Topology-aware resource allocation for data-intensive workloads. In Proceedings of the first ACM asia-pacific workshop on Workshop on systems (pp. 1-6). ACM.

6. Ferreto, T. C., Netto, M. A., Calheiros, R. N., & De Rose, C. A. (2011). Server consolidation with migration control for virtualized data centers. *Future Generation Computer Systems*, 27(8), 1027-1034.

7. Schaffrath, G., Schmid, S., & Feldmann, A. (2012). Optimizing long-lived cloudnets with migrations. In Utility and Cloud Computing (UCC), 2012 IEEE Fifth International Conference (pp. 99-106). IEEE.

8. Hermenier, F., Lorca, X., Menaud, J. M., Muller, G., & Lawall, J. (2009). Entropy: a consolidation manager for clusters. In Proceedings of the 2009 ACM SIGPLAN/SIGOPS international conference on Virtual execution environments (pp. 41-50). ACM.

9. Chen, L. Y., Birke, R., & Smirni, E. (2017). State of Practice of Non-self-aware Virtual Machine Management in Cloud Data Centers. *In Self-Aware Computing Systems* (pp. 555-574). Springer International Publishing.

10. Wang, H., Li, Y., Zhang, Y., & Jin, D. (2017). Virtual machine migration planning in software-defined networks. *IEEE Transactions on Cloud Computing*.

CHAPTER 11

DIFFERENT APPROACHES FOR LIVE MIGRATION

Abstract

Virtualization has become one of the key technologies in the era of cloud computing. It is loosely defined as an abstraction of the computing resources that can be achieved by either dividing the resources into multiple computing environments or merging various resource components into one. The division of the resources can be applied using various concepts and techniques such as time-sharing, hardware and software partitioning, simulation, emulation, etc. Thus, virtualization technology has enabled efficient utilization of hardware resources by abstracting away the underlying resources like processors, main memory, secondary storage and networking. In this chapter, two kinds of live migration techniques for hardware-assisted virtual machines (HVMs) are studied and implemented.

Keywords: Cold migration, hybrid live migration, migration types, scaling.

11.1 Virtualization

Today, with the help of virtualization [1], the data centers are continuously employing the virtualized architecture to execute multiple applications that are mapped onto the physical machines. This has been enabled with the help of VMs that form the software abstraction of a physical machine. This abstraction is achieved by the various virtualization techniques such as:

- *Full Virtualization:* It is defined as the isolated execution of the unmodified guest OS by simulating the hardware resources, including full instruction set, input/output operations, interrupts, and memory access, etc.

- *Paravirtualization:* It is defined as the isolated execution of the guest OS with modified resources in the form of hooks. The paravirtualized interface is used to decrease the performance degradation caused by the time spent by the guest in performing certain operations which are substantially more difficult to execute in a virtual environment compared to a non-virtualized environment.

11.1.1 Hardware-Assisted Virtualization

Hardware-assisted virtualization is defined as the execution of the guest OS with the capabilities provided by the hardware, primarily from the host processor. In this case, the resources can be either fully virtualized or para virtualized (See Figure 11.1). Therefore, the cloud providers that are providing the infrastructure resources completely rely on full virtualization with hardware assistance. This is because of the client requirements of unmodified guests as a part of the service level agreements (SLAs). Overall, virtualization helps in enabling agility, dynamism, and adaptability within a data center. VMs, therefore, form the basic building blocks of the IaaS with benefits such as flexible resource provisioning, monitoring and administration by the system administrators.

Resource provisioning allows the provisioning of the infrastructure-based resources either at the beginning or during the life cycle of a service. At the IaaS level [2], these resources consist of servers, network, and self-service for the clouds. Server provisioning, a part of resource provisioning, consists of well-defined configuration of the servers based on the requirements of the client. It consists of the following two types:

1. *Static server provisioning:* The configuration of the VMs at the beginning of the life cycle of a service constitutes the static part of server provisioning. During this process, a physical machine is selected from a pool of physical nodes. Today, a VM is instantiated by using the existing template-based provisioning before executing provisioning of other services, depending upon the requirements.

2. *Dynamic server provisioning:* Both from the client's point of view and cloud provider, the dynamic resource provisioning plays an important role in allocation or removal of the resources during the life cycle of a service. Currently, there are multiple ways to modify the resources either horizontally or vertically.

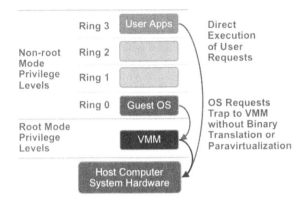

Figure 11.1   Hardware-assisted virtualization.

11.1.2 Horizontal Scaling

Horizontal scaling refers to adding multiple independent physical resources to provide more resources in terms of computing power, memory, disk space and even network bandwidth. This form of scaling employs multiple instances of the applications running on different physical servers.

11.1.3 Vertical Scaling

It refers to the addition of the resources on the same physical machine by adding CPUs, memory or even disk for that particular application residing on a single physical instance. Currently, vertical scaling is not supported by cloud providers as it requires changes to the guest OS or VMs running on the bare physical machines, which may result in several security issues.

A VM, which is a software implementation [3] of a physical machine, always uses the same physical resources (CPU, memory and I/O) utilized by a physical machine. At the beginning of the life cycle of a service, the initial provisioning of a VM is determined by the resource-usage profile provided by the client. These profiles also try to include the estimations to meet the future load requirements. But, either changes in the workload conditions on VMs or load on the physical machines can lead to hotspots, not enough resources to meet the load spikes/demands or cold spots, inefficient utilization of the provisioned resources.

Thus, to mitigate these issues, live migration of VMs plays an important role in the dynamic resources management of the physical machines inside a data center. Live migration is the process of transferring a running VM from one physical machine to another over the network. This will alleviate the hotspots to meet the SLA guarantee and handle cold spots for efficient resource utilization. Therefore, from a cloud provider's point of view, live migration plays a very important role in the following scenarios:

- *Server Consolidation:* With the help of server consolidation, the VMs residing on a lightly loaded physical machines can be packed onto a fewer physical machines while maintaining the SLA. This will not only lead to low power usage by the data center but also higher resources usage by a host.

- *Load Balancing:* The primary purpose of load balancing is to ensure the equal distribution of the resources, resulting in almost equal residual resource capacity across the physical machines. This can be achieved via live migration of the VMs which will mitigate the resource utilization discrepancy.

- *Hotspot Mitigation:* During the life-cycle service of a VM [4], if the resource utilization increases for some time window, it will result in a hotspot in the future. To mitigate this issue, either additional resources are locally allocated (*vertical scaling*) or globally, i.e., among the physical machines. If the local resources are not sufficient, VMs can be migrated to another physical node to offload the resources, thus resulting in hotspot mitigation.

- *System Maintenance:* In order to keep the servers running smoothly inside a data center, the physical resources need to be physically repaired, replaced or removed. Thus, during the maintenance, the cloud provider will try to migrate the VMs onto different physical machines while adhering the SLAs [5].

11.2   Types of Live Migration

Following are the three kinds of migration techniques that have been developed for migrating a VM from one host to another [6].

11.2.1   Cold Migration

In the case of cold migration, a powered-off VM is relocated to a new host. The attached disk and configuration of a VM can be migrated to a new location. This can also be used for migrating from one data center to another. In this approach, there is no notion of VM downtime, and performance degradation. A powered-off VM can be easily migrated to mitigate hotspots if there are any.

11.2.2   Suspend/Resume Migration

In this case, a live VM is first suspended and then it is migrated to a new host. Currently, this technique is not used as it will result in huge performance degradation and VM downtime if the VM is executing some task.

11.2.3   Live VM Migration

Live migration is the process of transferring an active VM's resources from one host to another over the network. The runtime information of VM consists of device states such as disk, memory, network, etc., that gets transferred to the destination. This process helps in dynamic consolidation of the resources by reallocating the resources on the fly. The migration approach which is derived from the process migration consists of the following three phases:

- *Push phase:* This phase is active on the source. In this phase, all the device states with large memory size, such as RAM and disk states, are transferred to the destination.

- *Stop-and-copy phase:* This phase begins after the push phase. In this phase, the VM at the source is halted and the dirtied pages of the disk and memory are transferred to the destination along with the other device states. The other device states are not transferred in the push phase not only because of the very frequent updates compared to memory and disk, but also being very small in memory size.

- *Pull phase:* This phase marks the resumption of the VM on the destination which might fetch the dirty pages if required.

Thus, depending upon the usage of the aforementioned phases, following are the performance metrics that are affected while a live VM is being migrated under different scenarios and constraints.

11.3   Live VM Migration Types

11.3.1   Pre-Copy Live Migration

The pre-copy live migration approach consists of the first two phases of the process migration. During the push phase, the memory data is iteratively transferred, followed by the transfer of the dirty pages along with the device states in the stop-and-copy phase (See Figure 11.2) [7].

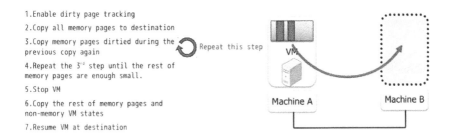

1.Enable dirty page tracking
2.Copy all memory pages to destination
3.Copy memory pages dirtied during the previous copy again   Repeat this step
4.Repeat the 3rd step until the rest of memory pages are enough small.
5.Stop VM
6.Copy the rest of memory pages and non-memory VM states
7.Resume VM at destination

Machine A   Machine B

Figure 11.2   Pre-copy live migration.

11.3.2   Post-copy Live Migration

In this subsection, we present the design, implementation and evaluation of the post-copy approach for the live migration of VMs in a LAN setup connected via gigabit switch. Post-copy utilizes the last two stages of a generic migration algorithm—stop-and-copy phase, and pull phase. This is in contrast to the classical pre-copy approach which iteratively transfers the memory state in the push phase followed by the remaining dirty pages and the device states' transfer in the stop-and-copy phase. With the introduction of the pull phase, the time taken to complete the migration process is undetermined.

1. Stop VM

2. Copy non-memory VM state
   to destination

3. Resume VM at destination

4. Copy memory pages on-
   demand/backgroundly

   · Async PF can be utilized

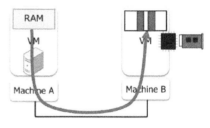

Copy memory pages
•On-demand(network fault)
•background(precache)

Figure 11.3   Post-copy live migration.

We resolve this issue by including a proactive background pre-paging technique which requests the memory pages from the source when there is no demand for the pages from the destination VM. This optimization coupled with block-based paging results in low network overhead as well as reduction in the major page faults. The post-copy approach proves to be effective by having the least downtime for all the workloads when compared against the pre-copy approach. We have implemented the post-copy approach on the top of QEMU/KVM and have demonstrated our results on the same.

Why post-copy? Pre-copy is the classical approach used by the vendors such as Xen, KVM, VMware etc.(see Figure 11.3) [8], that tries to keep the shorter downtime by transferring less data during the stop-and-copy phase. The pre-copy approach is effective in minimizing the two performance metrics, VM downtime and application performance degradation, only when the VM is executing a read-intensive workload. However, the effectiveness of this approach gets reduced for moderately write-intensive workloads.

11.3.3   Hybrid Live Migration

This approach incorporates all the three phases of process migration. During the push phase, the memory content is streamed to the destination once. After the conclusion of the push phase, the VM is stopped and all the device states along with the dirty bitmap are transferred to the destination. The VM is then resumed on the destination and the dirtied pages are obtained from the source when requested by the destination.

11.4 Hybrid Live Migration

The hybrid algorithm utilizes all three described phases of the process migration steps, namely push phase, stop-and-copy phase and pull phase. Thus, the basic hybrid approach tries to provide the better of two worlds pre-copy and post-copy, by outperforming the both of these approaches in terms of total data transfer, total migration time, and the application performance degradation (see Figure 11.4).

With the introduction of the push phase, the hybrid approach decreases both of the perceivable downtime as well as the number of network faults that are quite high in case of the post-copy approach. We have also introduced a histogram-based learning phase which not only improves the performance metrics but also reduces the resource consumption of the source. This phase is introduced prior to the push phase that assists the migration daemon in restricting the transfer of the writable working set, during the push phase. Depending upon the availability of the CPU and network bandwidth, we incorporate a compression technique using a real-time compression/decompression technique, lzo, as well as parallelize the push phase in order to utilize the unused bandwidth. We have implemented the hybrid approach on the top of QEMU/KVM and have demonstrated the results on the same.

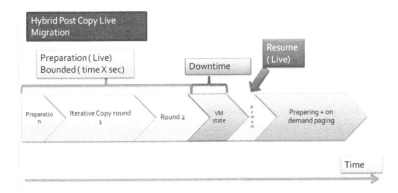

Figure 11.4   Hybrid live migration.

11.4.1 Hybrid Approach for Live Migration

In this section, we discuss the design of the basic hybrid approach along with the introduction of a new phase — learning phase, prior to the push phase and other optimizations incorporated in the push phase. The hybrid approach tries to optimally utilize the network bandwidth by a single transfer of the VM's memory to the destination in the push phase followed by only transferring the device state's along with the dirty bitmap in the stop-and-copy phase and then the dirty pages in the pull phase. The approach helps us to achieve shorter downtime when compared against the precopy technique, and drastic reduction in the perceivable downtime when compared against the post-copy approach.

11.4.2 Basic Hybrid Migration Algorithm

The various phases of the basic hybrid migration algorithm are as follows:

1. *Push Phase:* The entire memory is transferred to the destination without suspending the VM. There are no multiple iterations and hence no multiple page retransmissions across iterations. Only a single byte is transferred, if all the bytes in a page contain the same value.

2. *Stop-and-Copy Phase:* The VM is suspended and the dirty bitmap along with the device states are transferred to the destination. The dirty bitmap indicates the pages that got dirtied during the push phase. The VM is then resumed at the destination.

3. *Pull Phase:* Whenever the VM accesses a page that got dirtied during the push phase, a major page fault gets generated, which results in a network fault. This network fault is handled by retrieving the corresponding page from the source. The dirty bitmap transferred during the stop-and-copy phase is useful in deciding whether a page fault can be resolved locally or requires a page transfer from the source.

   A page gets transmitted in the push phase and gets retransmitted again in the pull phase, only if it gets dirtied again. During the stop-and-copy phase, no pages get transmitted. So a page gets transmitted at most twice. We introduce a learning phase before the push phase to minimize the number of pages that get transmitted twice.

11.5 Reliable Hybrid Live Migration

Reliability is considered one of the three related key attributes among system designers with modest resources. It is a key attribute providing consistency according to its specifications. The same is expected from the VMs, which are the software implementation of a physical machine and are responsible for executing programs like physical machine. But VMs tend to fail during the life cycle of their service. This can be attributed to the failure of the underlying physical machine on which the VM is running or the host operating system on the hardware failing. During the migration process, failure of either source machine or destination machine will have different implications depending on the phase of migration as discussed below:

11.5.1 Push Phase

This phase is active on the source in which the data is streamed to the destination. Failure of the source will result in permanent loss of VM. There will not be any effect if the destination fails as the source still has the current active state of the VM.

11.5.2 Stop-and-Copy Phase

Similar to the push phase, this phase is also active on the source, except the data is transferred when the VM has been suspended on the source. Thus, VM will be permanently lost if it crashes on the source while there will not be any effect if the failure of the destination occurs.

11.5.3 Pull Phase

During this phase, the VM is active on the destination machine. Since the state transfer is still under progress, the source machine may partially contain the current state of the VM. Failure of either the source or destination results in VM failure. Thus, pre-copy approach is tolerant to destination failure whereas post-copy and hybrid approaches are not. This is due to the presence of the *unreliable* pull phase. Therefore, pull phase becomes a critical state in ensuring destination reliability during migration. In order to mitigate the issue of VM failure during the pull phase, we discuss the approach and design of the *reliable* pull phase for the hybrid approach.

11.5.4 Network Buffering

Today, most of the applications rely on TCP connections which provide strong service guarantees. Thus, there is no requirement of the packet replication, since their loss will be accounted as a transient network failure. This fact simplifies the network buffering problem in which the packets get queued for transmission and are only transmitted after the VM state is successfully checkpointed at the end of each epoch. Thus, any VM state exposed to the external world can always be recovered from the checkpointed state. If the destination fails during the pull phase, the buffered packets can be reflected as lost state.

11.6 Conclusion

In this chapter, we studied and implemented two kinds of live migration techniques for the HVMs. The first contribution of this chapter was the design and implementation of the post-copy approach. This approach consisted of the last two stages of the process-migration phases stop-and-copy phase and pull phase. Due to the introduction of the pull phase, this approach becomes non-deterministic in terms of the completion of the migration. This is because of the only on-demand fetching of the data from the source.

REFERENCES

1. Salimi, H., Najafzadeh, M., & Sharifi, M. (2012). Advantages, Challenges and Optimizations of Virtual Machine Scheduling in Cloud Computing Environments. *International Journal of Computer Theory and Engineering*, 4(2), 189.

2. Salot, P. (2013). A survey of various scheduling algorithm in cloud computing environment. *International Journal of Research in Engineering and Technology*, 2(2), 131-135.

3. Vasani, M. P. P., & Sanghani, M. N. S. (2013). Resource Utilization & Execution Time Enhancement by Priority Based Pre-emptable Shortest Job Next Scheduling In Private Cloud Computing. *International Journal of Engineering Research & Technology* (IJERT), 2(9), 1649-1654.

4. Kaleeswaran, A., Ramasamy, V., & Vivekanandan, P. (2013). Host Scheduling Algorithm U sing Genetic Algorithm In Cloud Computing Environment. *International Journal of Advances in Engineering & Technology*.

5. Verma, A., Ahuja, P., & Neogi, A. (2008). pMapper: power and migration cost aware application placement in virtualized systems. In Proceedings of the 9th ACM/IFIP/USENIX International Conference on Middleware (pp. 243-264). Springer-Verlag New York, Inc..

6. Anand, A., Dhingra, M., Lakshmi, J., & Nandy, S. K. (2012). Resource usage monitoring for kvm based virtual machines. In Advanced Computing and Communications (ADCOM), 2012 18th Annual International Conference on (pp. 66-70). IEEE.

7. Mosberger, D., & Jin, T. (1998). httperfa tool for measuring web server performance. *ACM SIGMETRICS Performance Evaluation Review*, 26(3), 31-37.

8. Kratsch, S. (2016). On polynomial kernels for sparse integer linear programs. *Journal of Computer and System Sciences*, 82(5), 758-766.

9. Deshpande, U., & Keahey, K. (2017). Traffic-sensitive live migration of virtual machines. *Future Generation Computer Systems*, 72, 118-128.

10. Melhem, S. B., Agarwal, A., Goel, N., & Zaman, M. (2017). Selection process approaches in live migration: A comparative study. In Information and Communication Systems (ICICS), 2017 8th International Conference (pp. 23-28). IEEE.

11. Sun, G., Liao, D., Anand, V., Zhao, D., & Yu, H. (2016). A new technique for efficient live migration of multiple virtual machines. *Future Generation Computer Systems*, 55, 74-86.

12. Melhem, S. B., Agarwal, A., Goel, N., & Zaman, M. (2017, April). Selection process approaches in live migration: A comparative study. In Information and Communication Systems (ICICS), 2017 8th International Conference (pp. 23-28). IEEE.

13. Li, C., Feng, D., Hua, Y., Xia, W., Qin, L., Huang, Y., & Zhou, Y. (2017, May). BAC: Bandwidth-aware compression for efficient live migration of virtual machines. In INFOCOM 2017-IEEE Conference on Computer Communications, IEEE (pp. 1-9). IEEE.

14. Abali, B., Isci, C., Kephart, J. O., McIntosh, S. K., & Sarma, D. (2017). U.S. Patent No. 9,619,259. Washington, DC: U.S. Patent and Trademark Office.

15. Modi, A., Achar, R., & Thilagam, P. S. (2017). Live migration of virtual machines with their local persistent storage in a data intensive cloud. *International Journal of High Performance Computing and Networking*, 10(1-2), 134-147.

CHAPTER 12

MIGRATING SECURITY POLICIES IN CLOUD

Abstract

Network and cloud simulation has been around for a while. However, most of the network simulators are not capable of cloud modeling. On the other hand, most of the existing cloud simulators focus on performance benchmarking, cost-effectiveness evaluations and power consumption assessments. Hence, a majority of them lack modeling security boxes such as firewall, IPS and security services like VPN. Furthemore, in some experiments a real running VM and actual services which imitate the behavior of a real network are necessary. At the time of writing this chapter, there is no free cloud simulator available which mimics middleboxes and real services in simulations. This chapter covers the different migrating policies in cloud computing environments.

Keywords: IPS, VPN, cloud computing, firewall, migration security.

12.1   Cloud Computing

Perhaps the evolving nature of cloud computing [1] is the reason for not having a common and standard definition for it. However, when searching the literature, the NIST definition of cloud computing is the first choice of most researchers. Cloud computing is a model for enabling ubiquitous, convenient, on-demand network access to a shared pool of configurable computing resources (e.g., networks, servers, storage, applications, and services) that can be rapidly provisioned and released with minimal management effort or service provider interaction. In order to have a better understanding of this model, NIST described main characteristics of cloud computing and categorized it with deployment models and service models. The essential characteristics can be elaborated as follows:

- *On-Demand Self-Service:* Customer is able to manage resources remotely and automatically without the need to contact CSP.

- *Broad Network Access:* Customer access to capabilities through network and by standard mechanism. This feature has to be platform independent.

- *Resource Pooling:* Sharing of the providers physical and virtual resources among multiple customers.

- *Rapid Elasticity:* Described as an instant and on-demand possibility of scaling up and down the computing resources, by the customer.

- *Measured Service:* This characteristic enables pay-as-you-go feature with providing a complete report of resource usage for both provider and customer.

One important characteristic that is missing in above definition is multi-tenancy, which enables coexistence of different customers' data on the same storage medium. This might be implicitly deductible from resource pooling, but we would like to express this characteristic separately, due to its importance from security perspective and the research path. Cloud computing deployment models [2] are described as following:

- *Private Cloud:* In this model, there is only one organization that uses and manages cloud infrastructure. However, it is possible to hand over the responsibility of management and maintenance to a third-party company. This model gives the highest level of control to organizations, especially in terms of the security.

- *Community Cloud:* In cases in which organizations collaborate on projects or have shared data, the community model can be deployed to have a shared infrastructure between collaborative parties.

- *Public Cloud:* An infrastructure that can be managed by any organization in order to provide services and host for general public consumers. Since this model is public, control over that is limited and sometimes is partially shifted to the users for their own security.

- *Hybrid Cloud:* A combination of two or more aforementioned models can shape a hybrid infrastructure. This is the most complex method of infrastructure deployment and needs extra effort to make sure there is no security breach or lack of provision in different parts of infrastructure.

And finally, services are delivered to consumers based on the following service models [3]:

1. *Software as a Service (SaaS):* Customer can access applications that are running on cloud infrastructure with various interfaces. Microsoft Office Live and Google Docs are good examples of such services.

2. *Platform as a Service (PaaS):* Provider prepares a development environment including programming languages, libraries and different tools for customer in order to develop applications. Examples can be Microsoft Azure and Google App Engine.

3. *Infrastructure as a Service (IaaS):* In this model, customer is served by customizable desired resources such as processors, memory, network or even security appliances. Amazon Elastic Compute Cloud (Amazon EC2), Amazon Simple Storage Service (Amazon S3) and Rackspace Cloud servers are examples of this type of service. Our research is mostly in this scope since network-related issues come under this category.

In fact, cloud computing has enhanced the overall security. Concentration of infrastructure in one location and ease of management and control, separation of virtual infrastructures and isolation of VMs were major improvements in security although they were just remedies for mitigation of some attacks. Security is still an issue, because not only are most of the traditional attacks still applicable, but also some new cloud-specific attacks are manifested. In this section, we strive to categorize cloud- related security concerns and explain the most important methods of protection, with special focus on security appliance's role.

There is a rich literature on taxonomy of cloud computing security. Gartner, enumerates seven security risks as:

1. Privileged user access

2. Regulatory compliance

3. Data location

4. Data segregation

5. Recovery

6. Investigative support

7. Long-term viability.

While classification of cloud security concerns looks like an endless effort, it seems cloud security issues can be grouped into seven categories and then further grouped into three main domains, with respect to the most important key references. In order to safeguard a cloud, security should be applied in different layers. For instance, data security can be improved by using stronger encryption techniques, interface breaches can be mitigated by hardening the code, and compliance issues can be solved by revising SLAs [4].

Data centers, also known as server farms, require a huge amount of hardware and infrastructure facilities. On the other hand, due to the fast growing technologies that data centers hinge on and customers ask for, cloud service providers need to undergo major upgrades every few years. Therefore, data centers need to make the best use of their facilities and this is exactly where virtualization can inevitably help. Server consolidation is a great example of virtualization's impact on the improvement of data center efficiency. Hypervisors have different features and capabilities depending on their vendor. As it has been found in the literature, there are three main features, common between most of them and according to VMware, which is the leader in virtualization technology; these features are high availability (HA), fault tolerance (FT) and live migration. The first and the second features are dependent on the last one. A short description of these features follows [5].

High Availability: A technology that monitors all VMs constantly and in case of hardware failure immediately restarts the VMs on another server. This feature does not transfer the current state of VM and only loads the VM from the stored image in storage unit.

Fault Tolerance: This technology complements the previous feature. It runs identical copies of a VM in another place at the same time and in case of failure in origin location, duplicated VM will continue running without interruption. This feature is dependent on live migration of VM state.

Live Migration: This feature provides the means, to transfer a VM and its running state from a server to another in real time.

VM migration can be done in two ways; within a data center or across different data centers that sometimes are located in different continents. In addition to the mentioned motivation for migration that complements other features of hypervisor, there are more incentives to migrate a VM. One of the main reasons and motivations for VM migration is load balancing between servers. Sometimes a task needs more processor power and there are not enough resources available in the server; in this situation, a migration to another server can solve the problem. Periodical maintenance is another typical reason for VM migration. Reducing power consumption is always a desire for data centers. It happens once in a while that many severs have a minimum load and it is possible to shut down or hibernate them while transferring some VMs to another server; these migrations can significantly reduce power consumption and consequently data center cost. According to virtualization [6], security challenges can be categorized as follows:

Inactive VMs: Normally VMs receive daily updates and security patches. VMs that are offline, are not able to receive those updates and become vulnerable when they go active. As a result, they turn into security threats for the entire server.

VM Awareness: All security solutions and appliances are not compatible with virtualized environment. The hypervisor security is also another concern that should be taken into consideration.

VM Sprawl: VMs can be created with a click of a mouse. This is the key reason for the rapid growth of virtualization; however, not only can security be achieved as easily as that, many security weaknesses can easily duplicate and spread all over the network. Each VM needs special care and an administrator cannot apply the same solution to all VMs.

Inter-VM Traffic: Traffic between the VMs is not visible to traditional physical layer security appliances. Hence, monitoring and management of that traffic can be performed by an appliance that is integrated into hypervisor.

Migration: When a VM migrates from one cloud to another, the security policies that are associated with that VM remain in the place of origin.

12.2   Firewalls in Cloud and SDN

Network security that falls under architecture domain, can affect cloud security. Firewalling is one of the solutions that has a significant impact on improving network security. Firewall is a security appliance that filters packets and controls incoming and outgoing traffic. Still, there is not enough information that gives us a clear view of firewall. Therefore, it is necessary to go another level deeper and define what are main the purposes and benefits of using these devices on which data centers invest a huge amount money on. Middleboxes are essential intermediary devices in the network that mainly optimize performance and security of the network. Some of them, such as WAN optimizers and IDSs, specifically focus on one issue; respectively performance and security, and others can be helpful in both directions.

The term *middlebox* may mistakenly imply a physical existence of a separate device whereas, it can be a virtual appliance that is running on commodity hardware along with functionalities or even as a software solution. The authors in [1] state that security appliances can be distinguished by their types. Active devices can filter and modify the traffic. Common examples of active devices are antivirus, content-filtering device and firewalls. Passive devices basically monitor the network and make reports and alerts whenever they detect a suspicious activity, like IDS. Another type of device is a prevention one, such as IPS or vulnerability assessment tools that unveil threats before an incident occurs. Finally, there are unified threat management (UTM) devices that integrate multiple security features into one box.

Knowing the place of firewall among all middleboxes allows higher accuracy in giving a definition of the firewall. As a result, firewalls are software or hardware components that separate a network into different security levels by enforcing rules. These rules specify access level as well as limitations of each network entity or program. According to NIST, there are ten different firewall technologies [7] for production networks and two types for individual hosts and home networks.

- *Packet Filtering:* Most basic feature on any firewall that specifies ACCEPT or DROP of a packet, based on information in the header.

- *Stateful Inspection:* Keeps track of connection states in a table called state table and inspects packets by matching their state with connection state.

- *Application Firewalls:* Stateful protocol analysis, also known as deep packet inspection. Allows or denies based on application behavior on the network.

- *Application-Proxy Gateways:* Another deep inspection method that act as a middleman between two hosts and prevent a direct connection.

- *Dedicated Proxy Servers:* Placed behind firewall because they have very limited firewalling features and act as an intermediary between firewall and internal network.

- *Virtual Private Networking*: Uses additional protocols in order to encrypt and decrypt traffic between two gateways or a host and a gateway.

- *Network Access Control*: Grants access to a client based on his/her credentials and health check result.

- *Unified Threat Management*: Combination of multiple features like firewalling and intrusion detection into one system.

- *Web Application Firewalls*: A special type of application firewall for protecting web servers.

- *Firewalls for Virtual Infrastructure*: Software firewalls that can monitor virtualized network traffic.

While firewalls usually protect network to some extent, there are still some attacks that can pass through a firewall and reach the internal network. In order to protect the hosts in the network, there are firewalls designed to deploy particularly on host machines instead of network. Firewalls for individual hosts and home networks are as follows:

- *Host-Based Firewalls and Personal Firewalls:* Software firewalls that are installed on OS for servers and personal computers like Windows Firewall. They can have other capabilities such as logging, intrusion prevention and application-based firewalling.

- *Personal Firewall Appliances:* Small hardware firewalls that are used in home or small offices. They have more advanced features than host-based firewalls and add another layer of protection.

In a cloud environment there are high-capacity storage devices that store customers' information, plenty of high-performance servers that handle different tasks and VMs that are running on top of servers. Virtual network inside servers and sophisticated physical network that connects data center to the world are assets that should be protected very carefully. Firewalls are always deployed on the frontline of the network in order to safeguard the internal network. In a cloud, network can be extremely complicated due to the huge number of servers and also VM, which create a combination of virtual and physical traffic. Therefore, firewalling only on one layer cannot properly protect all assets. Moreover, virtual traffic is not visible to physical firewall. Co-tenancy of different customers on the same sever is another matter of contention because it may be owned by contender companies. Generally, different VMs in cloud are not considered as trusted to each other and there is a need for firewalling via VMs. In addition, security demand varies between different customers and in some cases, customized security services is demanded depending on the importance of their VMs. Thus, firewalling has to be applied in different layers from outside the data center to inside by physical firewalls with sophisticated features and within the virtual instances inside servers by virtual firewalls. In our work, we considered both physical and virtual firewalls since they share same the concepts in terms of access control, application filtering, state full inspection and other technologies.

Firewalling in a pure SDN network is shifted to the application layer. SDN application firewalls are similar to virtual firewalls from an implementation point of view, and are closer to physical firewalls, from the perspective of their scope and functionality. In general, SDN firewalls can rule and protect the portion of the network that is controlled by SDN controller and they follow the same main concepts of firewalling as traditional networks. However, it is very unlikely that we will see a pure SDN data center in the future; instead, it is more probable to have a hybrid architecture which is a combination of traditional network and SDN. Hence, virtual, physical and SDN firewalls will collaborate and protect the entire architecture. Our proposed framework in this chapter focuses on SDN firewall policy migration when a VM migration happens in relation to migrating security policies of VMs in software-defined networks.

VMM is an essential capability that supports cloud service elasticity. However, there is always a big concern on what happens to the security policy associated with the migrated machine. Recently, SDN has gained momentum in both research and industry. It has shown great potential to be used in cloud data centers, particularly for inter-domain migration of VMs. In distributed settings, where more than one physical SDN controller is used, particularly in different network domains, coordinating security policies during migration is an important issue. In this chapter, we present a novel framework to be deployed in an SDN environment that coordinates the mobility of the associated security policy along with the migrated VM. We implemented our framework into a prototype application, called MigApp, that runs on top of SDN controllers. Our application interacts with the VM monitor and other instances of MigApp through messaging system to achieve security migration. In order to evaluate our framework, the application integrated with the Floodlight controller and use it with a simulation environment.

Virtualization technology has become a commonplace in cloud computing data centers. Specifically, VM technology has recently emerged as an essential building block for such an environment as it allows multiple tenants to share the same infrastructure. The capability of VM migration brings multiple benefits such as high performance, improved manageability, and fault tolerance. While this mobility represents a valuable asset to the cloud computing model, it may introduce critical security flaws or violate the tenant's requirements, if the security policy does not follow the VM to the destination after migration. Manual reconfiguration of security policies is not an acceptable solution as it is error prone and is inadequate for live VM migration. To the best of our knowledge, existing works on VM migration have not addressed security policy migration in SDN.

In this chapter, we address security policies mobility with VMs in IaaS cloud computing, and demonstrate how to solve security policy migration in SDN-based cloud. Software-defined networking (SDN) is an emerging networking paradigm that aims at separating the control and data planes while offering logically centralized network's intelligence and state that are connected to the forwarding elements at the data plane. This architecture allows for a dynamic and flexible provisioning over the data plane and facilitates network management in a cost-effective way. Particularly, the network administrator can program and manage multiple network devices based on business requirements without the need to deal with each network device separately. At the management plane, the administrator can specify various policies, that are then used by a set of applications to program the controller through a northbound API. The controller, programs the forwarding devices at the data plane through a southbound API. The most popular protocol that offers an implementation of such an API is OpenFlow, maintained by the Open Networking Foundation (ONF). SDN provides new ways to solve age-old problems in networking while simultaneously enabling the introduction of sophisticated capabilities. For instance, GoGrid is an example of an IaaS provider that has adopted an SDN approach to cloud architecture. The configuration and control is put into customers' hands so that they can design their own cloud platform with virtualized services, such as firewalls and load balancers, managed using the management console or a public REST API. In order to deal with security groups, GoGrid implements security groups as global objects that are automatically synched across data centers. A recent IDC study projected that the SDN market will increase from $360 million in 2013 to $3.7 billion in 2016. There are several organizations worldwide, including Google, NDDI, and GENI, running and testing OpenFlow networks. A significant number of vendors, such as HP, Cisco, and IBM, are contributing by manufacturing SDN-enabling products.

Research initiatives supported by industry acknowledge the challenge and the importance of security context migration as a part of cloud elasticity mechanism. Many research initiatives have proposed to leverage the SDN paradigm to benefit cloud computing environments. Particularly, propose SDN strategy to enable live and offline migration of VM within and across multiple data centers. However, the reviewed solutions either circumvent the problem or do not fully address it, if at all. In this chapter, we design and implement a framework for migrating security policies along with the VMs within the same or between data centers based on SDN. Our solution, as opposed to vendor-specific ones, is meant to be open source, secure and interoperable with any SDN controller that provides a REST API and a virtual security appliance such as a firewall. To coordinate the migration, a distributed messaging system, namely RabbitMQ is proposed. The latter is based on advanced message queuing protocol (AMQP), a highly scalable publish and subscribe message protocol that is increasingly used in cloud architectures.

12.3 Distributed Messaging System

There is a need for a mechanism to coordinate the communication between the involved parties so that control messages and security policies can be exchanged. Constraints such as security, reliability, and performance have to be considered while selecting the right mechanism.

To this end, we opt for a distributed messaging system based on the AMQP. Interesting features of the AMQP protocol are that all resources used for storing messages are dynamically created and destroyed by clients as they need them, there is no need for static pre-configuration, and there are a number of free client libraries available in various programming languages. The RabbitMQ is chose, an open source broker implementation of the AMQP protocol. RabbitMQ is installed and used by clients on existing cloud services such as Amazon EC2. RabbitMQ is a message broker that basically accepts messages from a client program, called a producer, and stores the messages in a queue that works as a mailbox inside the server. Other client programs, called consumers, wait to receive messages from the queue. The queue can store any number of messages and it is a substantial an infinite buffer, which can run up to almost 30000 messages per second depending on the properties of the message. Many producers can send messages to one queue. On the other hand, many consumers can receive messages from one queue. A nice characteristic of such a system is that the producer, consumer, and the broker do not necessarily have to reside on the same machine. In fact, as distributed applications, they are scattered around different machines.

In RabbitMQ, the producer does not send messages directly to queues but to a specific entity called an exchange, which receives and pushes them to queues. Thus, one needs to first create an exchange, then creates the queues, and finally binds the exchange to the queue. A binding is a relationship between an exchange and a queue which means that the queue is interested in messages from that particular exchange. The exchange must know what to do with a received message: either to append it to a specific or multiple queues, or even to discard it. The fate of a message is determined according to the exchange type, which can be direct, topic, headers or fanout. Moreover, among various messaging patterns, publish and subscribe is one of the most used patterns in which messages can be received by multiple consumers with a fanout exchange that broadcasts produced messages to all subscribers. On the other hand, in some cases, the consumers are supposed to selectively receive some messages. It means that one message should be delivered to a specific consumer, whereas another message is destined for another consumer, and so on. In this scenario, the direct exchange will be used in addition to an extra routing key parameter that determines which consumer will receive which message. In our case, we use this latter exchange type so that any party only receives the messages intended for it.

With respect to a server's deployment, a RabbitMQ broker can be deployed in a centralized setting where multiple clients connect to the same server. However, it is also possible to use a distributed architecture, where multiple brokers are clustered and federated in order to ensure scalability and reliability of the messaging service and to interconnect multiple administrative domains. Particularly, a shovel may be used to link multiple RabbitMQ brokers across the Internet and provide more control than a federation. The latter deployment enables dealing with inter-data-center security rules migration. With respect to security, RabbitMQ supports encrypted SSL connection between the server and the client and has pluggable support for various authentication mechanisms. Thus, these specific features enable strengthening the security of the framework by only allowing authorized MigApps and hypervisors to produce and consume messages and protecting the underlying communications. In the next section we discuss the approach in more details.

12.4 Migration Security in Cloud

A framework and a prototype application to migrate security policies in SDN context. In order to test the viability of the prototype application, we used Minnie, which is a well-known simulator for SDN. Although there are many simulators for traditional networks and clouds, most of them are focused on performance and cost assessments. In this section, we strive to prepare a testing environment that supports VMM and focuses on security assessments.

Cloud computing is widely deployed all over the globe and its popularity is growing due to the benefits that it offers to both service providers and users. As the rate of adaption to the cloud increases day by day, cloud security is growing more important. Multi-tenancy is one of the main points of concern in cloud. Migrations are essential for cloud elasticity and security of data center and VMs should be preserved during and after migrations. There are many other examples that highlight the importance of security research in cloud.

In order to conduct a research, a test environment is a must for researchers. Benchmarking an application performance, testing the compatibility of a new protocol or analyzing the security of a new feature, all are examples that need a test-bed for evaluation. On the other hand, testing security on real world cloud environments is not a good idea. First of all, a real cloud needs a huge amount of money and time to deploy and it may not be safe to conduct a security testing on a production network. Furthermore, running multiple tests may need reconfiguration of the entire network that apparently takes more time in a real network. Thus, simulation environments are a good alternative to real employments, because they are cost effective, safe and flexible.

There are two ways to model a real network behavior, which are known as Simulation and Emulation, and each one has pros and cons. A network simulator is usually a piece of software that models network entities and the interactions between them, by using mathematical formulas. Simulators are typically used in research for studying and predicting network behavior and performance analysis. Most of the simulators model network devices, links between them and generate network traffic within the same program. Discrete-event simulation that models system operations as a sequence of events in time, is widely used in network simulators. Another method of simulation is using a Markov chain, which is less precise but faster than discrete-event simulations. There are many commercial and open-source network simulators with various features. For instance, OPNET[1] is a commercial simulator with GUI, NS2/NS3[2] are open-source simulators that accept scripts as input for network parameters and NetSim[3] is another example.

A network emulator is a piece of software or hardware to test and study a network that imitates the behavior of a production network. Emulators normally do not simulate endpoints such as computers; and therefore, computers or any type of traffic generator can be attached to emulated network. Normally, in emulation actual firmware runs on general purpose hardware. As a result, it is possible to run live applications and services on an emulated network, which usually is not feasible in a simulation. Hardware-based network emulators are more expensive and more accurate than software-based ones and are commonly used by service providers and network equipment manufacturers. Dynamips is a free emulator for routers and QEMU is an open-source hypervisor that can be used as a machine emulator.

Although, both simulators and emulators are applied for testing network performance, they are used for different purposes based on the capabilities that each of them offers. For example, simulators are good for scalability and performance tests while emulators can be used to test network applications and real services. Nevertheless, both simulators and emulators are crucial in network research.

Network and cloud simulation has been around for a while. However, most of the network simulators are not capable of cloud modeling. On the other hand, most of the existing cloud simulators focus on performance benchmarking, cost effectiveness evaluations and power consumption assessments. Hence, the majority of them lack in modeling security boxes such as firewall, IPS and security services like VPN. Furthemore, in some experiments a real running VM and actual services which imitate the behavior of a real network are necessary. At the time of writing this chapter, there is no free cloud simulator available which mimics middleboxes and real services in simulations. Hence, we decided to prepare a distributed testbed based on GNS3[4] that is mainly a network simulator. In order to use GNS3 for cloud, we introduced an architecture that models the deployment of standard data centers in a small scale but with real running services and security features. We also equipped the testbed with a set of free network and testing utilities that facilitate many experiments. In addition, we focused on VMM in cloud and first designed a migration framework and then improved it to a security preserving migration framework.

---

[1] www.opnet.com
[2] https://www.nsnam.org
[3] www.tetcos.com
[4] https://www.gns3.com

12.5 Conclusion

Cloud computing is a fast-developing area that relies on sharing of resources over a network. While more companies are adapting to the cloud computing and data centers are growing rapidly, data and network security is gaining more importance and firewalls are still the most common means to safeguard networks of any size. Whereas today data centers are distributed around the world, VM migration within and between data centers is inevitable for an elastic cloud. In order to keep the VM and data centers secure after migration, VM-specific security policies should move along with the VM as well.

REFERENCES

1. Ramkumar, N., & Nivethitha, S. (2013). Efficient resource utilization algorithm (ERUA) for service request scheduling in cloud. *International Journal of Engineering and Technology (IJET)*, 5(2), 1321-1327.

2. Khalid, O., Maljevic, I., Anthony, R., Petridis, M., Parrott, K., & Schulz, M. (2010, April). Deadline aware virtual machine scheduler for grid and cloud computing. In Advanced Information Networking and Applications Workshops (WAINA), 2010 IEEE 24th International Conference (pp. 85-90). IEEE.

3. Hatzopoulos, D., Koutsopoulos, I., Koutitas, G., & Van Heddeghem, W. (2013, June). Dynamic virtual machine allocation in cloud server facility systems with renewable energy sources. In Communications (ICC), 2013 IEEE International Conference (pp. 4217-4221). IEEE.

4. Kapil, D., Pilli, E. S., & Joshi, R. C. (2013). Live virtual machine migration techniques: Survey and research challenges. In Advance Computing Conference (IACC), 2013 IEEE 3rd International (pp. 963-969). IEEE.

5. Vignesh, V., Sendhil Kumar, K. S., & Jaisankar, N. (2013). Resource management and scheduling in cloud environment. *International journal of scientific and research publications*, 3(6), 1.

6. Rasmi, K., & Vivek, V. (2013). Resource Management Techniques in Cloud Environment-A Brief Survey. *International Journal of Innovation and Applied Studies*, 2(4), 525-532.

7. Ahn, J., Kim, C., Han, J., Choi, Y. R., & Huh, J. (2012). Dynamic Virtual Machine Scheduling in Clouds for Architectural Shared Resources. *In HotCloud*.

CHAPTER 13

CASE STUDY

Abstract

This chapter looks at different case studies that are very useful for real-life applications, like KVM, Xen, and the emergence of green computing in cloud. Finally, this chapter concentrates on one case study that is very useful for data analysis in distributed environments. There are lots of algorithms for either transactional or geographic databases proposed to prune the frequent item sets and association rules: herein an algorithm is proposed to find the global spatial association rule mining, which is exclusively represented in GIS database schemas and geo-ontologies by relationships with cardinalities one-to-one and one-to-many. This chapter presents an algorithm to improve spatial association rule mining. The proposed algorithms are categorized into two main steps: First, automating the geographic data preprocessing tasks developed for a GIS module. Second, discarding all well-known GIS dependencies that calculate the relationship between different numbers of attributes.

Keywords: GIS, data mining, distributed database, data analysis, green computing.

13.1   Kernel-Based Virtual Machine

Kernel-based virtual machine (KVM) is a hypervisor built right into the Linux kernel. It is similar to Xen in purpose but much simpler to get running. To start using the hypervisor, just load the appropriate KVM kernel modules and the hypervisor is up. As with Xen's full virtualization, in order for KVM to work, you must have a processor that supports Intel's VT-x extensions or AMD's AMD-V extensions [1]. KVM is a full virtualization solution for Linux. It is based upon CPU virtualization extensions (*i.e., extending the set of CPU instructions with new instructions that allow writing simple virtual machine monitors*). KVM is a new Linux subsystem (the kernel component of KVM is included in the mainline Linux kernel) that takes advantage of these extensions to add a virtual machine monitor (*or hypervisor*) capability to Linux. Using KVM, one can create and run multiple virtual machines that will appear as normal Linux processes and are integrated with the rest of the system. It works on the x86 architecture and supports hardware virtualization technologies such as Intel VT-x and AMD-D.

13.2   Xen

Xen is an open-source type-1 or bare-metal hypervisor [2], which makes it possible to run many instances of an operating system or indeed different operating systems in parallel on a single machine (or host). Xen is the only type-1 hypervisor that is available as open-source. Xen is used as the basis for a number of different commercial and open source applications such as: server virtualization, IaaS, desktop virtualization, security applications, embedded and hardware appliances. Xen enables users to increase server utilization, consolidate server farms, reduce complexity, and decrease total cost of ownership.

13.3   Secure Data Analysis in GIS

This is the era of the Internet, where every user wants to store and retrieve their private and public information according to an online storage survey. When the data is stored in the server, the problem comes when the user considers accessing their information, since a different number of techniques are available in the field of data mining, like association rule mining, classification, clustering, etc. There are also two main techniques: the first one is prediction [3], where the database admin predicts the relationship between the end users or a different number of attributes. And the second one is descriptive, where the database admin describes the users useful information. In data mining techniques, association rule mining techniques are very useful to find the relationship between the different number of database. And the second technique is clustering, where attributes are eliminated or grouped according to their values. The last technique is classification, where attributes are classified according to certain criteria of the users, it may be age, education, etc.

13.3.1   Database

A database is the collection of data, where data represent useful information gathered from the real-world object. The system which manages these collected data is called database management system. This system is a necessity for the organization, enterprise, etc. Consider the example of a university database which has the information about faculty members, staff members, students, courses, departments, etc, which will be changed very frequently. There are different types of database environments present in the network such as centralized and distributed. Dissimilar to the centralized database model, the distributed database model is fast but it needs some extra effort concerning privacy.

13.3.2   Data Mining and Techniques

Data mining is the process of finding out useful data or frequent patterns from the huge amount of database such as data warehouse. Data warehouse is the multidimensional database in which new information will be appended but editing of old information is not allowed. Data mining is a step of the KDD [6].

13.3.3   Distributed Database

Distributed database is a database in which data are physically located in different computers but connected through the controlled network. The distributed database system is the high speed, less memory required method of data connection, but apart from this it is also costly because security and more management tasks, such as care about duplication and replication, need to be provided.

Replication: In distribution database, whenever modification occurs on one site that modification must be synchronously done on all sites where the copy of it is stored so that all the copies will look alike. Software is needed for doing this replication [4].

Duplication: In the process of duplication in distributed database it is necessary to identify one copy of the original database and make that database as a master database and create a duplicate copy of that database for all sites as the local database of the site. In the duplication process any change in local database does not effect on the other copy of that database.

Horizontal Partitioning: In horizontal partitioning, disparate sites gather a similar set of information, but about unlike entities. Consider the example of the organization which has a number of branch offices located in different cities such as Mumbai, Delhi, and Kolkata. This organization has partitioned its central data in the form of horizontal data partitioning; now each branch has only their local data but can access other branch data by using distributed network. This causes a privacy problem, leading to the use of different algorithms for privacy-preserving data mining [7].

13.3.4   Spatial Data Mining

Spatial characterization is how objects vigorously connect in space throughout the world. Spatial data is an enumerated data which has the length, height, width, etc., attribute of an object in it. Spatial database is the database of this kind of enumerated data type which defines a geographic structure present in the world. This will be represented in the form of there pictorial views which will be the correlation of their pixel-position in three-dimensional structure. A database which is improved to store and access geometric space is called a spatial database. This type of data generally contains coordinates, points, lines, and polygons. Some spatial databases can deal with more complex data like three-dimensional objects, topological coverage and linear networks. Spatial data mining is the application of data mining to spatial models.

13.3.5   Secure Multi-Party Computation

Secure multi-party computation (SMC) works on the assumption that all the parties, which want to communicate each are not trusted by each other or they don't trust the communication channels. Still, they want computation of some common operations with the privacy of their local data.

The skeleton of secure multi-party computation provides a concrete theoretical foundation for privacy.

Trusted Third-Party Model: TTP model works on the assumption that the data will not be inferable from anyone else. The main aim of the secure protocol is to get that level of privacy. The TTP model works when the data is distributed in the distributed environment, and each database owner has their own private datasets, and no one wants to disclose their private information to other data owners. Therefore, one of them is selected as the trusted third party, who is responsible for calculating or managing all the private and secure information from all the other data owners presented in the environment.

Semi-honest Model: The semi-honest model is called the honest-but-curious model. A semi-honest party works with the correct input followed by protocol, but after the protocol is released it uses whatever it gets during execution of the protocol to compromise security or privacy.

13.3.6   Association Rule Mining Problem

In the last decade, researchers have found that association rule mining (ARM) is the one of the core processes of data mining. ARM is the most important data mining process for finding out about all the relations between the frequent patterns and it doesn't need any supervisor for that. ARM processes variable length data and determine comprehensible results.

Modern organizations have geographically distributed structure. Characteristically, every location locally stores its eternally increasing amount of day-to-day data. In such type of organize data, centralized data mining can't discover feasible useful patterns because of the large network communication costs that are incurred. This is overcome by using distributed data mining.

Let $I = I_1, I_2, , I_m$ be a set of m distinct attributes, T be transaction that contains a set of items such that T is a subset of I, D be a database with different transaction records T_s. An association rule is an implication in the form of $X \Rightarrow Y$, where X, Y sunset of I are sets of items called item sets, and $X \cap Y = \phi$. X is called antecedent while Y is called consequent, the rule means X implies Y.

There are two important basic measures for association rules, support(s) and confidence(c).

Support(s): An association rule is defined as the fraction of records that contains X ꟷ Y to the total number of records in the database. The count for each item is increased by one every time the item is encountered in different transaction T in database D during the scanning process. It means the support count does not take the quantity of the item into account. For example, in a transaction a customer buys three bottles of beers but we only increase the support count number of beer by one, in other words, if a transaction contains a item then the support count of this item is increased by one. Support(s) is calculated by the following Formula:

$$Support(X \cup Y) = \frac{Support count of X \cup Y}{Total number of transaction in D} \qquad (13.1)$$

Confidence(c): An association rule is defined as the fraction of the number of transactions that contain $(X \cup Y)$ to the total number of records that contain X, where if the percentage exceeds the threshold of confidence an interesting association rule $X \Rightarrow Y$ can be generated. Formula:

$$Confidence(X \cup Y) = \frac{Support(X \cup Y)}{Support(X)} \qquad (13.2)$$

Confidence is a measure of strength of the association rules; suppose the confidence of the association rule $X \Rightarrow Y$ is 80%, it means that 80% of the transactions that contain X also contain Y together. Similarly, to ensure the interestingness of the rules specified, minimum confidence is also predefined by users.

13.3.7 Distributed Association Ruling

Distributed association rule mining (DARM) finds rules from different spatial dataset located in distributed environment [5]. Conversely, parallel network connection does not have fast communication compared to the distributed network. So distributed mining frequently aims to minimize cost of the communication. Researchers desired high-speed DMA to mine rules from scattered datasets partitioned among three different locations. In each site, FDM finds the local support counts and prunes all infrequent one. After finishing home pruning, each site broadcasts messages to all other sites to request their support counts. It then decides whether huge item sets are globally frequent and generates the candidate item sets from those globally frequent item sets.

13.3.8   Data Analysis in GIS System

Nowadays, geographic data is used in different applications like planning development of urban areas, improvement of transportation, enhancement of telecommunications and marketing, etc. Normally geographic useful information is gathered in GDBMD and managed by GIS. Some new technologies have been developed which provide operations and functions for spatial data analysis, However, they are not efficient for the large databases because unknown knowledge cannot be discovered by GIS. Specialized techniques have to elaborate this type of knowledge, which is the base of the KDD. Data mining is a technique to retrieve useful information from the huge amount of database. There are two main goals for retrieving the data from the database; the first one is the prediction and the second one is the description. There are different mining algorithms available for mining data from the database, like ARM, clustering and classification, etc.; among these, the SARM concept is used in the geographical region, so the concept is spatial association rule mining, in which data is retrieved from the geographical areas. Spatial association mining concept is used to find the relationship between the different attributes by considering the threshold value of support and confidence and calculate the frequent item set in the distributed environment. In this process, we divided the entire region into three different regions, each having their own spatial database $SDB_1, SDB_2, ...SDB_n$ and their own key values $SK_1, SK_2, , SK_n$, or Select N number of region each having their own database $SDB_1, SDB_2, , SDB_n$. Each region calculates their frequent item sets and support value.

Each region is arranged in ring architecture then finds the partial support. Now region 1 sends their partial support (PS) value to region 2 and region 2 sends their value to region 3 and this process continues till region n, and after that region n sends their value to region 1. Region 1 subtracts all the Random Number value from the Partial Support value and calculates their actual support. Now region 1 broadcasts the actual support value to the entire region present in the distributed environment.

13.4   Emergence of Green Computing in Modern Computing Environment

In the modern computing environment many utility-based applications may be performed, relating to the case of backup and recovery which is highly required in a cloud computing service where many servers perform their task and the issues of duplicate infrastructure make no sense. However, SaaS is a cloud computing method. Whether it's a payroll or customer relationship management (CRM) system, there are times when delivering those applications as a service makes sense. A lot of times, the internal IT organization does not have the expertise required to run a particular application or that application may not be strategic enough to justify committing limited IT resources to managing it [9, 10]. There's no doubt that there are potential security issues when it comes to cloud computing, but like all things in life the risks need to be weighed against the potential benefits.

Algorithm . Encryption Process

BEGIN

    Step 1: Take the Spatial Database

    Step 2: Convert into the horizontally partitioned distributed database (N Number of datasets)

    Step 3: Calculate the support count of each database.

    Step 4: Calculate the support and confidence.

    Step 5: Calculate partial support and partial confidence.

        Partial Support (PS) = X. Support - DBMinimum Support

        Partial Confidence (PC) = X. Confidence - DB x Minimum Confidence

    Step 6: Add their own private key in all partial support and partial confidence.

        Partial Support(PS) = X. support - DBminimum support + Key

        Partial Confidence(PC) = X. Confidence - DBxMinimum Confidence+Key

    Step 7: Divide the partial support and partial confidence into the three different values.

    Step 8: Convert partial support, partial confidence and partial lift values into the ASCII value and compute the matrix Y.

    Step 9: Take the transpose of the matrix (YT).

    Step 10: Exchange YT into the Binary format.

    Step 11: Let own key matrix X

    Step 12: Exchange X into binary

    Step 13: Execute Ex-or among X and Y.

    Step 14: The matrix (Step 14) stored in associate memory.

    Setp 15: The resultant matrix is sanded to the protocol initiator Server.

END

Algorithm . Decryption Process

BEGIN

    Step 1: Let encrypted matrix M

    Step 2: Calculate transpose of M into MT

    Step 3: Exchange MT into binary

    Step 4: Let own key X (Matrix)

    Step 5: Exchange X into binary

    Step 6: Execute Ex-or among MT and X

    Step 7: The result (Step 6) is converted to the ASCII code (Original Matrix).

    Step 8: After receiving all the original values from the different databases, the protocol initiator takes the step for data analysis by calculating Global support and confidence.

    Step 9: After that, the protocol initiator broadcasts the results to all the database server admin present in the distributed environments.

END

Arguably, the next big thing in cloud computing will be more specialized application services. A lot of IT organizations can't afford to invest in supercomputer-class infrastructure. Yet, the business could benefit from access to some pretty compute-intensive analytic applications. None of this means that on-premise applications and infrastructure are going away. On a practical level, there are far too many existing applications that can't be cost-effectively rewritten to run on a public cloud. On a strategic level, there are hundreds of applications that are too fundamental to the business to run on a cloud. And finally, there are a number of legal and regulatory issues that may not make cloud computing practical in some cases [6].

Cloud computing is not an all-or-nothing proposition. What we are slowly migrating toward is a blended computing model that will combine the best elements of public cloud services with on-premise applications that will run on internal IT systems that use the same architectures as public cloud services. And once that happens, we'll enter a new era of IT flexibility that should for the first time really allow IT organizations to dynamically respond to the rapidly changing needs of the business, versus always trying to get the business to conform to the way IT works.

Abuse and Nefarious Use of Cloud Computing: The ease of registering for IaaS solutions and the relative anonymity they offer attracts many cyber criminals. IaaS offerings have been known to host botnets or their command and control centers, downloads for exploits, trojans, etc. There is a myriad of ways in which in-the-cloud capabilities can be misused; possible future uses include launching dynamic attack points, CAPTCHA-solving farms, password and key cracking and more. To remediate this, IaaS providers should toughen up the weakest links: the registration process and the monitoring of customer network traffic.

Insecure Interfaces and APIs: As software interfaces or APIs are what customers use to interact with cloud services, those must have extremely secure authentication, access control, encryption and activity monitoring mechanisms; especially when third parties start to build on them. The keys to solving those problems are a thorough analysis of the interfaces and quality implementation of the security mechanisms.

Malicious Insiders: The malicious insider threat is one that has been gaining in importance as many providers still don't reveal how they hire people, how they grant them access to assets or how they monitor them. Transparency is, in this case, vital to a secure cloud offering, along with compliance reporting and breach notification [7].

Shared Technology Issues: Sharing infrastructure is a way of life for IaaS providers. Unfortunately, the components on which this infrastructure is based were not designed for that. To ensure that customers don't thread on each other's "territory", monitoring and strong compartmentalization is required, not to mention scanning for and patching of vulnerabilities that might jeopardize this coexistence.

Data Loss or Leakage: Be it by deletion without a backup, by loss of the encoding key or by unauthorized access, data is always in danger of being lost or stolen. This is one of the top concerns for businesses, because they not only stand to lose their reputation, but are also obligated by law to keep it safe. There are a number of things that can be done to prevent such occurrences; from consistent use of encryption and quality disaster recovery to contractual specifications regarding backup and secure destruction practices.

Account or Service Hijacking: The attacker can gather information, change data, falsify transactions, and also redirect your clients to illegitimate sites. In this day and age, it only takes a credible phishing site or a good social engineering approach, and the keys to your castle have changed hands. Strong authentication techniques, security policies and monitoring should prevent this from happening.

Unknown Risk Profile: Security should always be in the upper portion of the priority list. Code updates, security practices, vulnerability profiles, and intrusion attempts are all things that should always be kept in mind.

13.5   Green Computing

With rising energy cost and growing environmental concerns, green computing is receiving more and more attention. Software and system architectures (in terms of concurrency patterns) play a crucial role in both computing and telecommunication systems, and they have been analyzed for performance, reliability, maintainability, and security. Yet, little work on analysis based on the amount of energy that the CPU/processor will consume has been reported. Since most communication systems have to run 24/7 (e.g., most server farms, servers in a cloud computing infrastructure), the energy consumption of a system based on a specific software architecture is of great importance. For example, high energy consuming always leads to higher operational cost of the system. High energy consumption also implies more heat produced, thus, more power is required for cooling down.

The greatest environmental challenge today is global warming, which is caused by carbon emissions. The energy crisis has introduced the concept of green computing, and green computing needs algorithms and mechanisms to be redesigned for energy efficiency. Green IT refers to the study and practice of using computing resources in an efficient, effective and economic way. The various approaches of the green IT are virtualization, power management, material recycling and telecommuting. The basic principle of cloud computing is to make the computing be assigned in a great number of distributed computers rather than local computers or remote servers. In fact, cloud computing is an extension of grid computing, distributed computing and parallel computing. Its forte is to provide secure, quick, convenient data storage and net computing service centered by the Internet. Currently, a large number of cloud computing systems waste a tremendous amount of energy and emit a considerable amount of carbon dioxide. Thus, it is necessary to significantly reduce pollution and substantially lower energy usage. The analysis of energy consumption in cloud computing considers both public and private clouds. Cloud computing with green algorithm can enable more energy-efficient use of computing power [8].

Green computing is defined as the study and practice of designing, manufacturing, using, and disposing of computers, servers, and associated subsystems such as monitors, printers, storage devices, and networking and communications systems, efficiently and effectively with minimal or no impact on the environment. Research continues into key areas such as making the use of computers as energy efficient as possible, and designing algorithms and systems for efficiency-related computer technologies [9]. There are several approaches to green computing, namely:

1. Product longevity

2. Algorithmic efficiency

3. Resource allocation

4. Virtualization

5. Power management, etc.

Need for Green Computing in Clouds: Modern data centers, operating under the cloud computing model are hosting a variety of applications ranging from those that run for a few seconds (*e.g., serving requests of web applications such as e-commerce and social network portals with transient workloads*) to those that run for longer periods of time (*e.g., simulations or large dataset processing*) on shared hardware platforms. The need to manage multiple applications in a data center creates the challenge of on-demand resource provisioning and allocation in response to time-varying workloads. Green cloud computing is envisioned to achieve not only efficient processing and utilization of computing infrastructure, but also minimize energy consumption. This is essential for ensuring that the future growth of cloud computing is sustainable. Otherwise, cloud computing with increasingly pervasive front-end client devices interacting with back-end data centers will cause an enormous escalation of energy usage. To address this problem, data center resources need to be managed in an energy efficient manner to drive Green cloud computing. In particular, cloud resources need to be allocated not only to satisfy QoS requirements specified by users via SLA, but also to reduce energy usage [10].

13.6 Conclusion

In this chapter, different case studies were presented that are very useful for real-life applications, like KVM, Xen, and emergence of green computing in cloud. Finally, this chapter is concentrated on one case study, that is very useful for data analysis in distributed environments. There are lots of algorithms for either transactional or geographic databases proposed to prune the frequent item sets and association rules; herein an algorithm was proposed to find the global spatial association rule mining, which is exclusively represented in GIS database schemas and geo-ontologies by relationships with cardinalities one-to-one and one-to-many. This chapter presented an algorithm to improve the spatial association rule mining. The proposed algorithm is categorized into three main steps. First, it automated the geographic data preprocessing tasks developed for a GIS module. The second step is discarding all well-known GIS dependencies that calculate the relationship between different numbers of attributes. And finally, in this chapter an algorithm was proposed to provide the greatest degree of privacy, when the numbers of regions are more than two, with each one finding an association rule between them with zero percentage of data leakage.

REFERENCES

1. Moschakis, I. A., & Karatza, H. D. (2012). Evaluation of gang scheduling performance and cost in a cloud computing system. *The Journal of Supercomputing*, 59(2), 975-992. DOI: 10.1007/s11227-010-0481-4.

2. Dash, M., Mahapatra, A., & Chakraborty, N. R. (2013). Cost effective selection of data center in cloud environment. *International Journal on Advanced Computer Theory and Engineering (IJACTE)*, 2, 2319-2526.

3. Abirami, S. P., & Ramanathan, S. (2012). Linear scheduling strategy for resource allocation in cloud environment. *International Journal on Cloud Computing: Services and Architecture (IJCCSA)*, 2(1), 9-17.

4. Majumdar, S. (2011). Resource management on cloud: handling uncertainties in parameters and policies. *CSI communicatons*, 22, 16-19.

5. Roy, N., Dubey, A., & Gokhale, A. (2011, July). Efficient autoscaling in the cloud using predictive models for workload forecasting. In Cloud Computing (CLOUD), 2011 IEEE International Conference on (pp. 500-507). IEEE.

6. Farooqi, A. M., Nafis, M. T., & Usvub, K. (2017). Comparative Analysis of Green Cloud Computing. International Journal, 8(2).

7. Masoud, R. I., AlShamrani, R. S., AlGhamdi, F. S., AlRefai, S. A., & Hemalatha, M. (2017). Green Cloud Computing: A Review. *International Journal of Computer Applications*, 167(9).

8. Piraghaj, S. F., Dastjerdi, A. V., Calheiros, R. N., & Buyya, R. (2017). Container-CloudSim: An environment for modeling and simulation of containers in cloud data centers. *Software: Practice and Experience*, 47(4), 505-521. DOI: 10.1002/spe.2422

9. Khosravi, A., Nadjaran Toosi, A., & Buyya, R. (2017). Online virtual machine migration for renewable energy usage maximization in geographically distributed cloud data centers. *Concurrency and Computation: Practice and Experience*. DOI: 10.1002/cpe.4125

10. Machen, A., Wang, S., Leung, K. K., Ko, B. J., & Salonidis, T. (2017). Live Service Migration in Mobile Edge Clouds. *IEEE Wireless Communications*. pp.2-9. DOI: 10.1109/MWC.2017.1700011

Printed and bound by CPI Group (UK) Ltd, Croydon, CR0 4YY

27/10/2024

14580478-0001